The Politically Correct Netherlands

Recent Titles in
Contributions to the Study of World History

The Politically Correct Netherlands

Since the 1960s

Herman Vuijsje

Translated and Annotated by Mark T. Hooker

Contributions to the Study of World History, Number 76

Greenwood Press
Westport, Connecticut • London

Library of Congress Cataloging-in-Publication Data

Vuijsje, Herman.
   [Correct. English]
   The politically correct Netherlands : since the 1960s / Herman Vuijsje ; translated and annotated by Mark T. Hooker.
      p.   cm.—(Contributions to the study of world history, ISSN 0885–9159 ; no. 76)
   Includes bibliographical references and index.
   ISBN 0–313–31509–4 (alk. paper)
      1. Social problems—Netherlands.   2. Netherlands—Social conditions—1945–   3. Netherlands—Social policy.   I. Title.   II. Series.
HN513.5.V8513 2000
306′.09492—dc21   99–462061

British Library Cataloguing in Publication Data is available.

Library of Congress Catalog Card Number: 99–462061
ISBN: 0–313–31509–4
ISSN: 0885–9159

First published in 2000

Greenwood Press, 88 Post Road West, Westport, CT 06881
An imprint of Greenwood Publishing Group, Inc.
www.greenwood.com

Printed in the United States of America

The paper used in this book complies with the Permanent Paper Standard issued by the National Information Standards Organization (Z39.48–1984).

10 9 8 7 6 5 4 3 2 1

Originally published as *Correct. Weldenkend Nederland sinds de jaren zestig*, Amsterdam, Uitgeverij *Contact*, 1997. Annotated and updated for the English edition.

Contents

Acknowledgments

Various people have helped me in various ways with this book. Andries de Jong (the Central Bureau of Statistics) and Gijs Beets (the Dutch Interdisciplinary Demographic Institute) were so kind as to provide detailed answers to my demographic questions. I have for years had a permanent exchange of ideas on the topics touched on in this book with H.J. Schoo, Cas Wouters and Carlo van Praag. Rob Bakker, Jos van der Lans, Hagar Peeters and Cas Wouters provided a critical commentary on parts of the manuscript, which led to important improvements. This book would not exist were it not for the exceptional patience of the Fund for Special Journalistic Projects and of Contact Publishers. To all of them go my sincere thanks.

I have devoted a number of separate publications to some of the topics in this book: *Vermoorde onschuld, etnisch verschil als Hollands taboe* [Innocence Murdered: Ethnic Difference as a Dutch Taboo] (1986), *Lof der dwang* [Praise of Coercion] (1989), *Mens erger je niet* [Sorry] (1992) and *Hulpeloze gladiatoren* [The Helpless Gladiators] (1996). These publications served as the foundation for this book.

From the Translator

This translation is aimed at the widest possible audience of English speakers around the world, not just at Holland-watchers. Because the examples used in the book are sometimes very Dutch, the text is fully annotated to make it accessible to readers who are not Dutch specialists. The first occurrence of an annotated word or term is marked in the text by the symbol [q.v.], which is the Latin abbreviation for quod vide. Subsequent occurrences are not marked, but the annotations are arranged in alphabetical order for ease of repeated reference.

All the book and article titles in the text were translated for the convenience of the nonspecialist reader, but the overwhelming majority of the source materials referred to in the book are only available in Dutch. The original title of books and articles can be found in the notes or in the bibliography.

My thanks to Herman Vuijsje for his active and enthusiastic participation in this project. He not only read the translation, letting me know when I had missed the point, but also updated the text especially for this English-language edition.

My thanks also to Maarten Carbo of Contact Publishing for his encouragement and support of the unconventional arrangement that allowed this book to be published in English.

My special thanks to my wife, Stella, born and raised in The Hague, who read the manuscript of the translation and helped me get the words right.

Prix des Ambassadeurs

The Politically Correct Netherlands Since the 1960s was the winner of the 1999 *Prix des Ambassadeurs*, which is a literary prize that was established in 1985 by the French ambassador to the Netherlands. Its original goal was to recognize a work in French by a Dutch author. In 1996 it was radically revised along the lines of the prize of the same name that is awarded in Paris, by the then-serving ambassador, Bernard de Montferrand. The *Prix des Ambassadeurs* is now awarded annually to a work originally written in Dutch that "addresses major contemporary issues, is universal in character and will advance intercultural dialog." The prize alternates annually between a work of fiction and a work of nonfiction. The prize for 1999 was for a work of nonfiction.

The *Prix des Ambassadeurs* is intended to convey the respect of the diplomatic community in The Hague for the literary, intellectual production of their host country. Its goal is to draw attention outside the borders of the Netherlands to what is being written inside them, by encouraging the translation of the winning work into French.

Nominations for the *Prix des Ambassadeurs* are submitted by Dutch publishers to the Selection Committee. For 1999 there were almost 60 nominations. The Selection Committee narrows the number of nominees down to a short list of five, which is presented to the jury of the approximately 25 French-speaking ambassadors to the Netherlands, who make the final choice.

The jury's official summary of *The Politically Correct Netherlands Since the 1960s* praised the author's criticism of the misdeeds of the ideology of intellectual conformity—political correctness—which originated in the revolutionary decade of the 1960s. The totems and taboos that originated from this ideology made it hard to deal with, or even signal the presence of, the real problems in Dutch society over the preceding 25 years. This often led to a worsening of the social position of certain groups, many times precisely the groups that society wanted to protect, like racial minorities.

The jury categorized Vuijsje's book as "a brilliant essay on the way that the Dutch government and its officials have functioned over the last twenty years and on the changing power relationship between the state and its citizens." "Vuijsje has the gift of analyzing a problem and reducing it to its essentials in a few sentences. He is also a perceptive polemicist, who can make use of deadly irony," they said. In typical diplomatic fashion, however, the jury also noted that it did not share the author's point of view on this controversial topic in all cases.

The jury calls special attention to the case studies with which Vuijsje's proofs are laced. Some are laughable in their absurdity, while others are horrifying, as in the case of the young Turkish girl who was murdered by her mentally disturbed neighbor, who, because of a politically correct taboo, could not be forcibly committed to a mental institution, despite repeated complaints.

In presenting the prize, Ambassador de Montferrand pointed to two reasons that were decisive in selecting this book as the winner. The first is the book's subject: "political correctness." It is a subject that has great topical value in each of the countries from which the jury members come and, therefore, is one, which gives the book a universal character. The second reason, in the ambassador's opinion, is the clarity with which the subject was treated. Vuijsje calls things by their real names, said the ambassador; this is an approach that he finds makes the book very lively and "literarily correct."

Vuijsje's book shows that, in the Netherlands, the pendulum has started to swing back from the extremes that it had reached, but, at present, only on an ad hoc basis. Nevertheless, the tide of social thought in the Netherlands is changing. His book offers a perspective that has been muted in the American discussions on these issues and that is especially refreshing. It is of interest not only to students of the Netherlands but to students of Western society as a whole.

A *Sur Place* [q.v.]

In the 1960s the Netherlands developed an iron-strong reputation. In that magical decade we let the world see once again how big a small country can be. Far and wide, the Netherlands became known as a laboratory for anarchistic and liberal ideas. In the 1970s and 1980s this trend toward individualism and increasing autonomy continued to progress unabated. The "un-nannying" of people's private lives is now as good as completed. Inasfar as individual freedom goes, the Netherlands has become a country worthy of envy.

The ideas of the 1960s also played an important role outside the private sphere of people's lives. Was its effect there just as positive? Asking this question in the 1970s and 1980s was not politically correct. The generation of the 1960s was in control of the mental climate. In that climate it was not done—it was even life-threatening—to put something in the way of the freedom and autonomy of individual citizens. Even the government was expected—except as a provider of "Fun Things" [q.v.] for the people—to take an extremely unobtrusive stance not only in people's private lives but also in the public domain.

The public debate on "sensitive" areas such as government coercion, privacy and race relations was caught in the power of some strong taboos. These taboos had sprung up in the 1960s but continued to increase in breadth and intensity in the 1970s and 1980s. They continued to dominate the mental climate for so long that they found themselves reflected in legislation and policy. Reports of undesirable side effects of these taboos disappeared under the table, even when it began to appear that primarily the weaker social groups were being affected by these side effects. The "time had not come" to disclose information about large-scale welfare fraud, crime rates for certain ethnic groups or the neglect of mental patients.

In the 1970s and 1980s the situation in the politically correct Netherlands seemed like a *sur place* in a bicycle race, where all the racers are in a technical standstill on the course, keeping their balance and watching each other closely. No one dares to be the first one to move, but if one of them begins to ride, then all the others have to go along. Things only got to this point in the 1990s, however. The riders took off in an unexpected and wild sprint, in which the inviolability of all the new commandments was quickly cast aside.

The first part of this book develops the picture sketched here. Politically correct patterns of thought have a strong, long-term effect on the Netherlands. The ideas of the 1960s were applied even in the area of public administration without much contradiction. Power had to be decentralized, and society had to be as "self-regulating" as possible. Even these administrative "totems" brought unwanted side effects with them. The first part of the book closes with a number of examples of groups that were affected by these side effects.

In the second part of the book, I look for explanations. Why were certain thought patterns from the 1960s so strictly interpreted in the Netherlands? Why did it take so long for the pendulum to begin to swing the other way? Special attention is paid to the trendsetting elite of the baby boom, the generation that had given the Netherlands a reputation for individuality and anarchy in the 1960s but that ten years later was preaching anxious conformism. What had gotten into them in the intervening period?

PART I

Totems and Taboos

CHAPTER 1

The Taboo on Coercion

In 1988 I did an interview with Rajendra Pradhan, a cultural anthropologist from Nepal who had descended on a village in the province of South Holland to study the customs of the indigenous farmers, who belonged to the Dutch Reformed Church. Pradhan biked happily to the Lingebos Woods and the Diefdijk Levee. "It's very pretty there, especially in the summer," he confided in me. "But I really feel that the polders [q.v.] are a man-made landscape [q.v.], because everything is so regulated and so orderly. The Dutch want to control and regulate everything: not only the landscape, but also relations and emotions." Pradhan meant that everything that cannot be controlled by mankind is a problem for the Dutch. According to him, that was the reason that the Dutch always talk about the weather. Maybe all their small talk about the weather is nothing more than an incantation, he thought, an attempt to exercise a certain degree of control over it.[1]

Other foreign observers also see the tendency "to plan" as characteristic of our national identity. Not one other European society is as wild about zoning and social planning as a "way of life," wrote the American Holland-watcher, William Shetter, in his book, *The Netherlands in Perspective*. Zahn, in his book *Regents, Rebels and Reformers*, also brings to the fore our "belief in the malleability of society," for which we draw on "an age-old tradition, acquired during the shaping of the land."

The picture of the level-headed, reasonable Dutchman, always looking for a systematic solution, may be ages old, but it has not always been so. Certainly, the Dutch still plan: their career, their children, their health and even the time of their death. Businesses and government departments also subject themselves to a strict regimen of scenarios, annual plans and quality standards.[2] But, in the last few decades, bringing order to society seems to take about as much effort as controlling the weather.

Since the 1970s, when the baby-boom generation took over the reins, directive and restrictive government intervention has fallen out of favor. The baby boom was raised in the shadow of the war and with terrifying visions of a police state. Big Brother, *Brave New World*, De Tocqueville's vision of the future were all variants of the same picture: a huge, patronizing government apparatus that foresees everything, regulates everything and keeps its subjects hopelessly fixed in a nanny state. That had to be avoided at any cost; a strong government was dangerous. The baby boomers would never dance around the law books the way the Jews do on the holiday of Simchas Torah [Hebrew: Joy in the Law].

In the meantime, administrators and civil servants could not just give up the pretense of regulation. What were they there for, then? This is how the Netherlands developed into an advanced school of *management by speech*. One policy speech after the other was fired off at reality without much being heard about implementation. In the 1980s, it became popular to make a policy statement in which plans were carefully attuned to the way that things were already heading. The government let others decide where the parade was going and limited itself to putting up barricades at the cross streets. In that way spontaneous developments could be presented as policy results. A textbook example of this was the way that Finance Minister Andriessen and the Central Statistical Bureau presented the forced cancellation of the census as a resounding victory (see Chapter 3).

Management by speech also made a new administrative jargon and officialese necessary. In the newspeak officialese, there could be no mention of "directing." Even "administering" was a bit dicey, while "heading" was still barely possible. The concept of "leading" was avoided like the fascist plague, and "supervision" was really also too patronizing. Guidance became the slogan now, the sort of leadership that takes place almost by itself and does not hurt at all! Inducement, of course, was even better yet.

It was obvious, following this line of reasoning, that the government was no longer using coercion but, at the most, "insistence." Even better, it could set itself up as a "facilitator." Naturally, in this style of leadership, talking about "upper" or "lower" levels of government was out of place! The governments in the regions and submunicipalities were not a bit less important than the one in The Hague: they were other governments! This newspeak delivered a number of words that have no equivalent in other languages. Throughout the world an "obligation" is an unambiguous concept. It is only in the Netherlands that there are two sorts of obligation. A *"resultaatsverplichting"* [literally: result-obligation] is an obligation to produce a result within a specific period of time. A person who takes on an obligation of this type can be held accountable for the "result." In addition to that, in Dutch there is also an *"inspan-ningsverplichting"* [obligation to make an effort]. This is an emancipated *"resultaatsverplichting."* This type of obligation contains only the promise not to do nothing. No one other than the person making the effort can measure the amount of effort expended on this promise. All these new concepts have one thing in common: they make it impossible to measure output and to check whether responsibilities have been lived up to.

THE APOLOGISTS IN POWER

In private relationships the traditional distributions of power could no longer be taken for granted. Women began to act "assertively" toward their spouses, as did children toward their parents and teachers. This assertiveness was justified on the grounds of the idea of emancipation and democratization from the rich 1960s, but in the 1970s and 1980s, with a declining economy, it turned out that a big mouth was a wonderfully useful tool for achieving other goals. The switch from emancipation and personal growth to self-interest was a question of swallowing hard a couple of times and pushing ahead. The weapons of the present-day struggle for existence were, therefore, forged in the heyday of the welfare state. This is a remarkable case of "paradoxical continuity" (see Chapter 15).

The mutation of ideological activism into the promotion of concrete interests can be clearly seen in the squatters' movement. In the 1960s, the Provos [q.v.] came out with the "White Housing Plan" and an illegal Housing Office. Fifteen years later, these benevolent initiatives degenerated into squatters' terror and crippled the municipal housing distribution system, which was intended to protect the weakest members of society. As early as 1996, Provo leader Roel van Duijn had a feeling that something was wrong when he had to spend two weeks in jail because of his use of inflammatory language in the paper *Provo*. To his surprise, he noticed that the movement was popular among his "cell mates, burglars, people with whom I felt I had very little in common."[3]

Provo, the poster movement of the 1960s, was primarily concerned with legitimizing the expanded limits on acceptable behavior. When problems arose from this expansion of the repertoire of acceptable behavior, they were dealt with by adding even more new, possible behaviors. That is how the Association of Law Violators came into being; the junkies began to press their demands via the Junkie Association; truants got the Truants Bus [q.v.], and Hell's Angels got a yearly subsidy.

The government was there to help its citizens—not to coerce them, to fine them, to exercise control over them or to hold them accountable. If its citizens did bad things, then the reasons for this had to be sought in their social conditions. Punitive measures were equated with treating the symptoms. "Opening a can of policemen" [q.v.] was proof of powerlessness. This is how the "socialization" of accountability and guilt gained momentum. More and more often the government picked up the bill for the consequences of undesirable behavior, while the idea of personal, moral responsibility crumbled. It seemed that, in the Netherlands, the "apologists" had come to power, the professional sympathizers, who were ready with an apology, an excuse, for every human failure. If a member of society did something that really should not be done, then he could not help it, and the government was not permitted to do anything about it.

While the apologists were on the advance, the officials, who of old had wielded the rod, retreated timorously. In every society there are professions that are held in low esteem, because those who practice them are busy with tasks that, while they are necessary, are viewed with revulsion by the populace. The tasks that are relegated to these "infamous professions" vary widely with the culture of the society viewing them. Sometimes it is the collection of trash and excrement; sometimes it is moneylending; often it is hangmen and whores. In the Netherlands in the 1960s and 1970s, it was the regulatory and oversight professions that came to stand in this "infamous" light. You did not want to have more of that sort of official than was absolutely necessary, and it was best if they did their jobs as unobtrusively as possible.

This led to a decision on 21 February 1968 by the Amsterdam Municipal Council—following the lead of Rotterdam and The Hague—to abolish the position of conductor on streetcars and buses. Practically the entire council was enthusiastic about the departure of the conductors. Only one deputy recalled their duty to maintain order: the Pacifist Socialist Party deputy Ten Brink, who raised the question of whether the driver, all by himself, would really be capable of dealing with the potential problems caused by "drunken passengers or other troublemakers."[4]

In the same period, during the construction of the Amsterdam subway, the new ideas about regulation and supervision were, so to speak, built into the project. The subway had to be "open," "integrated with the surrounding city." Narrow-minded arrangements such as checking tickets did not support that goal. Supervision of the platforms was placed in the hands of men behind monitors, somewhere behind bulletproof glass in a small office, which was well hidden by the architects, as if their "infamous" activities could not stand the light of day. This approach garnered appreciation: the designers were awarded the Merkelbach Prize, the architectural prize of the city of Amsterdam, in 1980.

In a few years, the Amsterdam subway had changed into a gruesome no-man's-land. One-half of the passengers were riding without paying, vandalizing the stations and the trains, using drugs and picking pockets. The other half subjected itself to this resignedly, but many preferred to avoid the subway instead. On the streetcars, too, riding without paying had become common practice. Only at the beginning of the 1990s were attitudes ripe for a reintroduction of the conductors.

FROM REGULATOR TO ADVISER

Before 1940, in the first movie theaters in Amsterdam the lights would regularly come on in the middle of the showing. Four men in uniform would walk along the rows, and everyone had to show their tickets. They were the entertainment-tax controllers, who were there to verify that the members of the audience were sitting in the seats to which their tickets [q.v.] gave them the right. At other times, the showing would be interrupted by people from the Movie Rating Board, firemen or policemen.[5]

Stern men in long leather coats is how people instinctively pictured these controllers. A half century later, the government's regulators have taken on a completely different attitude. That could be seen in 1995, for example, when the executives of the waste treatment company Tankercleaning of Rotterdam (TCR), were sentenced to prison. For ten years, the company had pumped huge amounts of poisonous waste right into the Maas River, without any questions being asked by the Ministry, the province, the regulatory organs or the inspection service. In the meantime, TCR had gotten an ISO certificate and 23 million guilders [± U.S. $11.5 million] in government subsidies. "Inspections, oversight and even investigations are always conducted with an assumption of good faith on the part of large companies," said the prosecutor during the trial. "Obviously, it has not yet dawned on civil service officials that companies and/or their directors are so sly, that everything you touch is doctored. What we have here is a trusting government."

In 1999 the European Commission issued a devastating report about two Dutch fat-processing plants that appeared to be mixing fat wastes from the sewers into animal food. Both firms had a Good Manufacturing Processes certificate. "Apparently this certificate does not mean anything at all," concluded the Commodity Board for Cattle, Meat and Eggs. "And the quality control of that certificate just as little."[6]

How can this trusting attitude among regulators and inspectors be explained? Many of them are caught in the "two-hats dilemma." There was perhaps a lot you could say about the stern men who entered the movie theater unexpectedly, but they had one thing going for them: they played an easily comprehensible role. In the 1960s and 1970s, the regulators began to feel that the "stern" aspect of their job was unpleasant or even "infamous." They were less quick to issue tickets, and when they had to, they preferred to do it over a cup of coffee. When I interviewed members of various oversight services in 1989, it turned out that a number of them had a distinct predilection for a citation with coffee. It seems that the Big Brother of the Netherlands enjoys a cup of coffee [q.v.].

The relationship between the inspector and the inspectee also underwent a change. All sorts of departments that had been set up to provide oversight and to inspect began to see their job more as one of giving advice. That was seen as a step forward toward "accommodation by negotiation" between adult citizens. At the same time, it was a step up for the officials it affected. By putting on their adviser's hat, the regulators were able both to make their job easier and to upgrade its social status.

"The adviser's hat is much better," said the chief of the field service of the Rotterdam Consumer Goods Inspection Service. "You get a pat on the back and you leave—but what's the effect? The danger is that you creep too far into the role of adviser, while the basis for your job is talking politely to the client about his responsibilities. . . . The desire to be seen as nice is greater now than it used to be. I always tell my testing specialists: 'I want to be seen as nice' is the beginning of letting yourself be bought off. . . . If you are nice first and then, all of a sudden, take hard action, that action is illogical from the point of view of both the inspector and the inspectee."[7]

The Netherlands can thank the period of prosperity, during which the government was busy distributing fun things [q.v.], for the advance of the apologists, for the idea that oversight is really something infamous and for the miraculous metamorphosis from inspector to adviser. In the second half of the 1970s, the government had to shift over to a fair distribution of things that were not as much fun, but the widespread expansion of the taboo on coercion within the culture of the government made the change difficult. In the interim period, the law and reality were bound together provisionally by the principle of the blind eye.

Turning a blind eye to things was more or less explicitly elevated to the level of policy in two areas: the environment and soft drugs. But it did not stop there. Not only did all sorts of government entities that dealt with these areas turn a blind eye to things, but also departments in completely unrelated corners of the government apparatus began to assume that turning a blind eye to things was apparently OK. All you had to do was recite the incantation of toleration. Repeat slowly after me: *"If I do not go along with this abnormal behavior just a little bit, then there is the chance that I will lose my grip on the affected party completely."* In the 1970s, this incantation was the Open Sesame of the Dutch welfare state. Every politician or leader who had problems with a difficult-to-deal-with deviation from the norms became a modern Ali Baba in front of Saint Peter's mountain [q.v.]. He mumbled his toleration incantation, the mountain opened in front of him and all the injustices, all the differences between fact and fantasy of the welfare state were shoved into the cave, after which the mountain discreetly closed again.

But in the 1980s, the cave began to bulge in an ugly way. There were cracks and holes in it, through which you could look inside. Close to the entrance you could see huge stacks of barrels with a skull and crossbones on them, the result of the decentralized oversight on compliance with environmental laws. There were a number of places where it seemed that local politicians had "tolerated" severe violations. The child pornography films and HIV-positive heroin-addict whores were stored in another cavern.

Wispy clouds of complaint came drifting out of a remote niche. It was the old women, who had pulled their hair out after their long-awaited homes had been squatted right out from in front of their noses by some big lummox. In the older districts of Amsterdam in the beginning of the 1980s, more than half of all the housing units that the city council had at its disposal for distribution were squatted when they became vacant, after which, with a few exceptions, they were "assigned" to the squatters.[8]

But luckily, there were also happy places in the cave. A little farther on, the cries of the old women were drowned out by the clinking of glasses. Here the fictitious WAO [q.v.] cases, who had been swept into the cave for years, were spending their time singing songs and telling tales of how they had been too smart for the Public Health Service. There was also a party going on in the lair of Hell's Angels, but you could not get in there as easily as you could in the WAO bar. The entrance was guarded by a sentry with a riot gun. Hell's Angels play an important role in international drug and weapon trafficking, but since 1980, the police have not dared to set foot in the lair again. The municipal government of Amsterdam has, however, faithfully paid them a subsidy of 20,000 guilders a year, furnished by the Department of Youth Activities.

By mumbling the toleration incantation in unison, not only did the exercise of leadership take a downhill path, but the threat of political apathy and social disintegration was raised. Increasingly, citizens have become dependent on corporations, stated H.G. van de Bunt in his inaugural speech "Organization Crime." Rampant violations of the law by scheming organizations can lead to the loss of trust in important social institutions. The sociologist Kees Schuyt comes to the same conclusion. According to him, it is possible to have a "half-hearted policy of both prohibition and permission," as long as it is "strictly and consequently implemented." If, however, as is the case in the Netherlands, "a half-hearted policy is implemented half-heartedly," then not only does the policy miss achieving its goal, but it creates an atmosphere of inequality and caprice.[9]

Whoever turns a blind eye to a problem can, up to a certain point, pretend that the problem does not exist. Blind-eye thinking was the path of least resistance in responding to the policy challenges that a shrinking welfare state presents. It was a failure. It impaired compliance with the norms. It undermined trust in the government and victimized many of those who are most dependent on government protection.

There is one area where the advantages of turning a blind eye to things appear to outweigh the disadvantages: where developments in individual lifestyles occur so quickly—quite often faster than they do abroad—that the legislation covering them cannot keep pace: sexuality, arrangements for living together, prostitution, abortion, soft-drug sales and use. These areas are discussed in Chapter 14 as the only ones in which an actual "fragmentation" of the norms is taking place.

THE 1990s

It is interesting that it was precisely the Dutch Left that so fervently defended the expansion of the taboo on coercion. The Left permitted itself to be caught in a double bind with regard to the government: it demanded rights and services on a large scale but cultivated a hostile image of the government when it came to responsibility and control. Even more interesting is the fact that the government reacted to this by taking an extremely unobtrusive stance in these areas. The government did not oppose the expansion of the taboo on coercion but went along with it and, in the end, became an important pioneer in this area.

In the 1980s, it became customary to see the relationship between the citizen and the government as one between a client and a commercial service provider. This comparison is valid for one aspect of the government's function: the actual delivery of services. As a sobriquet for the relationship between the government and the citizen as a whole—which includes policy making, implementation and evaluation—it is misleading. The customer, as we know, is always right. He is not a part of the store where he shops. Citizens, however, are a part of the government—they are the base of it. The government is, therefore, forced to make much greater demands of its citizens than store owners place on their customers. In addition, store owners do not have to decide on a customer-by-customer basis what the customer can buy, while the government has all sorts of criteria to separate its clients into groups, which define their right—or lack of it—to certain services. This is even more important in a welfare state, where the government's store has an unprecedentedly wide assortment of programs and services to offer its citizen-customers. In order to give everyone his due, the government-storekeeper will often have to be "customer-unfriendly."

The taboo on coercion reached its peak in the second half of the 1980s. After that, a new snag showed up. The PvdA [Labor Party—q.v.] came around after its defeat in the 1990 elections. The new, tougher positions initially applied to marginal groups like criminals and those defrauding welfare programs. Only later did the closed shops of the established interest groups come under fire, and oversight was also heightened in the stock market and the waste-processing and insurance industries.

In 1996—long after countries such as England and the United States already had them—the residents of the neighborhood of Abstede in the city of Utrecht formed a neighborhood watch. Together with the police they are going to keep the streets clear of aggressive young people. That same year, the Minister of Justice let it be known that "the time that young people just got a pat on the head, if they were involved in vandalism or petty theft is past." In 1999 the Council of Chiefs of Police declared that a fellow citizen's "boxing kids' ears" because they were "being obnoxious" can be justified.

There was a snag in the taboo on coercion for big people as well. The "purple" cabinet [a coalition of PvdA, D66 and VVD—q.v.] is running out of breath from opening cans of policemen, and is taking hits from the Parliament that it is not going fast enough. The number of detainees per inhabitant, which traditionally was one of the lowest in Europe, has doubled in the last ten years, thereby erasing this deficit in one fell swoop.

The police in the big cities have—in any event, verbally—shifted over to a zero-tolerance policy. "The officer on the street has to be strict and just," said the Chief of the Amsterdam Police, J. van Riessen, in 1998. Police officers in Amsterdam have to once again take a more "aloof" and a more "formal" attitude. They also have to learn to stick to the rules again, for example, when they are subjected to disrespect while "on duty," a criminal offense that has only been found in comic books since the 1960s. Beginning in 1999, every police office in Amsterdam had to write at least 1 citation a day. In 1998 the average number of citations per officer was 2.3 per year!

Social control is not a dirty word anymore. Closed-circuit television cameras are visible everywhere in the Netherlands, and after every violent incident, like the recent ones in the nightlife areas [q.v.], the authorities make a plea for even more cameras. Appeals for regulation and personal obligation are the order of the day even outside police and Ministry of Justice circles. There are also appeals for new forms of "censorship" on movies, television and the Internet.

Trendsetting politicians, both those in government and those in the opposition, are pleading for a return to political leadership. The PvdA caucus is studying resolutions to force the unemployed to accept a job or training and to force criminal junkies to kick the habit. A report by the CDA [Religious Coalition Party—q.v.] *New Paths, Solid Values* (1995), wants "more government in those places, where society has to be protected or where conflicting interests threaten to bring society to a standstill." The VVD [Liberal Party—q.v.] leader Bolkestein [q.v.] is pleading for government intervention to prevent concentrations of power in the media. Piet Reckman—the conscience of the Dutch Left in the 1970s and 1980s—is training policemen.

Even "turning a blind eye" is no longer holy. At the end of 1996, the cabinet published a paper entitled *Limits on the Blind Eye*: departments that turn a blind eye to things will, in the future, have to account for their actions to the people's representatives, the Office of the Budget or the ombudsman. Turning a blind eye to things because the regulations are difficult to enforce or because there are not enough resources to do so is "by definition, unacceptable."

The same newspapers that ten years ago saw the opening of every can of policemen as the dawn of the police state are now pleading for zero tolerance, heavier penalties and a police force with central leadership. On 21 July 1998, when the Netherlands was in the grips of a huge child pornography scandal, the editor in chief of the sedate *NRC Handelsblad* wrote, with barely concealed anger: "It is too often that the unparalleled Dutch culture of live and let live is used as a shield to defend the undesirable effects of it. But the reality of the situation is sobering. Yes: because of its liberal drugs culture, the Netherlands has become an important European producer and distributor of XTC. Yes: drug trafficking leads to murders. . . . Yes: because of its liberal policy on vice, the Netherlands has created a breeding ground for child pornography."

With this, the turnaround in public opinion making is as good as complete; but things are different with implementation. The administrative arrangements are strongly colored by the permissiveness of the last few decades. The "culture" of reticence with regard to supervision and oversight, both within the Establishment and among the public, is now drawing verbal fire, but real change in that area will take several more years.

NOTES

1. An interview in the *NRC Handelsblad*, 16 April 1988.

2. Aafke Steenhuis, "Wat Kok niet zegt" [What Kok Does Not Say], *TIJDschrift*, March 1996,   p. 4.

3. Roel van Duijn, *Provo, de geschiedenis van de provotarische beweging 1965-1967* [Provo: The History of the Provo Movement 1965-1967], Meulenhoff, Amsterdam, 1985.

4. *Gemeenteblad Amsterdam* [Municipal Record of Amsterdam], sec. 2, 1969, 5 February 1969 (the evening session).

5. Mariëlle Kempen, "Tuschinski en Royal in de jaren twintig" [Tuschinksi and Royal in the Twenties], *Ons Amsterdam* [Our Amsterdam], February 1996.

6. *de Volkskrant*, 24 June 1999.

7. Quoted in H. Vuijsje, *Lof der dwang* [In Praise of Coercion], Anthos, Baarn, 1989.

8. In 1981, the Amsterdam Housing Board (GDH) decided, except for the most extreme cases, to "legalize" all the squatters occupying housing units that the city council had at its disposal for distribution. The standards applied here deviated "strongly from the legal standards of the Woonruimtewet [Law on Housing]," declared director Jongejan. *Haagse Post*, 25 December 1982.

9. Kees Schuyt, "Het bleke mensbeeld van paars" [The Pale Portrait of Mankind by the Purple Coalition], *de Volkskrant*, 1 April 1996.

CHAPTER 2

The Ethnic Taboo

In January 1983 a number of welfare umbrella organizations, together with Utrecht University, organized a congress on "The Law and Racial Relations." There was also a women's working group, which reported (in somewhat condensed form) on a discussion between black and white women:

B: White women look for the problem somewhere else, with the blacks; they'll never find a solution that way.
W: Maybe that's because you are so busy with welfare work. Black women, on the other hand, speak from—maybe this is a strange way to put it, but I don't know another way to say it—the "position of a victim."
B: You can't show your solidarity, if you don't first look at yourself to see how free you are of racial conceptions and the like.
W: Black women have to take the lead. They know what pain is. White women only approach it, after all, intellectually.
B: I can't agree with you there. White women just have to take a look around themselves.
W: Can't the whites also have an opinion about the blacks' struggle?
B: I'll decide that for myself.

This tone was not exceptional in militant black circles of the time. The black researcher Philomena Essed, for example, let her white sisters have it: "What do you feel, when you sit (or have to sit!!) next to me, instead of next to a white woman, in a streetcar? Have you ever looked at my eyes? In my eyes? What kind of associations do you have, when you think about black women? Do you think that these are uncomfortable questions? Do you think that these are strange, unimportant questions? Do you shrug your shoulders, because you 'don't have anything against black women' and 'therefore' think that I'm being difficult?"[1]

Essed stated that the Netherlands was infected to the core with workaday racism: "The seat next to you in the streetcar that stays empty, while there are a number of people standing, is an everyday experience for us." Another crime-and-punishment preacher, Anet Bleich, knew about "the infamous empty seat in the streetcar next to passengers of color."[2] In 1977 Maja Daams took the trouble to investigate whether such statements were based on fact. She investigated the seating choice of white passengers on Utrecht city buses. Discrimination could not be demonstrated by her research. It seemed that white passengers, if they could choose, sat next to white passengers somewhat more often than next to black passengers, but this tendency was not statistically significant.[3]

When the stream of immigrants [q.v.] from the former colonies and from the Mediterranean area began, it appeared that the soil in the Netherlands was fertile ground for discrimination and racism. Reports of discrimination by people renting rooms, employers, housing associations and discos showed up, and they were confirmed in studies.[4] In 1969 and in the 1970s there were a number of outbreaks of anti-Moroccan and anti-Turkish riots in the old districts of the big cities. Virulent racism in the Netherlands produced fatal results: in 1976 the Turk Ibrahim Uysal was pushed into a canal in Amsterdam and drowned. In 1983 Kerwin Duinmeijer, of Antillean heritage, was murdered.

But, taken as a whole, the reaction was limited, when compared to the events in France and England and, later, also in Germany, where serious and widespread violence broke out.[5] In England, for example, between 1976 and 1983, 70 racially motivated murders were committed. The annual number of reports for racial violence for the whole of the Netherlands was lower than for some districts in London.[6] The smooth integration of 180,000 Dutch-Indonesians [q.v.] was an international success story.

In recent years, the number of incidents of racial violence and discrimination has unmistakably increased under the influence of the issues of asylum seekers, illegal aliens, *allochtoon* [q.v.] criminality and competition in the labor market. Nevertheless, the Netherlands continued to show up well in comparison to the rest of Europe. Racist politicians attract relatively few voters, Islamic fundamentalists can hardly get a foot in the door, real ghettos, of the kind found in France and the United States, do not exist.[7]

The tradition of Pillarization [q.v.] offered—both culturally and institutionally—a proven recipe for living with one another's deviate behavior: from a distance. With regard to the practice of religion and the availability of confessional education [q.v.], the immigrants could make use of the existing pillar structures and democracy by consultation [q.v.]. On the basis of the same tradition, they matter-of-factly took part in the general arrangements for social services, urban renewal and public housing. Because the majority of the housing park is rented by nonprofit organizations, the manner in which immigrants are housed in the Netherlands is, with the possible exception of Sweden, the best in Europe.[8]

This was all made possible as well because the Netherlands is a rich country. Serious tensions between ethnic groups could, effectively, be "bought off." This happened because the government implemented centrally agreed-upon policy principles. The question is whether this policy will be continued after decentralization and the spin-off of some government departments.

SPECULATING ON THE MARKET FOR RACISM

In addition to a relatively positive record in the area of ethnic relations, the Netherlands distinguished itself in the 1970s and 1980s with a growing and expansive ethnic sensitivity. A strong tendency in official public opinion was to see racism as a life-threatening bacillus that was hiding in wait in each of us. Every critical statement or action that concerned a foreigner, even a pure reference to the difference, could give rise to a serious epidemic of racism. Decisive intervention was, therefore, prescribed at the earliest stage; even though it seemed like a minor complaint, a generous amputation was, however, the safest treatment.

The "bacillus idea" was tersely described by Anet Bleich in her book *Dutch Racism* (1984). According to her, there was a "wave of racism" coursing through the Netherlands. It was growing rapidly and openly. Bleich defended the assumption that "the complaint about 'yoos' [q.v.] poor upkeep of the stairwell, and the gas chamber [q.v.], were two extremes of a single racist universe, and that there is a logic in racist thought and deed that, in principle, leads from a little to a lot."

For the government, the threat of racism became a source of concern and for care. The taboo on racism increased in intensity and expanded to become the cornerstone of official morals. This intensification produced desirable results. The strong taboo on racism and discrimination seemed to work as a buffer against the extreme Right. Antidiscrimination initiatives were also more strongly anchored in legislation and regulations than in other European countries.[9] The Netherlands was the first West European country where resident aliens can vote for, and be elected to, municipal councils—after five years of residence. But the expansion of the ethnic taboo resulted in unforeseen dangers. The "expanded" taboo, in some respects, promoted exactly what people wanted to avoid. Immigrants were stereotyped, because they, even when they did not want to be, were treated, first and foremost, as members of an ethnic group, dependent on state care and assistance policy.

The ethnic Dutch were also stereotyped as latent racists. They found themselves presented with a double bind: they had to respect "diversity" at any price, but, at the same time, they could hardly let it be noticed that they saw anything different at all. Mayor van Thijn—himself an important proponent of this political correctness—found out just how hard this was when he opened the Prinsenhof conference on racism in 1984. His speech began: "Citizens of Amsterdam and new citizens of Amsterdam . . .," whereupon he was drowned out by booing from the audience. Wrong: there is only one kind of citizen of Amsterdam. He had been confronted by an extreme sensitivity, which perceives any mention of a difference, no matter how well intended, as objectionable.

By stimulating the mutual formation of stereotypes, ethnic difference became a much more loaded concept than was justified by reality. "White" and "Black"—in the Netherlands artificial labels for heterogeneous groupings that overlap each other in a number of ways—were presented as coherent entities that, by definition, were antagonistic to one another.[10] Friction and conflicts between members of these groupings were not viewed as something that could be resolved by consultation and tact but as an expression of a deep-rooted contradiction that permeated the whole of society. Instead of the open forms of personal interaction that could serve as the yeast of a "multicultural society," the result was guarded and self-conscious behavior. Under these conditions, effective policy instruments aimed at combating specific instances that disadvantaged someone could not get off the ground.

What the government's concern about ethnic minorities did do was lead to the establishment of a vast network of welfare organizations—a separate branch of industry in which "business representatives" competed with each other for influence, position and money. Lots of money, because the government was prepared to reach deep in its pockets to compensate for feelings of guilt and to avoid problems. If the minorities network was a "business," then racism was its most important raw material. The more racism a business representative or fighter of racism could "claim," the greater his market share. In the Netherlands, however, there are very few incidents of overtly virulent racism. There was, therefore, a very strong demand for a product that was in short supply on the market. This created ideal conditions for a real speculative boom in feelings of guilt. It was a golden opportunity for anyone who could, nevertheless, supply racism, for example, by detecting it before it came to the surface. Prospectors went out in search of hidden veins of this valuable raw material and, at the slightest suspicion, staked their claim on a vein of racism.

Up until the 1980s, when other welfare organizations had already had the thumbscrews applied to them, the minorities' industry continued merrily on its way. There was no control. Cases of mismanagement were overlooked. Its chaotic structure was not addressed, and its budget kept on climbing. Within the soft sector, the representatives of the minorities' industry held out longer than the others. They could press the hot button of the Netherlands: the national sensitivity to ethnic issues.

Under this pressure, when the ethnic Dutch had to deal with immigrants, there was a great temptation to bend over backward to conform to the taboo, just to be on the safe side. The ways in which they did this point to a case of "anomie": a short circuit between cultural goals and the available forms of behavior. When goals and resources clash, people turn to divergent strategies to keep their confusion and uncertainty to a minimum.[11] Officials whose work brings them into contact with immigrants demonstrate a number of reactions typical of anomie. One of them is to retreat to a rigidly formal approach. This can make ethnic clients the victims of a sort of permanent, strictly-by-the-book strike. I came across an example of this in 1985, when I was doing an article on ethnically mixed bridal couples in Amsterdam. "Our wedding at City Hall really wasn't so nice," said a Moroccan groom whose bride was Dutch. "The justice of the peace didn't say more than a couple of words. He didn't say anything about Morocco. He only read the name of the city where I was born. I'd have liked it, if he had said something more about it. I thought that it was a bit dry."

In the Netherlands, especially in Amsterdam, a justice of the peace who performs marriages is expected to be a kind of master of ceremonies. The justice of the peace will often make a joke about the heritage or place of birth of the bride or the groom. But I seldom, if ever, heard jokes like these directed at the "ethnic" half of the bridal couple. The "front rank of tolerance," as Mayor van Thijn was pleased to call the civil servants in direct contact with ethnic minorities, approached them coolly in suits of armor.[12]

A second reaction typical of anomie is not holding immigrants to the same standards as others are held to. This can result in spontaneous "positive discrimination," for example, for ethnic store owners who do not have a permit or ignore closing times, ethnic cafés that disturb the peace, or ethnic truants. In fact, each of these instances is an act of desperation by an individual civil servant. In this case, too, the "broad" taboo produces the opposite result of the one intended: this sort of positive discrimination plays into the hands of negative stereotyping.

A third variant of a reaction typical of anomie and perhaps the most tried and tested, is simply avoiding confrontation. If we imagine that there is a social minefield between ethnic groupings, where the smallest misstep can lead to an explosion of racism, then it is safer just not to cross it. In this manner, a "broad" ethnic taboo can result in spontaneous "apartheid," a preference for sitting next to one of your own on a bus, for example.

At school, this fear impedes the contact between the teachers and *allochtoon* parents. The positive effects of a home visit by the teacher are indisputable, but for the teacher, it is an extra effort and a risk. He has to embark on a trip to a "foreign area," where people can hardly speak Dutch and, in the first place, may not react positively to his arrival and where it is easy to say something wrong.

CHANCES FOR *ALLOCHTOONS*

When the "guest workers" [q.v.] from the Mediterranean periphery arrived, the idea was to give their children lessons in "their own language and culture," because they would need this knowledge when it was time for them to return to their countries of origin. Instruction was provided during normal school hours, while the cheeseheads [q.v.] were busy with such typically Dutch subjects as math and language arts.

When it became clear that most of the "guest workers" were really immigrants, this only seemed to produce a change in the argumentation used to support providing instruction to preserve their cultural heritage. Immigrant children first had to develop skills in their own language and to feel securely rooted in their own culture before they would have a chance of success in Dutch society. This 180-degree turn in circumstances, with no change in policy for this area, was one of the most important feats of the minorities' industry. Appealing to the interests of minorities managed to persuade the outside world, the donor organizations, and themselves of this, thereby securing a continuation of their work and positions.

In the meantime, in the *Report on Minorities 1993*, the Social and Cultural Planning Bureau established that "a heavy accent on the student's cultural identity" can further reduce the effectiveness of school. The "already limited time that there is in school for improving results in the core subjects" is further reduced by "competition" with classes on the student's own culture. Study showed that there was no positive effect at all from instruction in the student's own language and culture on the results for Dutch language and other subjects. In the meantime, it has become clear that the learning shortfall for *allochtoon* children is, to a great degree, caused by the shortfall in their Dutch language skills.[13]

This awe for the student's own identity also meant that the teachers did little to combat the great increase in truancy, especially among *allochtoon* students. The taboos on coercion and on the invasion of privacy worked against that. Could you truly apply Dutch standards to children from another culture? An experiment in the 1980s at vocational schools showed that an effective antitruancy policy is possible. By applying uniform, immediate and systematic control, the number of truants was reduced by one-third. The hard-core truants reduced their truancy by one-half. The initial huge differences in the truant behavior of *allochtoon* and ethnic Dutch students disappeared.[14]

According to Z. Berdowski, who studied school absences in Amsterdam, a strict and consistent approach is the only way to get the cooperation of Turkish and Moroccan parents. "You cannot expect that they will just throw their own standards overboard. A father who keeps his grown daughter at home because he does not want her to be in a class with boys, therefore, has to be forced to comply. . . . If the teacher, on the other hand, continues to show understanding for absences, you cannot hold it against the parents, if they keep their child at home."[15] The same complaint, according to Berdowski, can be made against municipal truant officers, who have to ensure that the Compulsory Education Act is well enforced. "If a child does not come to school for a week and it takes six months for the truant officer to whom it is reported to react, then people at the school will also begin to think that it is senseless to report the absences. . . . I think that you cannot tolerate these kinds of absences from the very beginning. If a child does not go to school, then, as truant officer, you have to make it clear that you will come pick up the child. If necessary, you put a uniform on somebody and put a hat on his head."

The Compulsory Education Act has enough sanctions to make truants toe the mark, but in practice, they were seldom used: in 1992 the truant officers in the judiciary district of Breda wrote up 97 tickets for truancy, and in Amsterdam not even half as many. In The Hague it was a total of 2. In those few cases in which fines were levied, most of them were not collected. Where did this nonenforcement come from? In making the decision whether or not to do anything about truancy, every truant officer and every school was on its own. In the 1980s many tasks in the area of education were decentralized. The Ministry bothered itself less and less with the municipalities; the municipalities, less and less with the submunicipalities; the submunicipalities, less and less with the truant officer and with the school; the school board, less and less with the instructor.[16] With a series of shifts in responsibility such as this, the man or the woman at the end of the chain of responsibility can hardly be expected to be a sort of Lone Ranger who gallops into the blackboard jungle to restore law and order and to grab truants by the scruff of the neck.

It was not until the mid-1990s that time was right for a change. More and more cities are replacing the Truants Bus with a tit-for-tat policy. In 1994 the Compulsory Education Act was made stricter: children 12 and older and their parents can be prosecuted for missing school. There is now a special truant prosecutor in each judicial district. On one day in 1996 in Arnhem, 9 Turkish couples were fined up to a thousand guilders [±$500.-] each for keeping their children out of school. (Of all the students in Arnhem who were truant in 1995, 90 percent were *allochtoon*.) In the same year, the police in Amsterdam-West [a heavily *allochtoon* district of the city] began picking up truants off the street.

Truancy often leads to dropping out of school. Nineteen percent of Moroccan boys drop out of high school compared to only 5 percent of ethnic Dutch boys. Once they are on the street, many of these dropouts end up in the crime and drug circuits.

The fact that Moroccan boys account for a relatively large part of the petty crime in the big cities was anxiously left unpublicized for a long time. The same was true of the fact that a quarter of all the young people in custody in judicial institutions were of Moroccan descent.[17] Kees Loef, a municipal researcher, compiled the first report about the activities of Moroccan gangs in downtown Amsterdam. Mayor van Thijn refused to publish it. A gag order was placed on the researcher, and he was harassed with telephone calls that made him out to be a racist and a redneck.[18] This also kept it from being possible to outline an effective policy of assistance and prevention tailored to the specific background of young Moroccans.

The Netherlands offered young *allochtoons* an antiracist subsidy and classes in their own language and culture, but measures to increase their participation in school and in the job market and to open ways out of a life of crime were not forthcoming. In the early 1990s, things became more open, but by then it was too late for part of the second generation. They had had the bad luck to be at the crossroads of Dutch taboos: the ethnic taboo combined with the taboos on the invasion of privacy and government coercion.

Adult *allochtoons* also have trouble finding work. In the 1980s, the decade of "Minorities' Policy," *allochtoon* unemployment increased sharply. The numbers are two and a half times higher than for the ethnic Dutch, and for Turks and Moroccans it is even five times higher. *Allochtoon* unemployment in the Netherlands is higher than in the surrounding countries, almost twice as high as in Germany, for example.[19]

Adults also had to deal with considerable ethnic reticence. For them, every pressure or encouragement to acclimatize to Dutch society was rejected out of hand. When they chose acclimatization themselves, for example, by registering for a Dutch language course, they often ran into problems. In June 1992 there were 11,000 people—of whom 80 percent were foreigners—on the waiting list for a Dutch language course. The Ministers of Education and Domestic Affairs came up with an "action plan" that would eliminate the waiting lists within a year. The municipalities got more than a hundred million guilders [$50 million] plus the responsibility for implementation. Since then, the number of those waiting has grown to 13,000: the demand is increasing faster than the supply is growing. In Amsterdam in 1994, there were four times as many adults waiting for a Dutch language course as there were places. For those with little education, the percentages are even worse. In Amsterdam there are no more than 1,500 places available each year for those with little education. [20]

The fact that the Netherlands is not covered with a network of language schools where every immigrant can learn our national language for free is indicative of the manner in which the *allochtoon* problem is dealt with. While a speculative boom was under way in the minorities' industry, and neither costs nor effort was spared in the fight against workaday racism, the Dutch welfare state was apparently not able to get something so essential and simple as language study for immigrants off the ground.

The taboos on acclimatization and government coercion prevented the central government from making a clear choice and taking over control of the program. This effect was increased in the 1980s by the decentralization and the spin-off of government organizations. Every municipality, every organization had to decide for itself if and how language instruction would be offered to immigrants. Instead of a national network, a maze of organizations was created in which not only the clients, but the civil servants as well could lose their way.

THE IMMIGRANTS HAVE HAD ENOUGH

In 1970 the splinter labor party DS'70 [q.v.] pleaded for a restrictive admission policy for immigrants. That resulted in the party's being accused of racism. When, at the end of the 1970s, the researcher Marlene de Vries proposed not to offer any assistance in finding a job to foreigners who refused to learn Dutch, she was made out to be the "new Hitler" inside the minorities' world. The Socialist Party, which, in 1983, proposed to give departing migrants a bonus, was accused of the "de facto advancement of xenophobia."

In the late 1990s all the proposals listed earlier were instituted. Government support for immigrants to their countries of origin is not disputed; open immigration is no longer a topic of discussion. Beginning in 1997, all newcomers are legally required to take a citizenship course, under penalty of a fine or a 20 percent reduction in their welfare payments. The government wants lessons in the student's own language, henceforth, to take place after normal school hours. Criminality among immigrants can now be called what it is, and specific strategies can be sought to prevent it.

In 1999 the government announced that, in order to combat the disproportionately high crime rate and increasing marginalization of young *allochtoons*, it would put more pressure on their integration. The government concluded that the decentralized approach had not worked and that a new, nationwide minorities policy is needed. This includes the central registration of truants and the monitoring of school dropouts.[21]

Word usage is also becoming less constrained. Jan Kuitenbrouwer points to the rehabilitation of the word "Negro." "Nice schoolgirls talk about their 'Negro boyfriend.' . . . In the meantime, the word 'Negro' has apparently done its time and the word has been let out on probation for good behavior."[22] Even the wariness about Zwarte Piet [Black Peter - q.v.] is beginning to wear down. There is a temps agency in Amsterdam that provides Negro Black Peters around Sint Nikolaas time.

The new "snag" in the ethnic taboo is often attributed to the shock therapy introduced by the VVD leader Bolkestein in 1991. Certainly, just as important was the awakening of the immigrants themselves, who slowly but surely have had enough of the role of victim and noble savage that was forced on them. On their way from pity to self-respect, they began to strike out at the "expanded" taboos. In 1992 Ruben Gowricharn, a sociologist and economist from Surinam, reacted against the obligatory concept that the problems of immigrants are a result of the racism of the Dutch. In his book *Despite Knowing Better*, he said that this concept is based on an axiomatic assumption rather than on a scientifically founded conclusion. Coming from a country where nobody speaks guardedly of cultural differences, Gowricharn noted, to his surprise, that in the Netherlands, culture and people are supposed to be equal. If immigrants do things that are just not done, then external factors will immediately be used to explain and legitimize their behavior. Those involved are, by definition, "discouraged, discriminated against, hampered by government organizations, negatively influenced by their social surroundings, sick, too old, or use fraud in an attempt to counteract the effects of long-term unemployment on their self-esteem."

In January 1999 this "apologetic" inclination was vividly illustrated when two Dutch girls were shot dead by a group of Turkish boys. The parents of the murdered girls [q.v.] appeared on television, and their reaction there was one of surprising reticence. There was no anger or indignation, only sorrow and resignation. It seemed almost to be an act of God instead of a murder. The parents did their best to declare that they did not blame the Turkish community. It appeared that they were not the ones who needed to be consoled, but the Turkish community. Nonetheless, the crime rate among Turks is three to five times higher than among the Dutch. In 1997 Turks made up 7 percent of the perpetrators of first- and second-degree homicides, while Turks make up only 1.5 percent of the population of the Netherlands.[23]

Criticism of this whitewash attitude is also growing among the *allochtoons* themselves. In 1992 imam Bouyejrar, the spiritual leader of the largest Moroccan mosque in Amsterdam, made the short, but powerful statement that for Muslims, learning Dutch was "a categorical duty." More than 80 percent of the *allochtoons* agree with him and think that new immigrants should be required to learn Dutch.[24] In November 1995 Saïd Bouddouft and Halim El Madkouri, staff members of the Moroccan and Tunisian Cooperation Association, sounded the alarm about the continually strengthening grip of the drug cartels on Moroccans in the Netherlands. They wrote that criminals from the drug world have taken over positions in the boards of directors of mosques and welfare organizations. "Keeping silent about it, only makes it worse. . . . If no steps are taken, a large number of the young Moroccans are threatened with disappearing in the drugs circuit for good." What steps? Investment in education and jobs, says El Madkouri. But first of all, "the police have to take stronger action. . . . It has to be made difficult for the criminals. An end has to be put to turning a blind eye."[25]

Turkish immigrants are also beginning to revolt against the prohibition on hanging out their dirty laundry in public. Drug trafficking in the Turkish and Kurdish communities "has taken on an aspect of seriousness," stated former welfare worker Hassan Kaynak at the beginning of 1996 in the *NRC Handelsblad*. Drug dealers hardly ever or never get disapproving reactions from the community, and because of that they are threatening to become successful role models for the younger generation. "Even though the Turkish and Kurdish community is not collectively responsible for the increased drug trafficking, it can certainly collectively make a contribution to combating it."

In some areas, the change, which has finally gotten under way, is moving so fast that there is the threat of an overreaction. That is why asylum seekers from countries like Iran, Zaire and Iraq are being sent back to their country of origin. If they cause a problem, a private firm comes to Schiphol [q.v.] to help give them a tranquilizing injection. Whoever thinks about this for just a little while gets a good picture of the speed with which public opinion in the Netherlands can change, when the time is ripe.

While the Netherlands was mobilizing for battle with the racism bacillus, social problems and deprivation continued to grow rampant. This is how the paradox of the Netherlands' good reputation in the area of racism, but the poor social prospects for *allochtoons*, came into being. The government promoted relatively peaceful racial relations in the Netherlands by "handing out" things. When, however, it came down to prescribing and requiring, the government dodged the issue.

W.G.C. Mijnssen, for many years a public prosecutor for discrimination cases, has an explanation for this paradox. In his practice, he noticed that many judges were primarily concerned with what the person who allegedly committed the discrimination "intended." "We spend comparatively less time looking at how it is perceived by the person at whom it was directed. During the last few decades, the 'intention' has been elevated to a higher and higher level." The reason behind this is, according to Mijnssen, the fact that World War II has not been brought to closure. "People sincerely feel that it really is bad for the victims, but instinctively place the question of whether the perpetrator is 'good' [q.v.] or not at the top of the list."[26]

This preoccupation with the "intention" made it risky to view ethnic groups as separate categories, let alone to make them the object of a specific policy. This had a crippling effect. In a number of respects, good intentions brought about the things that they should have prevented.

NOTES

1. Philomena Essed, "Racisme en feminisme" [Racism and Feminism]. In *Socialisties-feministiese teksten* [Socialistic-Feministic Texts], 7, Sara, Amsterdam, 1982.

2. Anet Bleich, Peter Schumacher, et al., *Nederlands racisme* [Dutch Racism], Van Gennep, Amsterdam, 1984, p. 10.

3. Maja Daams, "Naast wie zal ik nu eens gaan zitten?" [Now Who Should I Sit next To?]. In Frank Bovenkerk (ed.), *Omdat zij anders zijn, patronen van rasdiscriminatie in Nederland* [Because They Are Different: Patterns of Race Discrimination in the Netherlands], Boom, Meppel, 1978.

4. See, for example, Frank Bovenkerk and Elsbeth Breuning-Van Leeuwen, "Rasdiscriminatie en vooroordeel op de Amsterdamse arbeidsmarkt" [Race Discrimination and Prejudice on the Amsterdam Labor Market], and Willeke Bolle, Henk van Dijk and Dieke Hetebrij, "Discriminatie bij het verhuren van kamers aan gastarbeiders" [Discrimination in Renting Rooms to Guest Workers]. Both in Bovenkerk (ed.), 1978.

5. F. Bovenkerk, K. Bruin, L. Brunt and H. Wouters, *Vreemd volk, gemengde gevoelens, etnische verhoudingen in een grote stad* [Strange People, Mixed Feelings: Ethnic Relations in a Large City], Boom, Meppel/Amsterdam, 1985, Chapters 6, 7.

6. Frank Bovenkerk, "Minderheden in Engeland: het zwarte antwoord" [Minorities in England: The Black Reply], *Intermediair*, 30 November 1984.

7. In the last few years there have been indications that employers in the Netherlands discriminate more than in other countries. M. Gras and Frank Bovenkerk repeated an experiment that had been done 20 years ago, in which two applicants would respond to a help-wanted advertisement: one "ethnic" and one Dutch applicant. In all other respects the two candidates had the same

background and qualifications. For low and midlevel positions, it appeared that the ethnic applicant did not have a chance in 35 percent of the cases. This "discrimination score" is almost twice as high as it was twenty years ago and twice as high as it presently is in Germany. M. Gras et al., *Een schijn van kans, twee empirische onderzoekingen naar discriminatie op grond van handicap en etnische afkomst* [The Illusion of Opportunity: Two Empirical Investigations of Discrimination on the Basis of Handicap and Ethnic Descent], Gouda, Quint, Arnhem, 1996.

8. Barbara Schmitter Heisler, "De Nederlandse ervaringen op de hobbelige weg naar een multiculturele sameleving" [The Dutch Experience on the Bumpy Road to a Multicultural Society], *Migrantenstudies* [Migration Studies], 1995, nr. 1. pp. 73/74.

9. Since the Algemene Wet Gelijke Behandeling [General Equal Treatment Act] came into force in 1994, the Netherlands is the "star" of Europe in this area, said the legal sociologist Cees Groenendijk at the Congress of European Democratic Lawyers in Munich on 11 May 1995.

10. This antagonism, strongly encouraged by segments of the business of defending minorities, was based on the assumption that black is everyone who is not completely white. This was precisely the way of thinking that was the foundation of racism in the American Deep South: prejudice of origin. Those who thought in terms of black or white had, in fact, taken over the approach of the racists. The sociologist Hoetink pointed out that, in America, this contrast is, in a certain sense, real. A colored middle class has long been unrecognized there. In Caribbean society, where a segment of the Dutch minorities come from, there is much less talk of this dichotomy. The prejudice that exists there is based on a number of shades of white or black: prejudice of mark. "This dichotomy only comes into existence when they get here," stated Hoetink in an interview in the *NRC Handelsblad* (2 January 1986). He warned of the danger that "a dichotomy would be created that, in practice, does not exist at all."

11. The concept of "anomie" was introduced by Durkheim (*Le Suicide*, 1897) and later developed by Robert K. Merton. The strategies for adapting to anomie are inspired by Merton's typology of forms of adaptation. See his *Social Theory and Social Structure*, Free Press, Glencoe/New York/London, 1949, 1957, 1968.

12. Willemijn Bos and Herman Vuijsje, "Trouwen, een verschil als uitdaging" [Getting Married: Difference as a Challenge], *Avenue*, April 1985. In abridged form, reprinted in Herman Vuijsje, *Vermoorde onschuld, etnisch verschil als Hollands taboe* [Innocence Murdered: Ethnic Difference as a Dutch Taboo], Bert Bakker, Amsterdam, 1986.

13. M. Weide, *Effectief basisonderwijs voor allochtone kinderen* [Effective

Grade School Education for Allochtoon Children], GION, Groningen, 1995, Sociaal en Cultureel Planbureau, *Rapportage Minderheden* 1996 [Report on Minorities], SCP/VUGA, Rijswijk/The Hague, 1996.

14. M. Mutsaers and L. Boendermaker, *Criminaliteitspreventie in het onderwijs, eerste deelexperiment: spijbelcontrole* [Crime Prevention in School, the First Partial Experiment: Truancy Control], WODC, Ministry of Justice, The Hague, 1990.

15. Interviewed in Remco de Jong, "De absolute verzuimers" [The Hard-Core Truants], *Het Parool*, 5 October 1991. It is conceivable that such a clear requirement would be silently applauded by some Islamic parents. Many of them feel bound by the norms of their group that decree that their daughters be kept home from school on certain occasions. Even if they feel differently about this inside, it is difficult to violate this norm. This changes if they can counter the other members of their faith with reference to clear "information" from government channels that truancy will not be tolerated. A comparable situation could exist among the members of the Orthodox Reformed Church, who reject vaccination against infectious disease. More and more of them are having their children vaccinated secretly in another village. A clearly communicated and consequently enforced vaccination requirement for polio would perhaps be welcomed with a sigh of relief by many Orthodox Reformed Church parents.

16. Herman Wigbold has pointed out that this pass-the-buck system can lead not only to indifference but also to the consideration of interests that are hostile to the students: violence at school and truancy are sometimes overlooked out of a fear that jobs will be lost. Herman Wigbold, *Bezwaren tegen de ondergang van Nederland* [Objections to the Fall of the Netherlands], De Arbeiderspers, Amsterdam, 1995, p. 145.

17. Scientific Research and Documentation Center of the Ministry of Justice, research report *Jongeren in justitiële behandelinrichtingen* [Young People in the Care of Judicial Institutions], The Hague, 1995.

18. Kees Loef, *Marokkaanse bendes in de Amsterdamse binnenstad* [Moroccan Gangs in Downtown Amsterdam], gemeente Amsterdam, 1988. See also *HP/De Tijd*, 22 September 1992.

19. Sociaal en Cultureel Planbureau, *Sociale en Culturele Verkenningen 1994* [Social and Cultural Investigations], SCP/VUGA, Rijswijk/The Hague, 1994, pp. 102-105. Tesser, 1993, *NRC Handelsblad*, 23 March 1996.

20. Z. Berdowski and E. van Schooten, research report *Waar een wil is en geen weg* [Where There's a Will and No Way], Bureau O+S of the municipality of Amsterdam/SCO-Kohnstamm Instituut, University of Amsterdam, 1995.

21. *Criminaliteit en integratie van etnische minderheden* [The Crime Rate for

and the Integration of Ethnic Minorities], report of the Ministers of Internal Affairs and of Justice, November 1999.

22. Jan Kuitenbrouwer, "Zwart" [Black], *Het Parool*, 27 September 1995.

23. *Elsevier*, 30 January 1999.

24. Bureau Infomart commissioned by Nederlands Centrum Buitenlanders [Dutch Foreigners' Center] and IKON, research report *Allochtonen over Nederland* [*Allochtoons* on The Netherlands], January 1995.

25. Saïd Bouddouft and Halim El Madkouri in *Contrast*, the organ of the Nederlands Centrum Buitenlanders [Dutch Foreigners' Center], 16 November 1995, *NRC Handelsblad*, 6 February 1996.

26. Interview in *NRC Handelsblad*, 19 February 1994.

CHAPTER 3

From the Privacy Taboo to a Taboo on Intervention

In the 1960s, privacy and self-determination became positive values. Each individual must be able to develop without interference from others and without being treated like a child by the state. In 1983 the right of respect for an individual's private life was registered in Article 10 of the Constitution. In 1990 the Personal Public Records Act came into force, which precisely defined who, for what reason and under which circumstances, can stick his nose into which files with personal data.

In the 1970s and 1980s, privacy and self-determination began to play a role in more and more areas, which stretched the envelope of these concepts even further. Individual citizens had to be in charge not only of their own bodies and their homes but also of their interaction with others and with institutions and with government programs. Hand in hand with this rapid individualization came a strong tendency to screen off as much as possible of an individual's private life and to make it accessible to others only if it was absolutely necessary, or if it offered some advantage.[1] This position was greatly strengthened by a trend toward "orthodoxy" among ethicists and jurists, which gained considerable influence in the social, medical and judicial debate. No one could force citizens to surrender any of their privacy, especially not the government.

A "broad" privacy taboo like this is attractive for the individual citizen, but the social costs are high. Until 1994, an alleged murderer or rapist could refuse to allow samples to be taken for DNA testing under this taboo. A disproportionate part of the social cost was paid by those who were not "assertive" enough to turn noninterference to their advantage and by those who were the victims of noninterference. An example is the social worker who was raped in 1990 and requested access to the medical file of her rapist because of the possibility of HIV infection. The perpetrator would give his permission only if she would visit him in the prison clinic. She refused and had to be tested herself.

This is how the "individual's private life" was strengthened into a bastion that for others—even if they were acting in the name of the government or in the name of the ill or of victims—was almost unassailable. The liberating idea of respect for personal privacy of the 1960s expanded in the 1970s and 1980s to a broad taboo on intervention. After a while, all the entreaties for anti-interventionism became trapped between our ears. As a result, the ideological goal of the freedom not to be treated like a child by the government gradually turned into a personal fear of any form of intervention without our noticing it. Public interference or admonition by strangers is nowadays quickly felt to be a form of unwelcome intimacy.

This is another case of "paradoxical continuity": what began as a movement for individual emancipation changed unnoticed into a pure and simple instrument for the advancement of self-interest. This trend fitted perfectly into the trend toward fewer rules, less government, less central intervention. The greatest common denominator of all the buzzwords and policy axioms of the last decades—self-determination, personal responsibility, decentralization, self-regulation, the spin-off of independent units, accommodation by negotiation—was a holy belief in nonintervention. To the accompaniment of the recitation of these maxims, Dutch citizens and politicians washed away old responsibilities into the cesspool of society.

JUST A LITTLE BIT MARRIED

You can still find them in the provincial papers, the personal ads of yesteryear, short and sober heartfelt cries like *Widow, 63, w/ own house, seeks nice man.* Sometimes there will be some extra information given as well, such as *Protestant* or *Not a dancer*, but, as a whole, the ad leaves but scant impression on the reader. What can you learn from this sort of text anyway? How can you decide, on the basis of it, if you will hit it off, even a little bit, with this widow?

The modern reader needs more data to determine what kind of pig is in the poke. Nowadays, a widow who places an ad like this often wants to say so much at once that, out of desperation, she stammers out a list of keywords. Back then, you did not need lists like that to be able "to place" one another. The keywords were there already. Widow, Protestant, man, dancer—those were the keywords in the time that the personals were still marriage ads. But today, if you lived together [q.v.] for 20 years without being married, and your partner has died, can you then call yourself a "widow"? If your primary religious activity consists of writing a check for the church's medical mission and a visit to the Christmas service, are you still Protestant?

The blurring of the tried-and-true category criteria brought about major problems for the government. It cannot really begin to implement a policy without dividing its citizens into clearly defined categories. The government is, says Kees Schuyt, in "digital" communication with its citizens. For the government, people and situations either are something or they are not. But reality, as it is experienced by an individual, is, to a great degree, "analog": diffuse, all encompassing and interwoven with feelings.[2]

The leadership is panting as it runs behind an ever more divergent social reality, trying to get a grip on it with nets, which have smaller and smaller holes. It gets even more out of breath due to the obstacles that it encounters on its way. If welfare programs are more and more precisely targeted at a more and more finely woven net of reality, then you aren't there yet. You also have to figure out where each citizen "belongs" in that extensive conglomeration of square and round holes. In doing that, you cannot trust the information that citizens make available about themselves. Nowadays the decision to get married, to get divorced, to live together or to say that that is what you are doing has less to do with romance than with taxes and rent subsidies. If, as a government, you want to be able to use your net effectively in this situation, then you need to know more and more about those involved. Just like the reader of a personal ad, nowadays the government has to have a whole series of keywords to be able "to place" someone.

The problem is that citizens see their relationship with the government differently than lonely gentlemen see their relationship with a merry widow. While the government needed to know more and more, for more and more reasons, the citizens found it less and less self-evident that an anonymous government department should enter their private lives with impertinent questions. Even the holders of Personal Public Records became more reserved when it came to making their data available. The next obstacle was that the government could not use the data that it received efficiently. Advanced methods of data collection, processing and collation were already widely available in the 1980s, but their application was held up by a broad sense of distrust by the public.

In the last few decades, the accumulation of information about citizens has become both more necessary and, in a number of aspects, more difficult for the government. The expansion of the right to privacy formed a serious barrier to the accomplishment of certain governmental tasks. An important role was played by the memory of a period in which the government misused personal data in the most brazen way: the war.

"THE WESTERBORK [q.v.] SYSTEM AND THE CENSUS OF 1971"

On 16 January 1941 Dr. Hans Böhmcker, the representative in Amsterdam of the German Reich's commissioner, Seyss-Inquart [q.v.], summoned the head of the Municipal Registry Office, Sydzes, and gave him the assignment of inventorying all the Jewish households, businesses and institutions in the capital. On 20 January, Sydzes began accumulating the data. The Municipal Register determined which districts were primarily Jewish. The estimate of the percentage that Jewish households formed in each district was made in cooperation with the Housing Service. For the percentage of Jewish businessmen, the Trade Registry was called in. The Department of Education provided an overview of the schools in the affected districts. The Department of Public Health and Social Support inventoried the data on the Jewish hospitals, poorhouses, old age and nursing homes. The Open-Air Market Service made an alphabetical list of all the market salesmen in predominantly Jewish neighborhoods. The municipal Statistical Bureau processed all the data onto meticulous maps that showed the distribution of the Jewish population by street, by neighborhood and by district. This bureau, using the 1930 census as a base, also calculated the total number of Jews in Amsterdam: approximately 80,000. An excellent estimate, it later turned out.

By February Sydzes could deliver the requested data to Böhmcker. Even after that, the civil servants at the Amsterdam City Hall continued to supply the Germans—without the Germans having to ask for it—new data; old information was corrected and made more precise. That very spring, mandatory registration for Jews was announced. The Municipal Register took on 30 temporary civil servants to deal with the job. The personal data cards of the Jews were tabbed with the code J (full-blooded Jew), BI (bastard Jew with two full-blooded Jewish ancestors), or BII (bastard Jew with one full-blooded Jewish ancestor).

Thirty years later, on 28 February 1971, the 14th Dutch census was held. The census caused a heated debate on the potentially threatening effect it would have on privacy. Primarily in the left-wing media, this was accompanied time and time again by the drone of Nazi jackboots; witness the headlines in *Vrij Nederland* such as "THE DUTCH NOSES ARE BEING COUNTED" and "THE WESTERBORK SYSTEM AND THE CENSUS OF 1971." A poster that received widespread distribution, calling for people to refuse to cooperate with the census, carried this quote by Lucebert [q.v.]: "Before you know it, it's gone so far, then he'll carry a whip and he'll wear a Jewish star."

Cooperation with the census was compulsory. Those who refused faced a fine of 500 guilders or 14 days in jail. In the end, the percentage of those who refused to cooperate was 0.2—a sharp increase compared with the census of 1960 (when only two people refused), but in the light of all the propaganda, a negligible percentage.[3] It was, therefore, difficult to maintain that the census of 1971 was "a failure." Nevertheless, that was the impression—most of all, among policy makers—that remained. According to Overkleeft-Verburg, this "failure" had considerable consequences. "Not only did this discredit the census as a method for the collection of data for statistical purposes and planning, and eventually cause it to be done away with, but, as a consequence of these events, the establishment and use of a central data registry in our country remains taboo even today."[4]

The authorities quickly decided that for the next census in 1981, they would make a number of concessions to the criticism. Up until 1971, it was customary to use the census data to check the data in the municipal registries for accuracy and completeness. That practice was done away with in 1981. In 1971 there had also been the question of which Church you considered yourself to be a member of. This was a much "softer" formulation than had previously been used. Up until 1960, the question was one of matters of fact, like which Church you had been baptized in. Despite this, action groups spoke of an unknown invasion of privacy and of a potential threat to fundamental freedoms. The authorities gave in on this point as well. The dangerous question of religion would no longer be asked in 1981. This superfast capitulation ignored the fact that it terminated a category of data that was valuable to social researchers.

In 1979 a test census showed that 17 percent of the respondents refused to cooperate. This result produced a panic reaction in the Central Statistical Bureau (CBS), which had already been alarmed by the events of 1971. The combination of a census and the computer was clearly generating a great amount of fear and discomfort among the public. Was it at all possible to hold a successful census under these conditions?

The Central Commission for Statistics, which determines the working schedule of the CBS and which in 1978 had expressed a preference for an integral enumeration, a year later stated that a more limited arrangement would also be satisfactory. Still a year later, it advised the government to postpone the census and to make do with a series of subprojects. In justifying its decision, the commission named, among other things, "the preliminary findings of the public relations consultants that it had engaged" and "the numerous indications that had reached the CBS from the publicity campaigns."[5]

The census of 1981 was postponed and eventually canceled. In May 1991 the government repealed the Census Act, which ended a data series that had begun in 1829. The "expected limited readiness of the public" to participate played an important role in that decision. The existing "fear and discomfort" had, according to the government, "created a social-psychological climate that is unfavorable for the conduct of a general census." In the First Chamber [Senate], Finance Minister Andriessen spread it on even thicker: the basic Dutch data were so good and the statistics so clean that we really had "a tremendous headstart." When viewed in this light, the great expense of a census would be throwing money away. In addition, the repeal of the Census Act "fit in well with the Cabinet's policy aimed at deregulation."

In its annual report for 1991, the CBS performed a death-defying leap. The overly hasty capitulation to the census rebels was presented as a resounding success: "The Netherlands and Denmark are the only two countries in the EC [European Community] that no longer need a census." The CBS, with the government and Parliament in its wake, continued an old Dutch tradition: withdrawing before a rebellious rabble, even before a shot has been fired—the tradition of the burgomasters and commandant of Amsterdam, who in January 1795 [q.v.] turned power over to the Batavian Revolutionary Committee without being pushed or struck, of King William II, who, in the revolutionary year of 1848 [q.v.], in his own words, "changed from conservative to liberal in 24 hours," of the mayor of Rotterdam, Zimmerman, who in 1918, when Troelstra [q.v.] declared a revolution "by mistake," had already invited the local socialist leaders to City Hall to discuss an orderly handover of power, and of the Dutch authorities who sent the mayor of Amsterdam, Van Hall, home when the Provos began to clear their throats somewhat too loudly in the last revolutionary year of 1966.

The social researcher Peter van Hoesel calls the reaction of the CBS "almost spastic." "People were very afraid of the census. And if you behave that way yourself, then those around you will naturally react to that quite clearly." In the 1990s, even the veterans of the earlier battle were putting the commotion of that time into perspective. In hindsight, the whole panic was really somewhat exaggerated, says Jan Holvast of the Committee for Census Vigilance (after 1974, the Association for Personal-Public-Records Vigilance), one of the champions in the battle against the census. "Very little has come of the fear that a whole web of personal data files would be woven over our heads by computerization." "In hindsight, the census itself was not such a big deal. . . . But the suspicion was there." Even the NRC Handelsblad commentator, Frank Kuitenbrouwer, who heatedly participated in the discussion at the time, gives a mild assessment after the fact: "The census, I don't think it was that bad."[6]

"If you were to organize a census in the Netherlands now, I could well imagine that it would come off rather well," says Peter van Hoesel. The climate seems fit for it: in the 1990s, one database after the other was being collated without anyone's saying boo about it. But the census is still taboo, because if we were to introduce it again, what would all the commotion have been good for?

THE INCREASING NONRESPONSE

In the meantime, the Netherlands is the only European country that has stopped using a census as a method for the provision of statistical data under the influence of social protest. As an alternative for the census of the population and housing park in 1991, the CBS produced an integral enumeration based on municipal civil registries, together with education/housing statistics and sampling techniques.

A year after Minister Andriessen had praised them to heaven, the usefulness of the data from the municipal civil registries came into a questionable light. During the air crash disaster on 4 October 1992 at the Bijlmer high-rise apartment complex, Police Commissioner Nordholt categorized the municipal civil registry of Amsterdam as "completely worthless"[7] for determining the number and identity of the victims. The municipal civil registry had not been checked for correctness or completeness using census data since 1971. In the same two decades, a sort of phobia had grown up around keeping the civil registry in good shape and using it as the criterion for requests for legal rights. Reviewing and examining everything, checking changes of address, asking for an ID when someone registered, let alone going to look at someone's house, were only dangers to privacy.

After the Bijlmer disaster, the housing corporation that rented the apartments was of equally little help. As landlords, they could not ask impertinent questions, let alone check their data with outsiders, and, therefore, they had no idea how many people were illegally living in their apartments. Only by combining address lists from mail-order stores, sports clubs and family physicians' practices was it possible to get a picture of who was living in the Bijlmer apartments stricken by the crash. In the publicity surrounding the incident, the problem was placed at the door of unregistered illegal aliens. In fact, the problem was one of all sorts of calculating citizens who preferred not to have their house address widely known. Research in Amsterdam and Rotterdam shows that in certain neighborhoods, one-third of the houses and apartments are illegally occupied, primarily via sublet, which in many cases is coupled with frauds having to do with national assistance payments and rent subsidies.[8]

Not only are data from the municipal registry a poor alternative to a census, but so are sampling and questionnaires. Research of this type is based on samples and, therefore, can provide only general data. "Because smaller social groups are underrepresented in the samples taken, it will soon, for example, be impossible to localize the target groups of minorities policy and to determine the success or failure of the policy," said the economist Flip de Kam. According to him, only an integral enumeration of the populace and housing park provides the data to combat the deprivation of certain groups in certain districts. By no longer holding a census, the Netherlands falls "into the category of a third-world country" in the area of statistics.[9]

Sampling, compared with a census, has another great drawback. The fact that participation is not compulsory has dramatic consequences in the Netherlands: on the average, half of the respondents refuse to cooperate or cannot be reached. Little or nothing is known of the people who are "missed" in this way, and, "if you are collecting data for administrative reasons, the respondents will, in general, take that into account," says H. van Tuinen, the director of Social Statistics of the CBS. "And that can be a source of distortion." The high level of nonresponse, therefore, introduces an unknown type of selectivity, so that the reliability of the results cannot be improved by statistical methods.

The response to social-scientific research in the last 20 years has shown a disquieting decline. The response figures in the Netherlands are now noticeably lower than in the neighboring countries. "For most questionnaires, they are presently not above 60 percent," said CBS director Van Tuinen. P. de Guchteneire, head of the Steinmetz Archive, reports response figures of "less than 40 percent for general polls." These figures are disquieting, because the modern welfare state is exceptionally dependent on polling. In the Netherlands more than 90 percent of the contracts for social-scientific polling are let by the government.

The business sector also has a strong need for polling. In this context it is self-evident that the obverse of the delivery of services is the requirement to deliver information. Even the government can require its "clients" to provide personal data. In reality, the pollsters go from door to door with their hats in their hands, humbly asking for cooperation. If doors are slammed shut in their faces, then they do not react angrily or even sadly, nor are they persistent, but they are, rather, full of understanding. Just like the census protest, the nonresponse is treated respectfully as an indication of genuine concern about one's private life. This is how it came to be that a country with one of the most "citizen-friendly" governments that have ever existed has a widespread social distrust of the same government. The distrust—which hampered the government in its efforts to help its citizens—was perceived by the same government as an expression of social engagement and is consequently respected and honored.

According to Flip de Kam, three-quarters of the refusals have absolutely nothing to do with imaginary fears about privacy but with "motives that, in my eyes, are not valid: people are just afraid that the government will find out about things that the people know very well to be in contravention of the law." Besides that, indifference seems to be an important reason for nonresponse. A completely "nonthreatening" questionnaire like the National Voters' Poll does not get more than a 40 percent response, says de Guchteneire.

A poll of those who, in 1979, refused to cooperate with the test enumeration for the census of 1981 pointed in the same direction. Those involved were asked why they had refused to cooperate. Only 7 percent named the fear of the invasion of their private lives or the misuse of data. The largest categories were those who gave "indifference to or lack of interest in questionnaires" as their motive (28 percent) and those who did not give any reason (22 percent).[10]

It is not only citizens who hamper the government in accumulating data for policy decisions, but also organizations that control databases with personal information. Database holders have a strong tendency to be "more Catholic than the pope" and to withhold more data from researchers than the law requires, due, for example, to exaggerated cautiousness, fear of negative publicity, laziness, frugality or because they would rather keep the data for their own use.

Overkleeft-Verburg, at the time acting chairman of the Chamber of Registries, the organization that oversees compliance of the Personal Public Records Act, said in 1992: "There are also cases in which the privacy argument is used out of laziness, because people just did not feel like it anymore. . . . You see wide-scale use of privacy legislation as an alibi for refusal to cooperate, that really has entirely different reasons. . . . I cannot always avoid the impression that the question of power is disguised in the question of privacy." The chances of this sort of improper use of the privacy legislation are considerable, because its implementation rests primarily on self-regulation (see Chapter 5).

Reservations are especially strong when it is a question of personal data having to do with ethnicity or with the police, data that are designated as "sensitive" in the Personal Public Records Act. When scientific researchers ask for access to this kind of information, database holders often show an apprehension that goes further than the law prescribes. This is how it happened that the CBS has not indicated any ethnic origins in arrest records since 1974 and in crime statistics since 1983. These data were called "reprehensible entries" by the CBS, as if these poor facts had the sins of the world resting on their shoulders.

Researchers had other thoughts about this. "Without the ethnic reference—anonymous, of course—I cannot conduct a rational discussion about the connection between ethnicity and crime," said the criminologist and minorities researcher Frank Bovenkerk in 1992. "I don't know if these are fairy tales, or, if it is really worse than some people think." In the early 1990s, the CBS abandoned this guideline. The CBS prison statistics for 1994 showed that *allochtoons* occupied 50 percent of the cells, while they make up only 8 percent of the populace.[11]

The expansion of the privacy taboo also had far-reaching consequences in another "sensitive" area: research on the spread of HIV and AIDS. Good, iterative data collection about the percentages of those infected in different groups of the population and the risk factors associated with them provides important insights into the course of an epidemic. The most reliable method is the testing of blood samples that are collected for other purposes. "You can do a study like this completely anonymously," emphasizes the epidemiologist Roel Coutinho. "You give every blood sample a number, send it to another laboratory, and analyze it together with the corresponding data that are routinely collected. What you get is only: this percentage of the clinic's patients is infected and the infection is primarily in this and that group."

In the United States, England and Sweden, anonymous, group-specific HIV surveillance has been in systematic use for years. In 1989 some government departments proposed beginning periodic, large-scale, anonymous HIV testing in the Netherlands, too. A protest immediately followed from the "orthodox" ethicists and jurists. Without the permission of everyone involved, they argued, a test of this sort would be in conflict with the constitutional rights to respect for everyone's personal lifestyle and the inviolability of the human body. The government agreed; a test of the populace to determine the spread of HIV continues to be viewed as undesirable in the Netherlands. Roel Coutinho has never "heard of another country in the World Health Organization that interprets the requirement for permission as strictly as we do."

THE CODE OF SILENCE

From whom will the Dutch still tolerate some kind of interference in their private life? From parents, children and a few good friends. Up into the 1950s, this list also included aunts and uncles. They had a sort of delegated parental authority. If your parents were taken out of the picture, then they were the first to be named to help or to take action. When it was necessary, they could also give you a strong talking to. But the new uncle would rather bite off his tongue than to get involved in the upbringing of his nieces and nephews. The new uncle is a big, good-natured guy with an inane smile who gives you a fat hand with a twenty-five-guilder bill in it. He has forgotten how to wave his hand threateningly and how to raise his heavy, deep voice. The proverbial 'Dutch Uncle' of world renown is gone.

In addition to close family members and intimate friends, we also permit doctors, professors, clerics and social workers a certain amount of interference in our private lives. They are being paid for it, after all, so it is "functional." But even within these professions, in the last few decades, privacy anxiety has taken off. Once, the Protestant newspaper *Trouw* would not report on suits against teachers, because this would have an undermining effect on their authority. In the long run it did not help much, as we have learned in the meantime. The idea that teachers could radiate moral leadership collapsed in the 1980s under the weight of noninterventionist thinking. "Obedience has been discredited as a virtue since the Second World War, disqualified by the collaborating obedience to the enemy of—unfortunately—the majority of the populace," said the educator Lea Dasberg in her speech "Hangers-on and Obstructionists." "In part because of this, pedagogy has shied away from the problem of obedience for decades and with that has kept the whole issue of moral education from being discussed." It was out of this fear that educators took refuge in rationalizations—for example, in a love of social and, therefore, also of moral "pluralism."[12]

In the 1980s, this sort of disengagement was so matter-of-course that some teachers and social workers did not even take action when they knew or suspected that the children entrusted to their care were being abused or mishandled. After a number of these cases came to light, the government, in desperation, decided to take steps. Schools and institutions for the mentally handicapped were legally required to report sexual abuse of the pupils by teachers and other employees.

The government has requested that workers in photo labs inform the police if they come across photos with child pornography on them. In March 1996 the State Secretary of Education called on teachers to be less disengaged if children were being pestered by others. These measures were necessary because an almost categorical prohibition on tattling had come into being in the politically correct Netherlands. "Tattling" to the higher authorities just was not done. If we ever begin with betrayal, preached the politically correct supporters of the code of silence, that would, almost certainly, place us on the slippery slope into a police state. Just look at the war. It was better to pretend that you had not seen anything.

It is not easy to explain how such a strong taboo on tattling to the authorities came into existence in the Netherlands. Every citizen makes up his own balance sheet when it comes to reporting crimes. One draws the line at murder and child abuse; another, at welfare payment abuse. Certainly, in a welfare state—which is not itself in a position to completely oversee all its programs—citizens should be expected to make a conscious choice on this point. In the Netherlands the opposite process was visible: as the welfare state was expanded, the readiness to make this choice diminished.

The memory of tattling on those in hiding [q.v.] during the war cannot explain the strength of this taboo by itself. The people who betrayed those in hiding turned over people who had not done anything and who were in the weakest imaginable position into the hands of the cruelest government you can imagine. Nowadays we are dealing with people who are violating democratically agreed upon rules and with a "kind" government and a low risk of arrest. Those who are arrested are far from defenseless, given the guarantees that a state of law provides.

Pointing to the war places tattling in an absolute context, whereby complete disengagement seems to obtain a noble hue. In fact, the Dutch recollections of the war show where disengagement leads. The fact that so many Dutch Jews were deported has less to do with betrayal than with the fact that the majority of the Dutch did not do anything at all. They took the same position to the German crimes as the one that is propagated by the supporters of the total code of silence: do not interfere in somebody else's business; you don't hear anything, you don't see anything, you don't say anything, you don't do anything.

It was not only the supporters of the code of silence whose arguments were anchored in the image of the slippery slope. Other taboo preachers also hammered on it: every undesirable statement or action put us on the slope, which would lead inexorably downward. There was always the same picture at the end of the slippery slope, drawn from the deep darkness of our collective memory: the Nazi dictatorship.

This scarecrow image was embellished and dressed up for each of the three taboos. As far as privacy, the code of silence and personal public records were concerned, Orwell had already painted a picture of the doomsday scenario. If we did not want to be slaves to Big Brother, then vigilance was called for to keep from making each and every first small step. The conduct of a census could, in the end, lead to the registration and isolation of minorities. In 1990 the Dutch Association of Lawyers equated the compulsory taking of blood samples from felony suspects with a threat of a fall in the standard of judicial civilization.

In the area of government coercion, the police state was waiting just around the corner. The image of this specter was thankfully held aloft by interest groups fighting to defend the rights that they had acquired. When, for example, the penalties for child pornography were strengthened, then pedophile leaders predicted the clear self-evidence of a witch-hunt for the love life of the entire country: "Now it's the pedo-s, soon it will be normal families."[13]

In the ethnic arena, the racism bacillus prompted the most extreme disengagement. Every critical statement or action that had to do with immigrants could result in the onset of a terrible epidemic of racism. In 1991, when Bolkestein began to criticize the exaggerated disengagement in the ethnic arena, businessmen in the minorities' industry and left-wing politicians immediately brought up the slippery slope argument. According to Van Koningsveld, a historian of Islam, Bolkestein was contributing to the creation of a breeding ground for hate directed at Muslims that could also turn against other groups, such as the Jews.[14]

Two things stood out in this apocalyptic mentality. In the first place, it demonstrates a limited faith in the resiliency of our democracy.

The Netherlands has a long and time-honored tradition of democracy. With the exception of a single "mistake" [q.v.], our democracy has never been threatened from within. Nevertheless, it is now being pictured as if it stood to reason that democracy is a greenhouse plant that would wilt if exposed to the slightest gasp of wind. If you did not know better, you would easily get the impression that, for the last few decades, the Netherlands had been teetering on the brink of dictatorship or weighed down under the reign of ultra-authoritarian zealots.

It is also interesting that, in the slippery slope mind-set, the leap from the public to the private domain is made so often and so easily. When implementing democratically agreed upon rules, the government could not set standards for fear of sliding into government oversight of our private lives. Even the collection and processing of personal data for policy making would lead to totalitarian control. In fact, it is unthinkable that today's modern democratic government would have such aspirations. The inclination of the powers that be to intervene in the private lives of citizens is extremely limited, because that is the way that the citizens want it and because the powers that be do not have the desire to do so anymore.

While one sermon followed another about the specters from the past, "real-live" slippery slope processes were under way at full steam. They, too, were visible in each of the three taboo arenas. The great strength of the privacy taboo made teachers and social workers slide into disengagement, even when there were victims at stake. The fear of the racism bacillus led to an exaggerated caution in placing requirements on immigrants to acclimate. The taboo on coercion, which was supposed to protect us from sliding into a police state, brought us onto the slippery slope toward a blind-eye state. This is where democracy showed its true vulnerabilities. It was not that democratic rights were breaking down but that democratic obligations were getting lost.

A NEW SNAG IN THE PRIVACY TABOO

The social and cultural changes described in this book have few milestones; it falls to the observer to drive a marker in the ground here and there. But in the history of the Dutch privacy taboo, 1 June 1995 can surely be called a momentous occasion. On that day, the Association for Personal-Public-Records Vigilance, which had stood in the breech for almost 20 years, defending the individual's private life, ceased its activities because it went bankrupt. On the same day, the Compulsory Identification Act, which was supposed to make it easier to track down illegal aliens, went into force. The draft of the law was one of the last proposals that the Association for Personal-Public-Records Vigilance had opposed—without creating a ripple of protest.

Compulsory identification had existed in all the countries around us for a long time; the Netherlands was the only European country where the introduction of this obligation had, for years, run into objections. But, in the early 1990s, when the issue of illegal immigrants could no longer be kept off the political agenda, times changed. Employees have to provide employers with a copy of an identification card, under penalty of being placed in a draconian tax bracket. Practically everyone complies with this requirement without a murmur.

On other points, too, the expanse of the privacy taboo hit a new snag. The Ministry of Justice is thinking about a law that would make compulsory HIV testing possible after a rape. The principals of elementary and high schools are insisting on a confidential register in which convicted pedophiles would be listed. School principals would be able to request data from this list when processing job applications.

As of 1994 those suspected of violent crimes can be forced to cooperate in a DNA test. The time was now ripe not only to respect the integrity of the body of the suspect but also to respect the victim who was raped. In 1996 a nationwide data bank with DNA data on sexual offenders was opened. It is also a goal to arrange the international exchange of DNA profiles, which will not be so easy, because the Dutch data bank is almost empty. In 1998 the Parliament agreed to a legislative proposal that made the taking of compulsory DNA samples possible for less serious crimes, such as theft. The Ministry of Justice is also investigating the possibility of DNA testing in cases of "family reunification" for those with refugee status [q.v.] to determine if the family ties that they claim do indeed exist.

Even in the area of the collation of data from databases with personal information, one barrier after the other is falling, and it is not just the incidental coupling of data. In a few years, an individual's social security number and municipal registry will have turned into a personal identification number, linked to the auto license plate registry, the auto safety inspection registry, the personal liability insurance registry, rent subsidy records, the municipal registry, the foreigner's service [q.v.], the police registry, municipal social services records, the Social Insurance Bank's records, the Internal Revenue Service's records, health insurers' records, hospital records, student scholarship and loan records, housing authorities' records, professional associations' records, public health insurance records, employment offices' records and the General Public Pension Funds' records.

Public opinion is not concerned about these developments; the Parliament has little control over them. Still, the dangers seem more real now than during the great privacy panic of 20 years ago. The rapid changes in information processing and telecommunications are leading to complex and dynamic forms of data collection and exchange. This is true not only for the government but also in the area that is neither the government nor the business sector, for example, in the shadowy, gray area of independent and semipublic organizations.

The risk of data misuse that comes out of this is much less "spectacular" than in the "big story" of Big Brother. It is a question of lots of Little Brothers who exchange personal data because they have real—often commercial—interests in doing so. This is how more and more public social insurance programs are being outsourced to (semi)private organizations, which will happily use the uncontrolled exchange of personal data to exclude "poor" risks. This can lead to the deterioration of the solidarity aspect of all kinds of social and employment programs—a danger that is much "closer" than the appearance of a mythical Big Brother in some distant future.

THE LESSONS OF SREBRENICA

The new snag in the taboos discussed here is moving quickly, but chaotically. This is not an unequivocal sea change but a number of spontaneous developments and ad hoc adjustments in areas where they cannot be avoided. Just because the government has retreated from the "broad" interpretation of nonintervention does not, for example, mean that the public is following the government's lead. For many in the Netherlands, nonintervention has become a self-evident conviction.

The events in Srebrenica in 1995 can serve as an extreme example of this. The murder of thousands of Muslim men taken from the safe area, guarded by DutchBat [q.v.], has saddled us with a whole series of incomprehensible memories: the strange statements by Colonel Karremans and Lieutenant General Couzy [q.v.]; the refusal to render assistance to seriously wounded Muslim civilians; Major Franken's signature on "Franken's list," which turned over local DutchBat employees without United Nations ID cards to the Serbs; the fact that Karremans "honestly had not thought" to inquire of the Serbian general Mladic about the fate of the Muslim men, who had been taken away; the festive boisterousness of the DutchBat troops and visiting dignitaries at the moment that thousands of men from Srebrenica were being murdered.

All these behaviors become somewhat less incomprehensible against the background of the culture of disengagement that has become self-evident in the Netherlands. DutchBat troops willingly transported wounded Muslims to the Serbian camp, made neat lists of those who could and could not be turned over and held on tightly to the classifications with bureaucratic intransigence. "The military is not any different than the people of the Netherlands," said Maarten Huygen, reporter for the *NRC Handelsblad*. "It has heard a lot about the Second World War, but it has not learned a lot from it." When push comes to shove, it reverts to "administering lists and reaching consensus with the occupier."[15]

In the light of this comparison, the Dutch reaction to Srebrenica—an enthusiastic heroes' welcome, followed by painful self-assessment—is nothing new. It was a quick replay of the manner in which the memory of the German occupation was dealt with. The Dutch position with regard to the persecution of the Jews was viewed initially as heroic, resolute and kindhearted, while, later, a strong, public feeling of guilt grew up around the fact that we had tolerated genocide.

Hasn't the memory of the war taught us anything, then? Srebrenica leads to the frightful question of whether we, perhaps, learned the wrong lessons. In the 1960s and 1970s, the lesson that was drawn from the memory of the war was primarily that the government should restrain itself from any desire to intervene. A government should never again gain so much power that it could destroy groups of its citizens. The taboos connected with this in the areas of privacy and intervention reached their height during the years in which the DutchBat-ers were growing up. Their "intervention" took place against the background of a conviction of the self-evidence of nonintervention that was so self-evident that innocent people fell victim to it.

NOTES

1. Peter Schröder, *Data-infrastructuur* [Data Infrastructure], Utrecht, 1990.

2. C.J.M. Schuyt, *Ongeregeld heden, naar een theorie van wetgeving in de verzorgingsstaat*, rede uitgesproken bij de aanvaarding van het ambt van gewoon hoogleraar in de empirische sociologie aan de Rijksuniversiteit te Leiden op vrijdag 11 juni 1982 [The Disorderly Present, Toward a Theory on Legislation in the Welfare State, a speech given on the occasion of investiture into the office of full professor of empirical sociology at the State University of Leiden on 11 June 1982], Samson, Alphen aan den Rijn, 1982.

3. Besides this, a small percentage of the populace could not be found by the counters. Gerard Visscher, "Kwaliteit statistieken lijdt onder ontbreken volkstelling" [The Quality of the Statistics Suffers due to Deficiencies in the Census], *Staatscourant* [Parliamentary Record], 28 February 1996.

4. G. Overkleeft-Verburg, *De Wet persoonsregistraties, norm, toepassing en evaluatie* [Personal Public Records Act, Standards, Application and Evaluation], Tjeenk Willink, Zwolle, 1995, p. 46.

5. *Jaarverslagen* [Annual Reports] for 1978, 1979 and 1980 of the Central Commission on Statistics, Voorburg, 1978, 1979 and 1980.

6. The quotes for Van Hoesel, Holvast and Kuitenbrouwer are taken

from Herman Vuijsje, *Mens, erger je niet, privacybescherming en wetenschappelijk onderzoek* [Don't Be Sorry, the Protection of Privacy and Scientific Research], Ministry of Education and Science, Zoetermeer, 1992, and *de Volkskrant*, 13 July 1988.

7. Unless otherwise noted, the quotes in this paragraph are from Vuijsje, 1992.

8. *Cebeon-onderzoek* [Cebeon Research], Amsterdam, 1993; *Het Parool*, 28 February 1996 and 7 December 1996.

9. Flip de Kam, *NRC Handelsblad*, 3 September 1988, quoted in Vuijsje, 1992.

10. Tweede Kamer [Second Chamber of Parliament], 1979-1980, 15 800, Chapter XII, nr. 36. Two investigations into nonresponse in 1994 produced the same results. N. Kalfs and E. Kool, *Ervaringen met non-respons* [Experiences with Nonresponse], NIMMO, Amsterdam, 1994. *Enquête non-respons VOI 1994, voorlopige resultaten* [Questionnaire Nonresponse VOI 1994, preliminary results], ITS, Nijmegen, 1994.

11. Auke Kok, "Onderscheid en onbehagen" [Difference and Discomfort], *HP/De Tijd*, 22 September 1995.

12. Lea Dasberg, "Meelopers en dwarsliggers" [Hangers-on and Obstructionists], lecture on the occasion of the 50th anniversary of the newspaper *Trouw*, supplemented by reactions to it by people from the world of education, *Trouw*, Amsterdam, 1993.

13. Frits Wafelbakker, chairman of the Working Group Pedophiles of the Dutch Society for Sexual Reform, quoted in *Het Parool*, 12 February 1996.

14. C.S. van Praag, "Bolkestein tegen de rest" [Bolkestein against the Rest], *Socialisme & Democratie*, October 1992.

15. Maarten Huygen, "Goed en fout in Srebrenica" [Right and Wrong in Srebrenica], *NRC Handelsblad*, 2 November 1995.

CHAPTER 4

Decentralization

In the 1980s that the mentality of the 1960s forced its way through into the organizational structure of public management. Citizens were certainly capable of fending for themselves. The center of power had to move closer to the people, and why shouldn't businesses and organizations regulate their own activities? These ideas seemed to be an excellent fit for the no-nonsense plans of the Lubbers [q.v.] cabinet: fiscal economies and a smaller government. Decentralization, self-regulation and spin-offs were, on the one hand, a reaction to the mentality of the 1960s and, on the other, a result of it. They were based on "soft" concepts, which, when implemented, were adapted to a harder world.

In this way, decentralization, self-regulation and spin-offs developed into totem poles that could be worshiped by all the parties. The left-wing parties danced around them like a maypole. The dance to the right praised the golden calf of the market and shrinking government. And even the Christian Democrats saw that it was good: the totem poles were planted firmly in "civil society." Ministers and senior civil servants jumped around enthusiastically, relieved that they could drop the hot potato of political leadership. Even municipal leaders and covenant partners, pleased with their new power, joined in the dance of joy. It seemed like this was a real "win-win situation."

A FIRE IN HOTEL GOVERNMENT

"Decentralization in the Netherlands makes me think of a fire in Hotel Government," a high-ranking civil servant once told me confidentially. "The ministers and civil servants are throwing everything out the windows, thinking that all these fine pieces of furniture will be caught down below. It is a very unorderly process and certain pieces of the furniture are not caught by anyone, so that they break into a thousand pieces. Others are being caught by the wrong person." Every now and again, you could hear some sputtering, when someone saw a particularly precious piece of furniture being smashed to smithereens, but only in the 1990s did bystanders begin to ask if any of the inventory would survive this way.

The prelude to this outbreak of fire began in 1964, when the Minister of Internal Affairs initiated the Council for Territorial Decentralization, with the task of making quick work of the transfer of administrative functions to the provinces and municipalities. The politically correct Netherlands was in the grip of participatory democracy. The "gap" between voters and elected officials had to be closed. In addition to that, the welfare state was getting more and more wealth to distribute, which could best be done as close to the citizens as possible. It took 20 years for this plan to produce results. It was only in 1983 that the long march through the hierarchy was completed and a concrete Decentralization Plan appeared. In the meantime, the Netherlands had become a completely different society. The welfare state was shrinking, and dwindling resources had to be allocated. Could administrative decentralization still meet the high expectations of the 1960s under these circumstances?

At the beginning of this century, no one had ever heard of decentralization. Nevertheless, socialist municipal administrators still managed to produce impressive results in the area of emancipation, in areas where the state remained passive. Wibaut in Amsterdam, Drees in The Hague and Brautigam in Rotterdam brought about not only public housing but also municipal unemployment insurance, employment offices, care for the elderly and scholarships. From the security of a sacred ideal, they were not afraid to take unpopular decisions. This is how Drees [q.v.] was able to apply an original approach to the problem of workers in the shadow economy [q.v.] during the Great Depression in The Hague. There were work camps in Drenthe where you could earn a little more than you would receive from assistance payments. Drees' target to send to Drenthe was precisely those of the unemployed, who did not want to go. If you were in Drenthe, you could not work in the shadow economy. Those who did not want to go to Drenthe, obviously, already had an income.

Can an equally unperturbed approach be expected now that ideological positions have given way to practicability and pragmatism? Lower administrative levels may be closer to the citizens, but they are also more sensitive to influence by their clientele and by interest groups. Often local civil servants are not sufficiently trained or equipped to offer resistance to the corporate force of large businesses. As more power comes into the hands of lower administrative organizations and officials, more people are exposed to temptation. Even simple municipal civil servants—the chief of the local trash dump, for example—have become interesting for the private sector.

"The retreat of the central government" also means a reduction in substantive and ideologically motivated leadership. Decentralization brings with it the danger that collective decisions, formulated by nationally elected bodies, will be overruled by the total effect of all sorts of local political considerations. This means that the first areas to get the ax will be those that do not have an effective lobby, because, for example, the interested parties are either too few in number or are too weak. A good lobby is equally impossible for areas, such as public health care, that are so diffuse that local politicians cannot "score votes" with them. In addition, national-level decisions can quickly be pushed aside if they come into conflict with local, short-term interests, as is often the case with environmental and zoning issues. This chapter provides examples of those areas of policy that are most vulnerable under decentralization.

THE LOBBY-LESS

The emancipation of minorities in the Netherlands is an important policy goal for the central government, but according to the minorities specialist Carlo van Praag, the state can hardly use the leeway that it has in this area anymore. "The transfer of powers to the municipalities and other local administrative organizations has gone too far for this."[1] This makes the expenditure of funds for the emancipation of minorities highly dependent on how successful the local minority lobby is. But where are the lobbies not successful? Precisely in places where the minorities are not emancipated, which is where a policy on minorities is the most necessary.

Minority policy is "ideologically" loaded, which is also true of public assistance policy and policy on the handicapped. These are areas where the provision of the basic necessities is affected, where the lower limit of what we find socially acceptable comes into view. The affected groups can usually not achieve much in the local arena. That is why the national government introduced binding regulations, to protect citizens nationwide.

A good example is the regulation of swimming lessons at school. In a country as rich in water as the Netherlands, learning to swim is not a sport but a dire necessity. Since World War II, completing swimming lessons to the "B" Diploma [q.v.] level has been a mandatory part of the elementary school curriculum. The cost for the program was covered by the central government. In the 1980s, the central government's program was abolished. Swimming lessons at school became dependent on the priorities of local politicians, and since then, many municipalities have partially or completely stopped the subsidies for this program.

For ethnic Dutch children, this is not such a big problem: most of them learn to swim when they are four or five years old. This decentralization, nevertheless, produced a number of victims, namely, children from the *allochtoon* community, where there is no tradition of swimming or no money for private swimming lessons. A study in 1997 showed that in prosperous neighborhoods 80 percent of elementary school pupils graduated from school with a "B" Diploma, compared to 14 percent of the pupils at "black schools." As a result of a number of incidents in which *allochtoon* children drowned, the National Council for Swimming Diplomas is pleading for a return to a national requirement for swimming lessons at school, in any event, at "black schools."

Even the physically handicapped were confronted with problems by the abolishment of the national guarantees for their welfare. This was in 1994, when the Handicapped Programs Act (WVG) was decentralized. Relocation and travel cost reimbursements, subsidies to adapt housing for the handicapped and grants for the purchase of wheelchairs have had to compete with the proverbial street lamp since then. This decentralization, as usual, produced a fiscal economy for the government: the target group was broadened to include those 65 and older, but the budget was not increased.

A study commissioned by the Ministry of Social Services and the Association of Dutch Municipalities showed that many municipalities' expenditures for WVG programs were far under budget. Of the 770 million guilders that they were entitled to spend under the WVG in 1994, 330 million was still on the books. Some municipalities spent the money that had been saved on completely different projects.[2] In addition, it seemed that the municipalities needed quite a lot of money to implement the regulations: out of the total of 440 million guilders that had been expended, 164 million went to administrative costs.

Since decentralization, the municipalities themselves determine the income level under which someone has a right to WVG benefits. In one municipality the copayment for a wheelchair was 60 guilders and in another it was 9,000. There were municipalities, that set the income level so low that people with a modal income had to pay the entire cost of their wheelchairs, while elsewhere, a millionaire got a wheelchair for free. Those with severe handicaps were primarily the ones confronted with the results of this uneven application of the policy. They had to economize on basic necessities and social contact, said the Social-Services and Association-of-Dutch-Municipalities report. Another study showed that reimbursement for travel costs was lower than before in 80 percent of the municipalities.[3]

Beginning in 1996, after much protest and publicity, The Hague tightened the WVG reins again. The copayment for wheelchairs was eliminated, and the copayment for other services was limited to 100 guilders.

PUBLIC HEALTH CARE: NO VOTES TO SCORE

Collective health care programs are of the most value to those who are least able to provide for their own health care with private insurance. It is, however, also important for the independent and healthy that they be surrounded by healthy people. In his book *Care and the State*, De Swaan describes how the increasing contact between social groups also makes it necessary for prosperous citizens to recognize the need of collective arrangements to counteract setbacks and deficiencies in health care. Steps to promote hygiene and to combat infectious diseases are in everyone's interest, because everyone is at risk.

In 1989, with the introduction of the Act on the Collective Protection of the Public Health, money for public health care lost its "earmark." Since then municipalities have decided how the money is spent. The consequences are often visible only after a long period of time, but in some cases they are immediately visible. The border area of the provinces of Brabant and Limburg is yearly stricken by a plague of oak processionary caterpillars (thaumetopoea processionea). The fine hairs of the caterpillar larvae are carried by the wind and lead to violent inflammations and irritation of the eyes and airways. In 1998, 30,000 people went to see a doctor with these symptoms. In 1999 the Central Provincial Workgroup for Caterpillar Control was disbanded, after which the municipalities had to make their own decisions in this area. The result is that practically no preventive measures are being taken now. Every municipality that does do something has a different approach. Even the research on control has come to a halt.

I spoke to Public Health Service (PHS) doctors and administrators about this new trend in decentralization, while working on a study in 1995.[4] One of them was Erik Lieber, the director of a PHS unit in the province of South Holland. For him, life after decentralization has not become easier.

Lieber's district covers 16 municipalities on four islands. The 16 municipalities belong to three different administrative districts, each of which looks to another province: Goeree-Overflakkee to the province of Zeeland, Voorne-Putten to the city-province of Rotterdam and Hoekse Waard to Southern South Holland. The tiny island of Tiengemeten does not have to choose, because it is being turned into a nature preserve. Financing for Lieber's PHS unit is based on four different sets of principles and funded from even more sources. It is administered by the elected officials of 16 municipalities, which all make their own decisions on health care. At most, each municipality has only a couple of hours per week that are available for public health policy making. Lieber talked with me about the tiring discussions on the question of whether the 16 municipalities should make financial contributions to the Tuberculosis Bureau in Rotterdam. Hadn't tuberculosis been eradicated on the islands? Lieber answered with the example of the municipality in the province of Friesland that wanted to stop providing fluoride to children because they hardly had any cavities anymore.[5]

"Nowadays everything has to be quantifiable, otherwise it won't fit into the accounting," explained Willem van den Ouwelant, then the deputy director of the PHS in Amsterdam. "But in public health care the time that elapses between an action and its result is a very long one. In addition, it is very difficult to demonstrate a causal relationship. That puts politicians under pressure." A lack of professional expertise in the municipalities is the greatest complaint that doctors and experts had against administrative control of the PHS's being given to the municipalities. "The concept was: you can better see what is happening at the local level and provide made-to-order solutions," said the epidemiologist P. J. van der Maas. "Yes, that is true, as long as the necessary expertise and political will are available everywhere. And with the technological advances in health care, the need for expertise is only increasing. You just cannot find this knowledge at the local level."

Another risk was outlined by Annette Wiese, a school doctor for the PHS in Amsterdam. Dutch children's health care is internationally renowned, she said. Inoculation coverage has reached a very high level. But the positive effects of children's health care are not something that you can express in a number that the local town councilor can use in the next election to score votes. And economies have to be made.

"Every PHS has its own way of implementing economies," said Wiese. "One municipality throws out the physicals for eleven-year olds, another the physical in the second year of secondary education, or in high school. In Amsterdam, you can see differences cropping up between submunicipalities within the municipality. . . . That means that you can no longer do a national study: there aren't any nationwide standards to compare the results to anymore. . . . If you drop the uniformity, then in reality, you are cutting the legs out from under the whole prevention program."

What do you need to do to prevent fragmentation? Legislatively establish, on the basis of a cost-benefit analysis, what has to be done. "At the same time, set qualitative criteria. Then things cannot be shot to pieces by local politicians."

THE ENVIRONMENT AND LOCAL INTEREST

Environmental protection is another area in which the short-term interests of those directly involved often clash with the common interest of all. An extensive set of environmental legislation has been enacted in the Netherlands, but implementation and oversight have been decentralized to the provinces and municipalities. Administration was moved closer to the citizens, but it soon turned out that in several places, "a blind eye was turned to" grotesque violations of the law, because that was better for local politicians.

The attorneys general complained in 1993 and 1994 about a lack of cooperation from municipalities and the police in enforcing the environmental laws. In 1995 it came out that municipalities were hesitant to make use of their ability to levy penalties on polluting firms. According to the Minister of Housing, Zoning and the Environment, many municipalities do not dare to initiate collections, because they are afraid of difficulties with the firm involved. These "psychological problems" stem from a fear of "making themselves unpopular."

That is understandable. Local politicians entrusted with upholding environmental laws are not in a hurry to saddle their voters with all sorts of strict regulations. Added to this is: if we don't do it, the next town will. An example of this is parking policy. According to W. Drees Jr., the ex-Minister of Transportation and Waterways, a stringent parking policy can greatly contribute to a reduction in the growth of automobile use.[6] But parking policy, too, has been decentralized to the municipalities, and they are not going to think about scaring away interested businesses with bothersome parking requirements. To the contrary, they compete with one another by offering discount parking rates.

There are also other ways in which the municipalities get around the central government's policy on reducing automobile use. According to the government's "location policy," labor-intensive employers should be located at public transportation junctions. In 1996 a Nijmegen study showed that most municipalities want to attract jobs so badly that they do not place any obstacles in the way of businesses that choose another location.[7] Municipalities are also even inclined to move economic activities to the town outskirts. Land is cheaper here, which, given their own budget responsibilities, is an important consideration for the municipalities. The relocation of jobs to the periphery of the town leads to an increase in automobile use, but its social and economic costs do not show up on the municipal books.

WHAT IS THE VALUE OF THE GREEN HEART [q.v.]?

Just how green the heart of Holland still is, is dramatically demonstrated when you approach Schiphol airport from the south: it seems like an endless mosaic of plots and fields, bound by water, in the middle of the most heavily populated area in Europe. This area of peat bogs and meadows is a typical, man-made landscape and a pearl in the crown of the Dutch zoning regulations: organically grown and afterward carefully nurtured and husbanded by a legion of pedantic little civil servants, each hammering on his rules and regulations. But recently, the annoying little civil servants have been cast in a bad light. Civil servants—provincial civil servants as well, the ones who have to oversee the proper implementation of the zoning regulations—do not want to be pedantic anymore, but rather customer-friendly. Formally, the provinces can put their foot down to the municipalities by issuing an "instruction," but the reputation of a strict overseer is what the provinces want to avoid! What they want most of all is to initiate, to stimulate, to inspire, to negotiate, if necessary, "to guide," but even more so, to play the role of a middleman or to act as a backstop. That being the case, putting on a stern face and showing off your oversight responsibilities are not the best advertisement.

The new Municipalities Act (1992) strongly restricts the authority of the province to withhold approval for municipal decisions. If the powers that be would keep their grabby little fingers to themselves, then 'Our Village' would return to the world of the heroes of childhood literature. When a problem would come up, then the village constable, the baron, the vicar and the oldest farmer would get together in the office of the mayor. They are all the salt of the earth, who, with a little give-and-take, can certainly reach an agreement. The big men from the city are about as welcome there as a toothache.

In this world, the village is bordered by an endless polder. There is no uncontrolled spread of greenhouse farming or agroindustry. Manure surpluses [q.v.] and environmental scandals are unknown, just as are spontaneous town and village expansion. In far-off The Hague sits a considerably reduced central government, which benignly oversees things and every now and again sends a delegate to Our Village, to pull up a chair with our top men in the mayor's office and have a good talk, while enjoying a superb cigar.

Another picture came to the fore in 1993, when the province of South Holland published a study on the enforcement of, and the compliance with, zoning plans for rural areas. In the 18 municipalities studied, one-third of the plans were neither being complied with nor being checked by the inspectors. "Throughout the rural areas of the province there is a creeping reduction in the quality of open space, due to the large number of violations and limited compliance with zoning requirements," stated the National Service for Environmental Planning in its report *Zoning Studies 1994*. "This has a negative effect on administrative credibility."

"If you look at a picture of the Randstad [q.v.] from 20 years ago and one from today, you think to yourself: we've been fooled somehow, there was a conspiracy somewhere that led to this," says the writer Koos van Zomeren in a recent interview. "But that is not at all true. The good intentions were there and the policy resolutions were precisely formulated, but when all the municipalities had their own mayors and their own executive committee chairmen, you didn't need a conspiracy anymore. Then things just went the way things go."[8]

It is not a law of nature that is subjecting the Green Heart to this development. The Green Heart is filling up, not by itself nor even because someone has decided that it should but because we have shoved responsibility down into the bog. A number of interest groups and lobbies are fighting for a place in the Green Heart. The municipalities are cooperating with them in every way possible. Every municipality wants to keep its residents, businessmen and jobs and, therefore, nibbles at the Green Heart bit by bit for housing construction or a business site.

The area of peat bogs and meadows is, in the most dramatic sense of the word, a "scarce" resource: there is only so much of it, and it can never be increased, only decreased. To a certain extent, nature can be "restored," but a man-made landscape cannot. An organically grown landscape is literally of inestimable value. No one can calculate the book value of the Green Heart as a treasure chest of landscapes. But, if the Green Heart is looked at as a collection of locations for housing, business, industrial farming, nature parks and organized recreation, then it is possible to place a value on it. It is for this reason that the Green Heart is defenseless, when private interests take the upper hand.

Regulation and enforcement are necessary, not only in the area of zoning but also in the surrounding policy areas, to preserve this man-made landscape. You cannot leave the regulation and enforcement to the private sector, to the interested organizations or to local or regional levels of government. Only the central government is in a position to make the consequent policy choices, to translate them into zoning policies and to oversee their implementation. The central government can do this, because it is "far removed from the people" and is, therefore, less vulnerable to influence by local or special limited interests, so that it can afford to take a long-range view.

AD HOC RECENTRALIZATION

In the mid-1990s a reassessment of central government became noticeable in the publications of zoning organizations. In its report *Zoning Studies 1994*, the National Service for Environmental Planning strongly criticized the policy implementation of lower levels of government. Especially in urban areas, it seemed that violations of the zoning plan were more often the rule than the exception. Municipalities do not follow their own zoning plans, there is too little inspection and there is a great deal of hesitancy when it comes to applying sanctions. In 1995 the RoRo, a consultative body of the four Randstad provinces, wrote that "continuing administrative splintering" was threatening the future of the Randstad.[9] A year later, in a report on the Green Heart, the Zoning Council pleaded for "a more aggressive approach." Clear leadership in zoning policy is necessary to preserve the Green Heart. An "administrative culture in which people bend over backward to be nice to each other" can have serious consequences in vulnerable areas such as the Green Heart.

The oversight role of the province can also be mentioned again now. More policy freedom for municipalities requires more coordination with the province, stated the Scientific Council for Governmental Policy in 1995, but in practice, the province is, in most cases, nothing more than one of the powerless actors.[10] In the meantime, various ministers have declared that the provinces need to show their teeth more often. The Minister of Housing, Zoning and the Environment wants to force the municipalities of the Green Heart to keep all construction inside rigid lines and demands that the provinces exercise oversight in this area. The Minister of Transportation and Waterways wants the provinces to ensure that the municipalities do not compete with one another over parking rates.

There were also other areas in which positive things could be heard about recentralization. In 1999 the central government decided to again take over the printing of new passports, something that had been decentralized to the municipalities only a few years before. The municipalities appeared not to be sufficiently well equipped to prevent fraud. That was also the year in which the Waste Products Service was recentralized. Municipalities, it turned out, were not well enough able to regulate the storage and processing of chemical wastes. They refused to take chemical wastes from each other; cooperation was not a success.

A similar sort of development became visible soon after decentralization in the area of public housing. In 1993 the municipalities became responsible for the oversight of public housing corporations. It was not long before various incidents came to light in which municipal administrators were so closely tied to local interests that they let their oversight responsibilities slide. In 1996 a study by the Office of the Budget showed that municipalities most often fail in their oversight of the social obligations of the housing corporations: the legal requirements that a certain number of their housing units be reserved for socially weaker target groups. More than half of the housing corporations do not report to their municipalities on their fulfillment of this social duty.[11] According to B. Kempen, the former general director of the National Housing Council, the department and the inspection service need to take a "more decisive" stand; if necessary, oversight should be recentralized. In mid-1996, the government introduced a draft bill that would take financial oversight of the corporations away from the municipalities.

Similar criticism can be heard with regard to the policy for combating the learning shortfall experienced by ethnic minorities. The central government wants every municipality to be individually responsible for the development of educational programs for minorities and for the compilation of plans to combat learning shortfalls. The Social and Cultural Planning Bureau (SCPB) had warned of this repeatedly in its annual Report on Minorities. According to the SCPB, the previously named tasks are outside the support and administrative capabilities of many municipalities. Continuing decentralization can, because of this, further decrease the program's effectiveness. The learning shortfall experienced by ethnic minorities calls precisely for more central and targeted direction by the central government.

Regarding the police and the courts: the same story. Since the reorganization of the police in 1994, 25 regional police corps have decided for themselves how they spend their money. The majority of the corps abolished the central teams for vice and youth crime. That dilutes the available expertise in these areas and makes it impossible to respond to serious cases with a large team. Other nationwide priorities also came under pressure. "Too much emphasis has been given to trying to bring the police closer to the people," said the director of the Dutch Police Institute in 1997. "The police are waiting for national guidance." The government announced steps to bring the police corps back under central direction that same year. Plans were made public in 1999 to restore central vice teams.

During a parliamentary inquiry on Investigative Methods in 1995, the committee established time and time again that responsibilities within the Ministry of the Public Prosecutor (MPP) were not clearly regulated, that lines of authority were not functional and that there were no clear standards on the admissibility of investigative methods. Consultation between the MPP and the police corps was already on equally shaky footing, resulting in each corps' going its own way. That was the year in which the Minister of Justice decided to implement a far-reaching centralization of the Ministry of the Public Prosecutor. There have to be "transparent administrative relationships," in which "powers, the chain of command and the chain of responsibility are clearly and strictly regulated."

In some cases, decentralization has been taken so far that it is only with the greatest difficulty and high cost that changes can be made or the process reversed. In 1991 the Employment Support Service was broken into three segments and decentralized. Since then 28 Regional Employment Support Services Administrations (RESSA)—each with a high degree of independence—serve a limited geographic area. While the labor market for those with advanced degrees, for example, turned out to be a national one instead of a regional one, decentralized RESSAs have no incentive to actively assist those with advanced degrees from outside their region. Now the RESSAs are trying to rebundle their services, but who can take the lead in this? How do you get 28 different computer systems connected to one another?

There is also a noticeable tendency toward recentralization among the submunicipalities of Amsterdam. In the 1980s local politicians—under the leadership of the Labor Party, which had wanted twice as many—shoved 16 submunicipalities down the throats of the citizens of Amsterdam. Ten years later, one municipal service after another is complaining that the intramunicipal decentralization has been a disaster, especially because of the large-scale loss and/or factionalization of know-how and experience.[12] In 1996 the municipality of Amsterdam announced tighter fiscal controls over the submunicipalities. In the meantime, a number of delegates to the submunicipalities have been pleading for larger administrative units. A merger of the submunicipalities in the south of the city is almost complete. This fusion cost the taxpayers of Amsterdam 14 million guilders. The D66 [q.v.] faction of the submunicipal council for Oud-West [Old West] has presented a unique idea: an "Association of submunicipalities in Amsterdam"!

An equally expensive and troublesome detour has been visible in other areas. An example is the fate of the Dutch elm, a majestic tree that contributes strongly to the special character of Dutch cities, polders and dikes. The elm is splendid, but it is also vulnerable: if a tree is infested by the elm bark beetle (Scolytus scolytus), then it is done for. The Netherlands has always had this disease well under control. It cost the central government 2 million guilders a year to keep an army of bark-beetle hunters in the field that reported infected trees so that they could be cut down. In 1991 this central subsidy was stopped with disastrous consequences. Since then, hundreds of thousands of elms have been infected and cut down. In some parts of the Netherlands the elm has completely vanished. Recently, a yearly allowance of 150,000 guilders was again made available to "report, coordinate, make policy and set up an organizational framework."

An even more gripping example is the decentralization of the responsibility for infectious disease policy. Up until 1989 combating infectious diseases was directed by the central government. Both the oversight and the direction of the implementation were the responsibility of three civil servants of the Central Government Inspection Service. With the introduction of the Act on the Collective Protection of the Public Health, the municipalities were in charge, so that policy was no longer made by three, but by nearly 600 civil servants. Unfortunately, the infectious diseases refused to take notice of the decentralization; they continued to ignore municipal borders as of old. In 1999 an outbreak of Legionnaires' disease took 23 lives. The victims had come from all over the country to visit a flower show, where they were all infected. Because little is left of the national reporting system, it was five days after the first death before a nationwide alarm was sounded.

During the first serious epidemic following decentralization, the polio epidemic of 1994, each of the 600 municipal civil servants was also on his own, because the new law had no provision for centralized leadership during crisis situations.

After the epidemic, all haste was made to establish a "national coordination center for combating infectious diseases." This coordination center does not have any power; its existence is based only on a memorandum of understanding between the inspection service, the Ministry of Public Health and another couple of organizations. To make their approach somewhat more integrated, the municipalities are now sending their well-paid civil servants to the Netherlands School of Public Health, where, under the supervision of the coordination center, they consult on a more uniform strategy. What was the purpose of the whole decentralization process again? Economy, efficiency and less bureaucracy.

While in a number of government sectors, (re)centraliziation is on the agenda, all the discussions and steps being taken continue to have a clearly ad hoc character. Make a mistake, then quickly fix it and keep moving with undiminished faith. The cleanup of a decentralization gone wrong is something of an embarrassing event in the Netherlands. People would prefer to do it through the back door. Cases like that are buried in the dark of night by hasty, silent men. If they are asked about the cause of the miscarriage, then they keep their lips tightly pressed together.

NOTES

1. Van Praag, 1992.

2. According to a study by the Socialist Party. *de Volkskrant*, 30 August 1995.

3. SWOKA, a study commissioned by *Konsumenten Kontakt* [Consumer Contact], June 1994.

4. Vuijsje with Bestebreurtje, 1996.

5. All the quotes in this paragraph are taken from Herman Vuijsje with Miriam Bestebreurtje, *Hulpeloze gladiatoren, haalt de openbare gezondheidszorg het jaar 2000?* [The Helpless Gladiators, Will the Public Health Service Make It to the Year 2000?], De Balie, Amsterdam, 1996.

6. W. Drees, *Openbare uitgaven* [Public Expenditures], 1994, nr. 2.

7. Study by P. Drenth, Catholic University of Nijmegen, 1996. The quote is from *de Volkskrant* of 30 July 1996.

8. Interviewed in Herman Vuijsje, *Vergezichten, tien visies op recreatie en beleid* [Panoramas, Ten Visions of Recreation and Policy], Voorlopige Adviesraad voor de Openluchtrecreatie/Op Lemen Voeten, Amersfoort/Amsterdam, 1994.

9. RoRo-Project Team, *Evaluatie Interprovinciale Verstedelijkingsvisie op de Randstad* [An Evaluation of Interprovincial-Urbanization Visions of the Randstad Conurbation], Haarlem, 1995.

10. Scientific Council for Governmental Policy, *Orde in het binnenlands bestuur* [Order in Domestic Administration], SdU, The Hague, 1995, pp. 30, 36, 43.

11. Office of the Budget, *Toezicht op woningcorporaties* [Oversight of Housing Corporations], The Hague, 1996.

12. See, for example, the New Year's speech of director Oskam of the Zoning Service, quoted in *Het Parool*, 8 January 1996.

CHAPTER 5

Self-Regulation

In the 1970s Dutch political scientists began to complain about the administrative obscurity surrounding the "fifth power"—the interest organizations set up along industry lines—and its linkage to public administrators. In their book *Crisis in Dutch Politics* (1974), Van der Berg and Molleman stated that these conglomerates of umbrella organizations, clubs and councils were holding the centers of democratic decision making prisoner inside an "iron ring." Large parts of the policy-making process were placed outside democratic control by the relationships between parliamentary staffers, civil servants and the interest organizations. Ten years later, in the same breath that announced the goal of bringing administration closer to the people, the iron ring was drawn even tighter. Together with administrative decentralization, a "functional decentralization" was also introduced. All over the Netherlands, interest groups, industry organizations and affinity groups concluded agreements with the government in which regulatory powers and authority were transferred to "civil society."

What was it that had changed since the time that the inclusion of interest groups in the equation of political power was discussed with trepidation? Perhaps the primary policy achievement, hidden behind all the hocus-pocus about administrative responsibility, was that, without notice, the somber tone of the 1980s had made way for a cheerful one. Wasn't the government in a position to keep the center in line anymore? Just hitch the horse up behind the wagon, let go of the reins and pretend that everything is all right.

The self-regulation of the past few decades was made up of a multicolored pallet of covenants, agreements to turn a blind eye, codes of conduct, administrative agreements, gentlemen's agreements, good-faith efforts, declarations of intention and other constructs, the common denominator of which is that they lack any legal basis and, therefore, any chance of being controlled or amended by the Parliament and of being appealed to public administrative bodies.

The Netherlands already had a number of "self-regulating" departments, which had come out of the previous corporate round: business associations, for example, which were their own supervisors, the Central Government's Aviation Service, which, as a result of a "gentlemen's agreement," investigated its own role in air crashes, the Specialist Registration Commission, a closed shop of medical specialists that set the quotas for the number of students who could study medicine.[1] In the 1980s a new batch of tasks was presented to the interest clubs of the center by the graceful means of a covenant.

THE UNBEARABLE LIGHTNESS OF THE COVENANT

Compared to an ordinance, a covenant very clearly lays out the equality and personal responsibility of both parties. This is why covenants are better than regulation imposed from without. That is how Marcel van Dam—a well-known Labor politician—articulated the general feeling of the last ten years in his plea for a "do-it-yourself welfare state." "Everyone has the inclination to rebel against prohibitions. Responsibilities that you accept for yourself, are something that you find it easier to adhere to."[2]

At first glance, covenants have a lot going for them: the appearance of a reasonable discussion among equals and pragmatic advantages, such as rapid implementation and minimal enforcement. But the advantages of a covenant over a long legislative process also give covenants an unbearable lightness. Something that can be implemented so flexibly does not automatically produce the desired result but is limited to a "commitment to make an effort": the definition of an agreement, the implementation of which cannot be legally enforced. Political oversight is tenuous, and democratic control is weak. "Everything about a covenant is half-way," said the political scientist Ries van der Wouden in 1992. "In one case, it is half a responsibility, without sanctions, in another case, it is half a decentralization or half a turn-over of responsibilities." He sees the covenants as a halfhearted imitation of the business world. The covenant suggests a series of characteristics that the business world is thought to have, such as speed, pragmatism and the equality of the sides participating in negotiations. In general, this imitation of the business world is bad for public administration.[3]

In 1995 Rob van de Peppel, another political scientist, concluded from a study of paint manufacturers that the environmental covenants—which, a year before, had been presented by Marcel van Dam as an enlightened example—were ineffective. Only one in five of the manufacturers was complying with the covenant on environmental policy inside the plant gates. In other areas, too, it turned out that a majority or a large minority of the manufacturers were not taking the slightest notice of the agreement. "It seems primarily to be window-dressing," said Van de Peppel. "The government is being led down the garden path. . . . A commitment to make an effort does not offer anything that you can hold onto." He believes that the government should resume its classical task of making rules and granting permits. The old one-sided policy instruments, which were based on coercion, had a much better compliance rate. This is especially true in areas where serious environmental problems have to be resolved, such as the rapidly increasing CO_2 emissions. Covenants can play a role only where the efforts they require are limited or where they serve as a prelude to legal regulation.[4]

A similar opinion was expressed in 1996 by Professor G. Bruinsma, who, as part of the parliamentary inquiry on investigative methods, studied illegal practices in the waste treatment industry. The government's goal, says Bruinsma, is to remove the influence of public administrators from the process. "Civil servants and leaders dine with waste treatment officials in the evening to make good agreements to protect the environment. The next day, the same waste treatment companies are dumping their rubbish in the sewer again." Bruinsma recommends that public administrators resume direct control of waste treatment again. Self-regulation does not work in this branch of industry. Covenants delay finding a good approach to waste treatment.[5]

GENTLEMEN AND VIOLENCE IN THE MOVIES

In 1995 the Office of the Budget determined that half of the covenants that the ministries had concluded with businesses and institutions were too informal: the goals are vague, the effective period is often not clear and there is no legal obligation to comply with the agreement.[6] Despite this, the preference for the covenant approach remained strong, as I will illustrate with the case of violent movies and videos.

The video series that now numbers six parts, *Faces of Death*—a succession of torture and death, not acted out but filmed live—has been a best-seller in the Netherlands for years but has never been on the official top-ten lists: a "blind eye" is silently turned toward it. The Germans, on the other hand, have recognized that *Faces of Death* exists, and in 1991, they prohibited both its performance in movie theaters and its sale and rental on video.[7] In the early 1990s other Western countries were reining in violent movies. Official censorship of violent movies was introduced in England: the sale or rental of such movies to children carries a two-year prison term. In America a debate had broken out on the introduction of a rating system for television programs, while in the Netherlands, people were getting ready to abolish the board of movie censors: it was time to finally put an end to the busybody interference of dear father state.

In reality, there was not so much left to abolish. By 1977 movie ratings for adults had been ended. The new Movie Performance Act provided only for "classification": a sort of jury of independent volunteers decided if a movie was or was not harmful for young viewers. The Netherlands had come from "censorship" via "rating," to the "classification" of movies.[8] In 1983 the preventive censorship of movies was constitutionally prohibited, except for public performances for young people under the age of 16. The government had no business at all concerning itself with the content of the media; that was dangerous.

Then, in the 1980s, when video appeared, the system of classification by an independent commission was also found to be too paternalistic. In 1991 the Dutch Retail Video Organization concluded a covenant with the Minister of Welfare, Health and Culture in which it agreed to a system of "conditioned self-regulation." The movies would be supplied with age-group classifications by the importers and by the producers themselves. P. Nikken of *The Children's Closet*—an organization that provides information and advice on children's television—described the course of events: "Someone working for the importer watches the video with a form in front of him. The age-group classifications are set depending on the film's scores in the areas of porno and violence. A one-man rating commission always agrees—the baker is rating his own bread."[9] In its 1995 report, the Office of the Budget panned the covenant with the video industry.

Formally, the classification is based on set criteria, with background support from the Supervisory Council for Video Public Relations, which is comprised primarily of representatives from this sector of industry. This council has concluded a gentlemen's agreement with the video rental companies in which the latter promise to observe the age-group classifications. The council has no way to check to see if they observe the classifications or not, nor does it have any sanctions to apply if they do not. In addition, the sale of videos by gas stations and tobacconists is not covered by this agreement. The same is true of movies from importers who are not members of the industry association.

In 1995 a journalist sent a 13-year-old girl to seven video stores to rent *Faces of Death*. In six of the seven stores, she got the tape with no problem.[10] This is logical, because without external controls and sanctions, each retailer has every reason to doubt whether his competitors will interpret the agreement so narrowly. If he observes the gentlemen's agreement, then he is "stealing his own billfold."

In their report *Movies and Government Policy* in 1991, the researchers Van der Burg and Van den Heuvel recommended that the system of self-regulation used in the video industry also be introduced for performances in movie theaters. It is true, they reported, that a large number of video retailers were not living up to the gentlemen's agreement, but that was not an insurmountable problem. Movie ratings were, in fact, quite unnecessary: the public was not interested in them, and, in addition to that, it had not been proved that movies can have a detrimental effect on children. Modern society is, after all, a "diversity of values and standards" that are expressed in "the individual blossoming of the rights of men, including the consumption of culture."[11]

The researchers had reached their conclusion without asking Dutch children and parents for their opinion. Others, however, did that in 1992. It appeared from this study that 81 percent of young people and 91 percent of parents think that the existence of an independent movie rating system is important.[12] Even though the report by Van der Burg and Van den Heuvel was not notable for its empirical foundation, it was in complete conformity with the ideas prevailing in the administrative Netherlands and in the Ministry of Welfare, Health and Culture, which had commissioned the study.

In 1993 the government submitted a proposal to the Parliament to abolish movie ratings and to introduce self-regulation in the movie industry. Only the Christian Democratic Party and the small, conservative Christian parties continued to hold on to the importance of legislative regulation to counter violence. Their perseverance was rewarded when concern about sexual violence against children began to increase among the rest of the politically correct Netherlands. In early 1997 the government announced that the article on child pornography in the penal code would be applied to the movie and video industry. Showing or renting movies to those under 16 that are rated to be shown only to those 16 years old and older, is punishable by a year in jail or a fine of 25,000 guilders.

REREGULATION

Since the "purple" [q.v.] government came to power, external control over civil society has been increased in other areas. The same maxim applies to this (re)regulation as to recentralization: "the sea wall first has to change the course of the ship" [Dutch proverb]. An example is the oversight of business in the financial world. This oversight is exercised for the government by the Chamber of Insurance, the Association for Securities Exchange Oversight (STE) and the Dutch National Bank.

The STE, which ensures that transactions on the exchanges are made properly, was, up until recently, dependent on the supervisory bureaus of the exchanges, but, at present, the roles are being reversed.

The STE started its own supervisory bureau in 1996 and is going to direct the activities of the supervisory bureaus of the exchanges. The supervisory bureaus are resisting the change, under the motto that supervisors need to be "close to the market," but both the director of the options exchange and the director of the largest market maker at the stock market think that the government should supervise the exchanges.[13] Even the new president-director of the Amsterdam exchanges—the option and stock exchanges—pleads for supervision by outsiders. "We are no longer bound by traditional ethics and morals," he said in his first New Year's Day speech. Before, you had the individual "member of the exchange," who felt himself constrained not only by the regulations but by moral considerations "to oversee the actions of those who worked under his authority. Patriarchal or not, it has been missing since yesterday."

This remarkable unanimity cannot be viewed as separate from the serious stock market scandals that became public in the early 1990s. In the world of the stock exchange, it is the sea wall that changed the course of the ship: the limitations of self-regulation are threatening the industry. The same thing happened to the Chamber of Insurance, which exercises control over the insurance companies and pension funds. The Chamber of Insurance tightened its controls in 1994 and 1996. This was also preceded by a shocking scandal: the bankruptcy of the Vie d'Or [French: Life of Gold] Insurance Company.

A scandal or a "disconcerting" event has, up until now, been the prerequisite for (re)regulation. That can be seen in other cases. First there was the Bijlmer air crash disaster; then came the questions about the "gentlemen's agreement" with the Central Government's Aviation Service, which had been spunoff a few years earlier under circumstances that made it unclear who was responsible for what. First there was the WAO [q.v.] debacle, and then only afterward there were the studies of whether industry associations are, indeed, the best ones to police themselves. First a 23-million-guilder subsidy had to go to a hazardous waste treatment company like Tankercleaning of Rotterdam, which let the filth run into the harbor, before the government started to ask itself if the cleanup of chemical wastes was perhaps better done by a public institution, as had been the case in the past.

Just like recentralization, reregulation is still a question of ad hoc decision making. Even those who denounce self-regulation in one industry refrain from drawing a more general conclusion. An exception is G. Overkleeft-Verburg, an expert in the area of administrative law, who published an evaluation of the Personal Public Records Act in 1995. Self-regulation plays an important role in the implementation of this act, which, since 1990, has protected citizens against disclosure and misuse of personal data. The holders of databases concluded an agreement on codes of conduct among themselves and then interpret the codes as they see fit.

According to Overkleeft-Verburg, this is a disservice to equal treatment under the law. In addition, there is a danger of decisions being made for the wrong reasons. The holders of databases can always have interests of their own, which make a certain interpretation of the code of conduct attractive (see also Chapter 3). She also points out that the reception for arguments of this kind is very cool. "There has to be self-regulation, self-regulation is good" because that was the slogan of the day. "In practice, the problems that have been reported seem not to make much impression." According to Overkleeft-Verburg, there is too little recognition of the fact that a lawmaker who incorporates elements of self-regulation into a law is making himself dependent on the readiness of some sector of society to cooperate with him. That readiness is there only, if those affected can also make hay from it.

The main idea of Overkleeft-Verburg's case study is not that self-regulation per se is an overrated concept but that it has been too matter-of-factly used as a template and that, in general, its effectiveness is overrated. Self-regulation has important inherent limitations and risks and, therefore, cannot be used as "the standard solution to a leadership deficit on the part of the legislature." The question has to be asked on a case-by-case basis if good results can be expected from self-regulation. Self-regulation needs to remain a made-to-order solution.

Overkleeft-Verburg uses the concept of "made-to-order" in an original sense. In the 1980s, "made-to-order" was always one of the most popular, politically correct slogans. The government had to adjust its services to match local conditions and also to give up as much decision-making power as possible. Self-regulation was a typical result of this made-to-order approach. The made-to-order solution that Overkleeft-Verburg is pleading for could be described in that same trendy jargon as a "complete made-to-order" solution. Not only are public services delivered to order, but also the degree of freedom that the government gives the service providers is examined on a case-by-case basis, not from the viewpoint of one or another administrative totem, but from the viewpoint of the simple question, What works?

NOTES

1. This is officially done because of considerations of quality, but it opens the door to the creation of artificial shortages. The Health Council is pleading for a central organization, like the one in England, with independent experts who can set training capacity for medical specialists without consequences or rebuttal. Thus far, their entreaties have been in vain: the sea wall and the ship have not met yet.

2. Marcel van Dam, *De opmars der dingen* [The Encroachment of the Things], Balans, Amsterdam, 1994, pp. 165/166.

3. *De Volkskrant*, 6 February 1991.

4. R. van de Peppel, *Naleving van milieurecht, toepassing van beleidsinstrumenten op de Nederlandse verfindustrie* [Compliance with Environmental Legislation, the Application of Policy Instruments to the Dutch Paint Industry], Kluwer, Amsterdam, 1995. The quote is from *de Volkskrant*, 19 September 1995.

5. *De Volkskrant*, 11 May 1996.

6. Algemene Rekenkamer [Office of the Budget], rapport *Convenanten van het Rijk met bedrijven en instellingen* [Report on Central Government Covenants with Businesses and Organizations], The Hague, 1995. The 154 covenants that were studied were primarily on the environment and education.

7. Jan van Gils, director of Palma Video International, quoted in M. van der Stoel, *e=md2*, Middelburg, 1991, pp. 96/97.

8. C.C.N. Crans, "In de marge van de tolerantie, filmkeuring op weg naar de 21e eeuw" [On the Margin of Tolerance, Movie Ratings on Their Way to the 21st Century], *Sec*, Ministry of Justice, April 1995.

9. *Het Parool*, 11 May 1995.

10. Margo Vliegenthart, "Niemand zou geweldsvideo's mogen zien" [No One Should Be Allowed to See Violent Movies], *de Volkskrant*, 13 May 1995.

11. J. van der Burg and J.H.J. van den Heuvel, *Film en overheidsbeleid, van censuur naar zelfregulering* [The Movies and Government Policy: From Censorship to Self-Regulation], Sdu, The Hague, 1991.

12. Frédérique Aben, *Heeft de Nederlandse Filmkeuring recht van bestaan?* [Does the Dutch Movie Rating (Board) Have the Right to Exist?], M.A. Thesis, University of Leiden, July 1992. A summary of the results of this research can be found in Frédérique Aben and Marcel Vooijs, "Opvattingen van jongeren en hun ouders over de Nederlandse Filmkeuring" [The Views of Young People and Their Parents on the Dutch Movie Rating (Board)], *Jeugd en samenleving* [Youth and Society], May 1993. The study was based on a select sample (of students from a few school communities and their parents). The conclusions were, in general, confirmed by a representative opinion poll of the Dutch populace commissioned by the television program *De Stelling* [Posing the Question], which is produced by the Evangelical Broadcast Corporation. The program was broadcast on 17 February 1993. [Translator's note: The Evangelical Broadcast Corporation is one of the public corporations that provide content for Dutch noncommercial television.]

13. Hans Kroon, director of Van der Moolen Securities, quoted in *de Volkskrant*, 10 January 1996.

CHAPTER 6

Spin-Offs

In 1977, in my book *The New Professionals*, I described how the "Jeans Proletariat" had managed to carve out a unique position for itself in the Netherlands. Instructors in higher education, policy-making civil servants in the welfare sector and other functionaries in the semipublic sector combined the income and legal position of a civil servant with the freedom of a business professional. They were hardly called upon to accept responsibility for their professional activities, because they could legitimize them by referring to the needs of their clients. The general answer to any attack on the privileges of their position was that it was really an attack on a welfare mother.

Twenty years later, the new professionals are silently enjoying the rights that they have won for themselves. But in the meantime, a new sort of professional has made an appearance on the stage. These new professionals do not pose as chain-rattling proletarians, like their predecessors from the 1960s and 1970s, but they, too, combine a privileged, government-protected position with the advantages of an independent professional and the money and aura of a businessman. Not only do these "calculating contractors" cost the government a great deal of money, but, according to the political scientist H. Daalder, the fact that they work in a shadow area and have no concept of the ethic of office as a public duty is, certainly, equally as bad. They are not responsible for anything, but those letting the contracts can certainly shove responsibility off onto them. The recommendations that they give can "become an alibi for adopting a policy one wants to adopt, but it is an alibi, that does not exclude the possibility that the choice of adviser was made, based on an anticipation that the adviser would make a recommendation which would correspond to one's wants."[1]

The advance of these "new regents" [q.v.] went hand in hand with the growth of the totems of the 1970s. Because policy responsibilities were decentralized, there are, for example, civil servants in policy positions in every municipality, in every organization who write mission statements and policy papers. These are often written with the help of external advisers. This market is incredibly profitable: with a few changes, the same story can be sold to new clients again and again, and society foots the bill.

The wave of "spin-offs" that has washed over the Netherlands in the last few years has also created previously unknown opportunities for these policy entrepreneurs. An area has sprung up between the public and the private sectors that is neither one nor the other. It is made up of spin-off organizations, the competences of which are often not regulated by legislation and that are not subject to parliamentary control.

The spin-off of government tasks to independent units—where the government spins off the implementation but officially retains its influence and responsibility—is far and away the most commonly used form of privatization in the Netherlands. In the 1980s, in a number of areas, the government spun off tasks to "independent administrative organizations," known in Dutch as ZBOs (*zelfstandige bestuursorganen*). ZBOs shot up like mushrooms all over the Netherlands. There are now at least 160 of them, and they take in about 160 billion guilders a year.

During this process, all sorts of half-baked responsibility and rickety authority were tried. One ZBO would hold a de facto monopoly, like the pilotage system; another would be financed as it always had been—by the government—like the labor exchange; a third could continue to make use of the infrastructure that was owned by the government, like Dutch Rail. In reality, very few ZBOs were subjected to true "market discipline."

This can also be seen in the fact that a part of the 160 billion guilders is being used for a considerable management expansion, coupled with a sizable salary increase. In the pilotage system, the salary increases were simply passed through in price hikes: that was not a problem; it's always been a monopoly. Part-time directors were sometimes paid full-time salaries, a fact that only came to light when conflicts broke out.

FROM ZBOs TO ZomBOs

Spin-offs were intended to increase efficiency, better quantify production and introduce competition. In his doctoral thesis at the University of Groningen (1998), in which he analyzed six spun-off governmental organizations at various levels, H. ter Bogt found that hardly any of these things have come about. The politicians did not have the information they needed to determine if things did work more efficiently. The causes? Among other things, they included a lack of competition, tasks that were not suited to industrial approaches and the strong legal position of the organization's personnel, which holds back change.[2]

In 1992 an official commission was formed to study each proposed spin-off. The chairman, A. Oele, quickly came to the conclusion that nearly all the managers involved wanted a place in the free market, but with government protection: "The more freedom you give to the manager of a service that has been spun off, the more he identifies with his product."[3]

Similar statements have quickly followed one another since then. The adoration of the independent spin-off totem got under way very quickly in the early 1990s. In 1992 the Scheltema investigatory commission concluded that it had become a mess. Every ministry had the leeway to slap together little pieces of legislation as it saw fit. "There has hardly been any overall leadership. (. . .) No one has been maintaining oversight, no one saw how thoughtlessly the phenomenon was being applied, how much the means of political control were being damaged."[4]

In September 1994 the Sint commission brought out its report *Responsible Independent Spin-Offs*. Creating independent spin-offs has become fashionably trendy, said Sint. This approach was often applied thoughtlessly, and political authority was often given up at the drop of a hat. This was not the correct approach: where public tasks are being carried out, you have to choose statutory legal forms. "Creating an external, independent spin-off cannot be an end-run around both market and government discipline."

The hardest blow was dealt by the Office of the Budget in its annual report for 1994. The Office of the Budget studied 160 of the 625 ZBOs. For half of them, the government had never justified why spinning them off was necessary. Hierarchically, 59 of them did not fall under any supervisory authority. For 49 of them, there was no obligation to send the minister an annual report. For the remainder that were required to submit annual reports, in practice, half of them did not supply the reports. Not one of the ZBOs studied had a regulation that fulfilled all the requirements levied by the government.

The devastating report of the Office of the Budget alarmed the "purple" government, which had taken power in 1994 with a resolution to restore "the primacy of political responsibility." The cabinet announced a review of all ZBOs and is preparing a framework law that will clarify the position of the ZBOs. In 1997 members of Parliament of all political colors complained about the proliferation of the ZBOs, and demanded stronger oversight by the ministries and, if necessary, the return of tasks to the central government.

So, a few years after the professional and administrative Netherlands was unanimously blowing the horn for ZBOs, it has become fashionable in those same circles to place tongue in cheek and call them "ZomBO-s." This quick and sharp turnabout in attitude could almost lead one to forget that it was not the idea itself that came under fire in the 1990s but the careless, matter-of-fact manner with which it was broadly applied and the absence of an appropriate structure defining responsibility.

In the meantime, a considerable, but delayed, bill has been presented for payment for the erection of the privatization totem pole. The first installment—the costs of the salaries that have gotten out of hand and the golden parachutes for incompetent managers and administrators—is being paid now. The second installment—the costs of partially dismantling it—is to follow.

NOTES

1. H. Daalder, "Van oude en nieuwe regenten, of: Politiek als beroep" [Of Old and New Regents, or: Politics as a Profession], speech made on the occasion of his retirement as a professor of political science from the University of Leiden, 2 April 1993, Leiden, 1993, pp. 33 et seq.

2. *de Volkskrant*, 21 January 1998.

3. Quote in Tom-Jan Meeus, "Privatisering leidde tot bureaucratie der dubbele loyaliteiten" [Privatization Led to the Bureaucracy of Dual Loyalties], *NRC Handelsblad*, 19 November 1994.

4. *Steekhoudend Ministerschap, rapport van de externe commissie Ministeriële Verantwoordelijkheid* [Convincing Ministership, Report of the External Commission of Ministerial Responsibility], Tweede Kamer [Second Chamber], 1992-1993, 21 427, nrs. 40 and 41. Quote in Tom-Jan Meeus, *NRC Handelsblad*, 19 November 1994.

CHAPTER 7

The Helpless Gladiators

Specialists in administration science like to refer to the area in which social forces interact as an "arena." They do not mean anything bad by that: it is a democratic arena in which self-sufficient citizens and their organizations confront one another and give form to their mutual arrangements themselves. According to this arena model, the role of the greatly slimmed down government is to withdraw to the sidelines and graciously watch the game. In old-liberal style, it is assumed that the free interplay of social forces will of itself lead to the optimum solution.

In recent years this Dutch variant of "grassroots" administration has become known as the "Polder Model." The name refers to the battle that the Dutch have been waging with the water for centuries to keep their land from being flooded. That is an exceptionally common interest. This battle to keep their feet dry has led to the typically Dutch culture of consensus and negotiation. The underlying idea is that if everyone contributes to the discussion and listens to everyone else, then the government can keep its distance. The original "Polder Model" was the *Waterschap*: a democratic organization of all those who owned land or buildings in a polder. *Waterschap*s had been established in the Netherlands as early as the Middle Ages and are among the earliest democratic organizations in the world.

With the emergence of "arena thinking," accompanied by decentralization, self-regulation and privatization, elements of this model were also introduced into public administration. World leaders such as President Clinton, the British Prime Minister Blair and the German Chancellor Schröder are singing the praise of this approach in unison. The Dutch economy is doing well because of the Polder Model. The

Dutch prefer not to think that it might be the other way around. If everything is going well, and there is enough for everybody, the Polder Model works fine. It is less certain that this is also the case when there are shortages, crisis or conflicting interests. In cases like that the readiness to listen is considerably less, and there is a great danger that the weak parties will be outvoted. The danger also increases that all the discussion that is necessary to come to agreement on a single line will undermine the decisiveness of the decision-making process.

The Polder Model has some of the characteristics of a good-weather model, and that is because there was a "copying mistake" made when translating the original water-control model into a general administrative model. Besides being democratic, a *Waterschap* is also exceptionally efficient and decisive. A great number of parties participate in the discussion, but there is also strong leadership, which, having heard all the opinions, makes decisions: the *Waterschap* board, led by the dike warden, overseen by the Crown Ministry of Water.

Even in times of economic prosperity, the arena hides—in addition to an *invisible hand*—another appendage: an *invisible foot*, which tramples the weak and the vulnerable.[1] With the introduction of "arena legislation," the government has given up its pretensions of leadership. Citizens have lost the chance to turn to the government for help and to make claims based on binding rules.[2]

Decentralization, self-regulation and privatization are important components of arena thinking. The helplessness of the underprivileged groups that ended up in this arena was magnified when their problems involved one or more of the new taboos. That made some of the causes that made them underprivileged literally unmentionable. In the chapters that follow, I offer some examples of groups that had the misfortune to land squarely at the intersection of some of these totems and taboos.

In the jargon of social rejuvenation [q.v.], "underprivileged groups" are often pictured as a sort of monolithic whole: a collection of victims. In reality, the inhabitants of poor neighborhoods are, in many respects, not standing shoulder to shoulder but are in a face-off. You can find groups of underprivileged, marginalized young people and groups of marginalized older people who no longer dare to go out at night for fear that they will be harassed by a gang of the aforementioned marginalized young people. You can find *allochtoon* inhabitants who feel that they are being discriminated against by the established Dutch. But you can also find ethnic Dutch inhabitants who, in less than ten years, have seen themselves surrounded by immigrants with a totally different lifestyle and who could not say anything about that without being made out to be a racist. And you can find Islamic women who are trying to get out from under the control of their fathers and husbands.

You can find squatters [q.v.] but also old people who had to look on helplessly as the council housing to which they had a right was stolen right out from under their noses; the theft was "legalized" by the municipality, and the housing was sublet by the residents for a multiple of the price that they were paying. You find long-term unemployed who show their displeasure by going for a walk with a pit bull, but also welfare mothers who do not dare to go for a walk with their stroller out of fear of terrier terror. Each and every one of them is certainly an underprivileged group.

Underprivileged groups do not form a homogeneous category of people who need only help. What they have in common is that, more than others, they have to turn to the public sector to fulfill the necessities of life. But they are not standing united, shoulder to shoulder, in the public sector, because there is a scarcity of resources there. They are also street fighters in an arena in which might makes right, when neither local government nor another local organization feels called upon to intervene between the combatants.

Public housing corporations do not like to be patronizing and have hoisted the privacy flag high up the mast. For municipal administrations it is much easier to treat underprivileged groups as a sort of uniform whole than to make difficult and partially tabooed choices in a social minefield. The closer you are to the citizens, the harder it is to be strict. The price for this is that the weakest members of underprivileged groups can no longer get government protection from those who are less weak.

THE LESSONS OF HAPPY STREET

When I hear someone singing the praises of the "civil society," I think about the Transvaal neighborhood in East Amsterdam, where my father grew up. The first workers' apartments designed by Berlage were completed there in 1913. The inhabitants were, almost without exception, members of the Social Democratic Workers' Party (SDAP) [q.v.] and, in large part, had come from the slums of the Jewish quarter of Amsterdam. Out of the window of the train on its way to Amstel Station, I always look at that proud complex that belonged to the Friends of the Workers housing corporation. There it stands like a safe stronghold with its pretty, stylized emblem in the gable. When leaders of the social democratic movement held speeches here, it was not from a podium but from the bay window of the Smalhout family's apartment. People danced around the maypole in the early morning of the first of May in the middle of Transvaal Square. There was a common where the Voice of the People and Art after Work gave concerts. Once a year there was a balcony decoration contest, and then the whole of Transvaal Street was festooned in streamers and flowers.

Not far from the fort of the Friends of the Workers, just across the train tracks, is Vrolikstraat [Happy Street], where, on 23 March 1993, a 12-year-old Turkish girl named Zülbiye Gündüz was beaten to death by her mentally ill neighbor. In the preceding months, 13 complaints had been made to the police about the neighbor. Lawyers had been engaged, and petitions had been circulated. Finally, the Gündüz family had requested to be moved to other housing.

Why had the New-East housing corporation not done anything? They had indeed called, they stated after Zülbiye's death, but the police and the Regional Institute for Out-patient Mental Health Care (RIAGG) refused to give them any information: privacy! Housing corporations are not friends anymore; they do not pay attention to their tenants, but to their market position. Why did the "visiting psychiatrist" not do anything? Because no one had asked him to. "We sit behind out desks until we get a call," explained a psychiatrist from RIAGG-East in the newspaper *Het Parool*. Our welfare state had them all: the submunicipality, the police precinct team, the RIAGG region, the social workers, the housing corporation, but they could not save Zülbiye.

Zülbiye and her neighbor were surrounded by social workers and organizations but were nevertheless left to their fates. Through a fatal combination of totems and taboos, the organizations were not prepared to exchange information or to exercise oversight, let alone to intervene. For the Gündüz family the state turned out to be the thing that we want to avoid at all costs: a Moloch against which you cannot defend yourself. It is just that this Moloch does not look the way that we had expected: he is not huge, monolithic and overpowering but slimy and elusive. He isn't "them," but us.

MENTAL HEALTH CARE:
NO TREATMENT WITHOUT NEGOTIATION

The reports of Zülbiye's death included photos of the inside of her neighbor's apartment. It looked like a total garbage dump that had repeatedly been set on fire. Anyone could see that the resident of this apartment was mentally disturbed; why did the powers that be not do anything?

In the mid-1970s the expansion of the taboo on intervention led to considerable reticence to forcibly commit and treat mental patients. Even in mental health care the autonomy of the "client" was elevated to the norm. According to "antipsychiatry," the client had to be seen as a "potentially autonomous individual" who—with his own free will and proven motivations—had to be assisted.[3] Coercion, therefore, had to be limited to situations in which there was a fear of "danger" to the client or to those around him. In fact, it became customary for treatment to be preceded by extensive "negotiations" on whether the client would indeed permit the treatment, said Henrie Henselmans, a psychiatrist from Rotterdam.[4]

This approach, a result of the optimistic 1970s, made victims of people who needed psychiatric help but who, because of their illness, did not have the autonomy and motivation to cooperate in committing themselves. This is the way in which a number of schizophrenic patients ended up on the street or in jail, said Alexander Achilles, a psychiatrist on a crisis team with RIAGG, "while they would have benefited from commitment." The Epsilon Association, whose members include the parents and family members of chronic psychotics and schizophrenics, has been trying for more than ten years to combat "the problem of a total lack of direction, which, with regard to the patients, is nothing more than total neglect," said Liesbeth Gerris of the Amsterdam Epsilon Work Group. She blames the psychiatrists, who not only abandon their patients to their own fate but also blame the patients for it by saying that the patients "chose to be on the street," of an even more coarse negligence. "One of the very common symptoms of schizophrenia is that you live in a delusional world: you are not sick; it is the rest of the world that is crazy. How can you ask someone like that if he "chooses" to be treated?"

The model of nonintervention is tailored to citizens, sound of mind and body, who are adequately equipped to take part in vital negotiations. If we view society, as became fashionable in the 1980s, as an "arena," then drifters and schizophrenics are among the most helpless of the gladiators.

In the 1990s it was the sea wall that changed the course of the ship here, too. "Now you see more and more care givers who are not afraid of a little paternalism," said Henrie Henselmans, the originator of the term "intrusive care."[5] "Really, that is very old-fashioned social-psychiatric work. Sticking your nose into everything, very practically. In the last few years that has not been done in mental health care." Alexander Achilles also sees something in intrusive care. According to him, easily two-thirds of the street people are "stark raving mad and the rest are, for the most part, retarded or heavily addicted. Looking back, I have to admit that we went along too easily with the general culture of reticence."

Interestingly enough, the emergence of this new consensus coincides with the entrance into force of the Special Admittance to Mental Hospitals Act (Bopz), in which the optimistic thinking of the 1970s is codified. In the Bopz, which, in 1994, replaced the Idiots Act of 1884, forcible commitment "for the patient's own good" has been shoved aside as being too patronizing; only the criterion of danger remains valid. Its long march through the legislative institutions took so long that the new law, as Henselmans expressed it, "could not anticipate the counter movement towards intervention."

Still the Bopz offers psychiatrists a lot of leeway for forcible commitments: the criterion defining danger has been considerably stretched by the judiciary.[6] The Supreme Court has decided that forcible commitment is possible if the danger exists that someone will "fall to the bottom of society" or will "neglect himself." Because quite a few social workers continued to hold on to the total autonomy of the client, the Inspector General's Office for Mental Health Care took an unusual step in 1995. All the psychiatrists, public prosecutors, judges and mayors in the Netherlands were mailed a brochure in which their attention was drawn to the possibility of forcible commitment in the event of serious self-neglect and, in fact, were encouraged to interpret the concept of "danger" more freely.

Even in the area of mental health care, the question is justified whether some other interest is hiding behind all that respect for the autonomy of the client. The Bopz was intended to protect patients from overactive caregivers, said Rob Smeets, Chief Inspector for Mental Health Care, shortly after the brochure had been sent. "Now they use the Bopz so that they do not have to do anything. This laissez faire attitude has led to serious injustices on the street."[7]

AT THE END OF THE CHAIN

According to the sociologist Paul Schnabel, beginning in the mid-1980s a "second institutional wave" has swept over the Dutch welfare bureaucracy. The first wave, between the two world wars, was the wave of the Pillars [q.v.]. The second wave was inspired by the professionalism of the caregivers and the autonomy of the institutions.[8]

There is yet another difference between the two periods. In the first half of the century, the "civil society" was firmly embedded in the vertical lines of responsibility of the Pillars. When there was a resurgence of the civil society via the deregulation, decentralization and privatization of the 1980s, that foundation was missing. The Netherlands was full to overflowing with tuned-in policies, with integrated leadership and leadership by committee, with platforms, networks and made-to-order projects at the neighborhood level. But who was really responsible for it all?

Since 1982 the Netherlands has had a Chain of Responsibility Act. Contractors who subcontract with third parties or who borrow workers from third parties remain responsible for wage taxes and social insurance premiums that are due on the income of those workers. They can be held responsible for what happens "at the end of the chain," an effective weapon in the battle against workers in the shadow economy [q.v.]. For the organizations that go together to form the chain of responsibility for social welfare and administration, there is no such provision. Over the last few decades, it has become less clear for clients at the end of the chain just who they can turn to. The government handed over care and supervision to a multiplicity of organizations, often without ensuring clear lines of responsibility.

The chain of organizations, connected one to the other with the clients at the end, can be viewed as a food chain that is slowly being poisoned. The farther that the organism finds itself down the chain, the more poison that is heaped upon it from the links before it. In this instance, the poison is the refusal to accept responsibility.

The splintering that is sketched here has also inspired other authors to create metaphors. According to Henri Beunders, the Netherlands is beginning to look more and more like a pan of spaghetti that has been cooking for too long. A. Oele, the chairman of a commission that advised the Council of Ministers on new, independent spin-offs, saw the building complex that is the government sprout "countless balconies and arbors" during the last few years.[9]

A very good characterization comes from Bram Peper, who in his book *The Formation of Welfare Policy*, speaks of "organizational involution." The concept of "involution" was thought up by the American anthropologist Alexander Goldenweiser, who used it to describe how more and more complex decorative patterns develop in "primitive" cultures. Involutionary processes are distinguished by a progressive increase in the intricacy of the forms, without the introduction of any significant new elements to the pattern. As an example of involution in Europe, Goldenweiser named the excessive use of ornamentation in the flamboyant Gothic style of architecture.[10]

The anthropologist Clifford Geertz was the first to use this concept for the study of social change. He describes how, in nineteenth-century Java, the number of people was really too large for the available means of existence. The populace reacted to this by continually adapting both the spatial and social organization of rice growing to the presence of more people. This made everything more complex; Geertz speaks of an "inwardly directed refinement." With never-ending virtuosity, everyone was ensured a place under the sun. But this addition of progressively more detail prevented fundamental changes. The basic patterns of the economy, society and technology displayed an increasing rigidity.[11]

The fact that similar processes were under way in the administrative and institutional Netherlands was given still more credence in 1991 by a study done by the Dutch Economic Institute (NEI). The NEI made a comparison between large urban areas in northwestern Europe. They found an overabundance of plans and discussion clubs in the Randstad [q.v.], combined with an absence of real change. Every administrative level has enough of a say to delay the plans of others but not enough to get its own plans put through. According to the NEI, "the Dutch situation in this regard can be called unique."[12] A similar observation was made by Arthur Docters van Leeuwen, who, in the late 1990s, was named "Super Inspector General" to put an end to the splintering of the decentralized justice system. When he took office, he counted 57 external consultants and consulting organizations that had in a short period of time been engaged by the Ministry of Justice. It reminded him of "the sickbed of a monarch in the Middle Ages" who was practically being smothered by "the layer of gentlemen in waiting, courtiers, and personal physicians."[13]

This "organizational involution" began in the Netherlands in the rich 1960s and 1970s, when you could afford not to solve problems but to "define them away" by adding more institutions and hierarchical levels. After that, the process continued, hitching a ride on the new trends of decentralization, self-regulation and independent spin-offs. It was, therefore, not so strange that even the organizations in the neighborhood where Zülbiye Gündüz lived were carried away with a game of hot potato over responsibility. Were they to blame? They were following the example and the invitation of the government. No one has any certainty; no one is in charge: *panta rhei* [Greek: everything is in flux—Heraclitus].

NOTES

1. Dorien Pessers brought my attention to this concept, taken from William Ophuls, *Ecology and the Politics of Scarcity*, Freeman and Co., San Francisco, 1977.

2. Paul Kuypers, *Overheid, bureaucratie en nieuwe ontwikkelingen, een paar notities voor het debat* [The Government, Bureaucracy and the New Developments: A Few Notes for the Debate], De Balie, Amsterdam, 1992.

3. Paul Kuypers and Jos van der Lans, *Naar een modern paternalisme* [Toward a Modern Paternalism], De Balie, Amsterdam, 1994.

4. Unless otherwise noted, the quotations in this paragraph are taken from Vuijsje in cooperation with Bestebreurtje, 1996.

5. Henrie Henselmans, *Bemoeizorg, ongevraagde hulp voor psychotische patiënten* [Intrusive Care: Unrequested Care for Psychotic Patients], Eburon, Delft, 1993.

6. A schematic overview of the Judiciary can be found in Paul van Ginneken, "Een zodanig gevaar" [Such a Danger], NcGv-reeks 93-21, Utrecht, October 1993.

7. Quoted in Gerlof Leistra, "Gedwongen opname" [Forcible Commitment], *Elsevier*, 2 December 1995.

8. Quoted in Vuijsje in cooperation with Bestebreurtje, 1996.

9. *NRC Handelsblad*, 19 September 1992 and 19 November 1994.

10. A. Goldenweiser, "Loose Ends of a Theory on the Individual Pattern and Involution in Primitive Society" in R. Lowie (ed.), *Essays in Anthropology, Presented to A.L. Kroeber*, University of California Press, Berkeley, 1936, pp. 99-104.

11. Clifford Geertz, *Agricultural Involution, the Process of Ecological Change in Indonesia*, University of California Press, Berkeley/Los Angeles, 1963, pp. 80-82.

12. Kees Bastianen and Marcel van Lieshout, in *de Volkskrant*, 23 November 1991.

13. *de Volkskrant*, 19 April 1997.

CHAPTER 8

Why the Hemophiliacs Had to Bleed

In the Western world two groups were disproportionately heavily hit by HIV and AIDS: homosexuals and hemophiliacs. The former were infected by sexual contact; the latter, by blood transfusions that they have to have because of their illness. Hemophilia is a defect in the blood's ability to clot quickly that primarily affects men. Between 1979 and 1985, approximately 170 Dutch hemophiliacs were infected with HIV by contaminated blood products. Since then, more than a 100 of them have contracted AIDS or have died from it.[1]

The homosexual victims of HIV are also almost all men, but there is a huge difference between the two groups. The first is in the numbers: the Netherlands has hundreds of thousands of homosexual men and 1,300 hemophiliacs. While homosexuals make up almost 80 percent of the HIV and AIDS cases, hemophiliacs are only 3 percent. The second difference is that Dutch homosexuals are very well organized and can strongly defend their interests. They were very influential in the national coordination team that, until 1987, largely determined AIDS policy and the obligation of funds from the budget that the Ministry of Welfare, Health and Culture made available. The primary characteristic of hemophiliacs, on the other hand, is their reserve and caution, inspired by their understanding of how fragile the human body is. A method to provide hemophiliacs with clotting factors via blood transfusion was only discovered in the 1960s. Up until then, their life expectancy was much lower than the average, and they had to contend with long periods of immobility and with increasing disability.[2]

These two differences turned out to be of major importance when these two groups had to face each other in the interest-group arena, where the government primarily restricted itself to the provision of funding, leaving the formation of policy largely to the "experienced specialists" from the field. Within the organized world of homosexuals, people talked enthusiastically about a "Dutch model of disease self-management."[3] But for the hemophiliacs, this model offered less reason to be happy.

THE "BLOOD DEBATE":
EXPLOITATION OF THE TABOO ON DISCRIMINATION

In early 1983, when the first reports of AIDS infections in hemophiliacs came out, a stormy "blood debate" broke out in the Netherlands. The Dutch Association of Hemophiliacs wanted the best possible protection of the blood supply. The blood banks, following the example of the United States, proposed to remove all homosexuals—the most important risk group for AIDS infection—from the donor lists.

The homosexual organizations refused to go along with this, for fear of being stigmatized. In the end a compromise was reached: the blood banks would request that persons belonging to the "risk groups" not volunteer to be donors. The homosexual organizations promised to strongly support this request. But as a condition, they insisted that not all homosexual men be viewed as members of the "risk group," but only those with multiple partners. After a stormy discussion, a definition of "multiple partners" was agreed upon: five or more partners in the preceding six months. Eight partners a year was, therefore, no reason to refrain from donating blood.[4] The hemophiliac organizations did not dare refuse this offer. "A conflict about blood donation fought out on the street could scare off other potential donors, which would lead to a shortage of blood plasma," said the chairman of the Dutch Association of Hemophiliacs, Cees Smit, "to the great disadvantage of hemophiliacs."[5]

This more or less forced compromise formed the basis of donor policy from early 1983 to early 1985, when it became possible to test donor blood for HIV contamination. Beginning in 1985, tests showed that approximately 15 HIV-positive donations were made a year out of a total of 400,000 to 700,000. Many of these donations came from donors who belonged to a risk group.[6] It can be assumed that for 1983 and 1984 approximately the same was true. This means that in those two years a couple of dozen HIV-positive blood donations were made, an important part of which came from homosexual donors.

In the meantime, a number of blood banks have come out with a declaration in which the donor declares to have read the AIDS information packet and, to the best of his knowledge, not to belong to one of the listed risk groups—including all men who, after 1980, have had sexual contact with another man. The Dutch Association of Homosexuals-COC [q.v.] was furious and talked about a "not-a-homo declaration," a reference to the not-a-Jew declaration that the occupying German forces had demanded during the war.[7] With this statement, the battle reached its absolute low point, and the memory of the victims of oppression was misused in the most cynical manner. From this comparison, the conclusion could be drawn that a valid justification existed for the exclusion of the Jews, which indeed is the case for the barring of donors from risk groups. At the beginning of the epidemic, the hemophiliac associations had reached this conclusion themselves by asking partners and helpers of hemophiliacs to refrain from donating.

A similar carefulness could not be detected in the attitude of the homosexual organizations. In the debate about whether members of the risk groups should have themselves tested—in some countries homosexuals were required to do so—the homosexual organizations were able to exercise so much power that initially the balance of the scales tipped all the way to the opposite side. In 1985, primarily at their insistence, a campaign was waged among homosexual men that was aimed at discouraging them from taking the antibody test. It was reasoned that both HIV-positive and HIV-negative homosexuals had to change to safe sex. The test results would, therefore, not provide any additional information about the required change in behavior. In addition, a negative result could generate a false sense of security.

In the second half of the 1980s, the policy discouraging the test came under increasing criticism. Studies showed that HIV-positive homosexuals were more likely to alter their behavior than HIV-negatives and those who had not been tested. In addition, there were more and more possibilities for early treatment. At the end of the 1980s, the policy discouraging the test made room for a more neutral position that offered advice of the advantages and disadvantages of the test in a businesslike manner.[8]

Hemophiliacs' survival depends on a reliable blood supply. They cannot avoid the chance of HIV infection if the government does not live up to its responsibility to ensure the purity of blood products. On these grounds the governments of a number of countries are paying huge sums to AIDS-infected hemophiliacs. A financial arrangement had to wait a long time in the Netherlands. AIDS-infected hemophiliacs were treated exactly the same as people who had been infected by sexual contact. The government was afraid to create a "precedent" by giving one of the groups a financial concession. The others could then also demand money, and the rejection of the demand could create the impression that the others were infected "through their own fault."

Every proposal to help the hemophiliacs stranded on objections from the Dutch HIV Association, the interest group of HIV-positives and AIDS patients, the majority of whose members are homosexual men.

Supported by the well-organized homosexual lobby, for years they managed to drown out the interests of the small group of hemophiliacs in the interest-group arena.

It was not until 1994 that the government created a contingency fund from which hemophiliacs with AIDS could draw a payment of 25,000 guilders. The payment for damages offered by the Netherlands was the next to the lowest on the list of 20 countries compiled by the World Federation of Associations of Hemophiliacs.[9] In 1995 the Minister of Welfare, Health and Culture, prompted by the National Ombudsman's report (discussed later) granted a payment for damages in the amount of 200,000 guilders to all 170 hemophiliacs who had been infected by HIV-contaminated donor blood. For the 30 who had already died, the grant was too late.

After the outbreak of the epidemic, the homosexual organizations succeeded in stretching the taboo on discrimination to the point that being a homosexual could not be treated as a risk factor. Even the term "risk group" was almost taboo. "In the Netherlands, you have to speak of 'risky behavior,'" said AIDS specialist Roel Coutinho. "But with sexual contact, it is not only the behavior, but the person with whom you do it: how great is the chance that he is a carrier of the virus? In Amsterdam, the chance for a homosexual male is perhaps 25 percent and for a heterosexual perhaps one in a thousand. But a statement like that would almost be considered discriminatory."[10]

The antitest campaign among homosexual men, the refusal to completely refrain from donating blood for transfusion and the resistance to compensation for hemophiliacs were, after a number of years, reversed or overruled. Public organizations had needed all that time to screw up their courage and to step into the arena where they had exposed these two minority groups to facing each other in unequal combat. By then, the bigger one had already done a lot of damage to the smaller one. The fact that there was intervention at the end of the 1980s was also due to the fact that the "spirit of the times" had changed. The weapons that the homosexual lobby had used—a "stretched" taboo on discrimination, a strong aversion to government intercession and a powerful call to nonintervention—began to show some wear after all the years.

AIDS BY BLOOD TRANSFUSION:
DRACULA AS DIRECTOR OF THE BLOOD BANK

In 1983, when it became clear that there was a danger of AIDS infection via blood transfusion, another possibility for protecting the blood supply—besides calling on donors from risk groups to refrain from giving blood—came in sight. Publications began to appear about a method of cleansing blood products of HIV by heating them. The effectiveness of this heat treatment was demonstrated in 1984. That same year, the Dutch Association of Hemophiliacs urged the state secretary of Welfare, Health and Culture to introduce heat treatment as soon as possible. It took the Ministry until 1988, however, to come out with compulsory guidelines, which nevertheless were ignored by some blood banks. The Dutch Association of Hemophiliacs submitted a complaint about this to the National Ombudsman, who issued a report on the matter in July 1995.

The largest supplier of blood products in the Netherlands, the Central Laboratory of the Blood Transfusion Service, began delivering heat-treated blood in the summer of 1985. It took until the beginning of 1986, however, before talks got under way with the 22 regional blood banks, which could also prepare blood products. After that, six months was lost before "consensus" could be reached on a requirement to apply the heat treatment. Why the consensus? Because the central government's Inspection Service, which exercised oversight over the quality of public health care, operated, as a matter of policy, on a consensus model. "This is the way it went: look to the responsibility of the field," summarized chief inspector Verhoeff. "If, at a certain moment, the majority of the field says: this is good, then at a certain moment, we'll talk with the stragglers."[11]

When consensus was finally reached, a "transition period" of a year was agreed to on top of that. The requirement would go into effect in June 1987. It took until July 1987 before the state secretary addressed the blood banks. He let them know that he found the proposed regulations to be "of especially great importance." Unfortunately, the proposed deadline had passed, but not to worry: 1 January 1988 was the new deadline. In December the requirement was indeed made law. "But later, it turned out that a number of blood banks went on for years without using the heat treatment," said Jan van Wijngaarden, the central government inspector for combating infectious diseases.[12]

In his report, the Ombudsman established that in a number of aspects, the government had not acted "appropriately." The state secretary took too "passive" a stance and had to repeatedly be prodded by medical organizations to take action. The government should have clearly made the risk of using blood that had not been heat-treated a topic of discussion or prohibited it. Further, it was evident that the government let an unacceptably large amount of time be lost before it took steps to compel action. Other countries had made the heat treatment of blood mandatory earlier; the Federal Republic of Germany, for example, did so in 1985.

The organization of the blood supply in the Netherlands is an example of self-regulation before the term existed. There are indeed guidelines, but the blood banks—independent associations—can make "justified" deviations from them. That is how, according to Cees Breederveld, chairman of the Collegium on Blood Transfusion, there are blood banks that do not adhere to the guidelines that donors from risk groups should be refused, because they think that it is "harmful" for the donors involved.[13]

Critical memoranda on the fragmentation of the Dutch blood supply have followed one another for at least ten years. In August 1982, shortly before the problem of AIDS came on the scene, ex-minister Ginjaar stated in a report that the blood banks had shortcomings in their control, cohesion and cooperation that endangered the usefulness of the medical blood supply.[14] But these calls of alarm did not produce results. The Hague trusted the blood banks to exercise "their own responsibility," said Dick Dees, who became the State Secretary for Health in 1986. First there had to be an extensive discussion with all those in the field who were involved so as to come to a "consensus."[15] The Dutch Association of Hemophiliacs expressed itself much more clearly and spoke of "a failure of self-regulation."

As a result of these events the transfusion system finally came under review. "The system of blood bank oversight has been sharpened," said government inspector Van Wijngaarden. "Much more supervision is being applied." Breederveld pleads for centralization and strong regulation: replace the 22 associations with "one centrally managed organization, with a board of directors, that can compel agreement and cooperation."[16]

HEMOPHILIACS: VICTIMS OF TOTEMS AND TABOOS

AIDS cases do not have to be reported to the inspection service in the Netherlands; voluntary, anonymous reporting is considered sufficient. As a result of this choice, which was made primarily to protect the privacy of the patients, the government cannot make any concrete statements about the number of infections from blood products. The absence of a requirement for mandatory reporting contributed, according to a specialist engaged by the National Ombudsman, to an "inadequate infrastructure" for government oversight.

The government could have gathered information on the scope of contamination among homosexual patients in another manner: by research. But here, too, as the government informed the Ombudsman, the privacy interests of those affected prevented that. The government had consciously abandoned this idea, because with such a small group, the anonymity of those affected could not be sufficiently guaranteed. The specialist was devastating in his evaluation of this point as well. A complete picture could now be achieved only through the extrapolation of samples done by third parties: an "inefficient manner for quickly gathering the desired epidemiological information" and, moreover, "insufficient for the timely formulation of a 'pro-active' policy."

Since 1985, when the screening of donor blood became possible, as far as is known, no more hemophiliacs have been infected by blood products. Of the 170 infections that had taken place before that, at least 11 came about through the use of non-heat-treated Dutch blood products in the period 1983 to 1985.[17] If the government had taken a less passive stand and had forced an earlier implementation of heat treatment, the number would have probably been lower. The Ombudsman did not make a statement on the question of guilt; and there is equally little chance of a judicial inquiry. Hereby, guilt is being implicitly laid at the feet of the "consensus" of the time: the taboo on compulsory intervention and the inviolability of self-regulation.

The number of victims could have also been lower if the homosexual organizations had not taken such an intransigent position. We have seen earlier that, in 1983 and 1984, dozens of HIV-positive blood donations were made, of which a major part came from homosexual donors. This number would have probably been lower if the homosexual organizations had asked all their members to refrain from donating blood, and if the tests had been encouraged instead of discouraged.[18]

The fate of the hemophiliacs paints a somberly complete picture that shows how totems and taboos can affect small minority groups that are suddenly confronted with a great danger. The blood banks could continue to deliver dangerous products for years, because the government dared not break the self-regulation and consensus axioms. Even when that finally happened, some blood banks refused to comply, with an appeal to "blind-eye think." Dracula had become the director of the blood bank, and the government was not holding up a cross in front of his nose. The most important risk group, male homosexuals, remained a danger for years by appealing to a greatly expanded taboo on discrimination and not being afraid of making reference to the war.

Hemophiliacs, due to their limited numbers and the specifics of their illness, were not inclined to make a fuss. They asked the government privately for help, but the government had retreated behind the sidelines and was watching the tumult of the battle. The fashionable enthusiasm for negotiation-think left no room for an appraisal of the relative strength of the combatants. The fact that the government did not have an adequate overview of the seriousness of the problem played into the hand of this standoffish position. On the grounds of a privacy taboo that had been stretched to the extremes, the government had forgone mandatory registration of HIV cases as well as studies of hemophiliacs. The government indicated to the National Ombudsman that the latter was for the good of those involved. The patient died, but privacy was maintained: a further expansion of the privacy taboo was really impossible.

NOTES

1. In addition, estimates are that another 150 recipients of blood transfusions were infected with HIV; in the meantime, 47 of them have been confirmed to have AIDS. Jos Hulst and Cees Smit, in *de Volkskrant*, 22 February 1996.

2. Cees Smit and Frits Rosendaal, "Hemofilie en aids: een andere werkelijkeheid" [Hemophilia and AIDS: Another Reality], in Herman Vuijsje and Roel Coutinho (eds.), *Dilemma's rondom aids* [Dilemmas about AIDS], Swets and Zeitlinger, Amsterdam/Lisse, 1989, pp. 47-66.

3. Simon Rozendaal, *Blus de brand, gesprekken over de Nederlandse aidsbestrijding* [Put out the Fire: Conversations on Dutch AIDS Control], Stichting Aids Fonds /Uitgeverij Jan Mets, Amsterdam, 1996.

4. Roel Coutinho, "Een terugblik vanuit het beleid" [A Look Back from within the Policy], in Vuijsje and Coutinho, 1989, p. 17.

5. Smit and Rosendaal, in Vuijsje and Coutinho, 1989, pp. 47-66.

6. In 1985 there were 15 HIV-positive donations out of a total of about 400,000; in 1986 there were also 15 (742,000) and in 1987, 16 (737,000). The figures are taken from the magazine *Concept*, 22 March 1994, quoted in the report of the National Ombudsman, p. 71. See also Smit and Rosendaal, in Vuijsje and Coutinho, 1989, pp. 55 and 56.

7. Smit and Rosendaal, in Vuijsje and Coutinho, 1989, pp. 64, 65.

8. A similar situation occurred in the assistance organizations for drug addicts. They, too, were initially taken with a policy of discouragement. It was only in 1987, when one-third of the injecting drug addicts surveyed in Amsterdam were found to be infected with HIV, that their attitude changed.

9. An overview from *Information Clearinghouse* of the World Federation of Hemophilia, May 1994, quoted in the report of the National Ombudsman, pp. 33/34. The highest payment for damages was made in France: 660,000 guilders. The only country on the list that made payments that were less than the Netherlands was Hungary: 15,000 guilders.

10. Quoted in Herman Vuijsje, *Keuzes in het Nederlandse Aidsbeleid* [Choices in Dutch AIDS Policy], gemeente Amsterdam, Amsterdam, 1992.

11. Quoted in Vuijsje in cooperation with Bestebreurtje, 1995.

12. Ibid.

13. Quoted in Petra de Koning, "De macht van de bloedkoninkrijkjes taant" [The Power of the Little Blood Kingdoms Is Waning], *Vrij Nederland*, 2 September 1995.

14. L. Ginjaar, *Nota bloedtransfusiebeleid van het Nederlandse Rode Kruis*

[Paper on Blood Transfusion Policy by the Dutch Red Cross], August 1982. Quoted in *National Ombudsman*, 1995, p. 36.

15. Quoted in De Koning, 1995.

16. Ibid.

17. Study results reprinted in the report of the National Ombudsman, p. 115. Another study for the same years comes to at least 36 cases of infection, but this includes infections via imported blood products. E.P. Mauser-Bunschoten, *Complications of Hemophilia Care*, Ibero, Houten, 1995.

18. The situation in the Netherlands is, in fact, considerably more serious, because in addition to the 170 hemophiliacs, apparently 150 other people were infected with HIV via blood transfusions. A third of them have since developed AIDS. Jos Hulst and Cees Smit, *de Volkskrant*, 22 February 1996.

PART II

In Search of the Causes

CHAPTER 9

The Public Memory
of the War

The social images that I have referred to as totems and taboos were not an exclusively Dutch phenomenon. Decentralization, privatization and self-regulation are being worked on elsewhere as well. An increased sensitivity in the areas of privacy, ethnic relations and government coercion is to be found in other Western countries also. Nevertheless, Dutch attitudes were a cause for surprise outside the Netherlands.

The sad story that Maurits Schmidt dished up in *Het Parool* in 1992 is an example. In the early 1990s, a series of friendly contacts had grown up between the Hageveld high school in the Dutch city of Heemstede and the Stiftsgymnasium, attached to the Benedictine cloister in the Austrian city of Lambach. The two schools decided to initiate an exchange program, and a delegation from Heemstede visited Lambach that same year. After that, the rector, Anselm Mayrl, did not hear anything further, until, in mid-December, a letter from Heemstede arrived in the mailbox. It was a good-bye letter: in the intervening time, the Hageveld high school had become aware that the young Adolf Hitler had gone to school at the Stiftsgymnasium, which was the reason that an exchange between the two schools was no longer desirable.

Hitler went to school in Lambach from when he was seven until he was nine, not to the Stiftsgymnasium but to the nearby public school. The cloister's only crime is that Hitler sang in the choir. During the war, the Nazis confiscated the cloister and established an elite school there. Two of the fathers from the cloister lost their lives to the Nazi regime. The Stiftsgymnasium does a lot against the resurgence of fascism and racism with programs that bring in Jewish concentration camp survivors and others. A group of students went to Mauthausen [q.v.]. But there was no trip to Heemstede.[1]

In the preceding chapters, I demonstrated that in the Netherlands this sort of political correctness developed a high level of intensity, sharply expanded its scope, and was dominant for a long period of time. That being the case, the question is which specifically Dutch factors are responsible for this. In the following chapters I look for these factors. In my search, I do not look for one, all-encompassing origin but for a confluence of developments that came about at the same time and reinforced one another.

One factor comes immediately to mind. It is impossible to examine the taboos on the invasion of privacy, ethnic differences and government coercion without immediately thinking of World War II. Especially in combination, these taboos bring out memories of the worst things that happened then. These memories are also perpetuated elsewhere in Europe, but there are few countries where this has had such far-reaching effects as in the Netherlands. In the Netherlands, the memory of the war was strongly developed and remained so. Can any links be found in recent Dutch history that can explain this?

If there is one country that can be compared to the Netherlands in this respect, it is Germany. The memory of the war that the Netherlands' eastern neighbors [i.e. Germany] have, led, in a number of areas, to "broad" taboos that were anchored in government regulations. Still, the origins are not easily comparable. It is understandable that the Germans are wrestling with a feeling of collective guilt. In the Netherlands the past offers much less reason for preoccupation with racism and state coercion. Democracy in the Netherlands has never been threatened from within, and instances of collective persecution of foreigners within Dutch borders have been rare. There are no Dutch groups before the twentieth century that are known to have written a hate of foreigners into their platform. Ghettos, pogroms and other expressions of virulent antiSemitism were only known in the Netherlands in the Middle Ages.

Even the colonial past [q.v.] does not provide sufficient explanation of the strong expansion of taboos in the past few decades. Colonialism is far away; it did not play an important role as a yardstick for personal behavior. No one ever invokes the image of a "new Van Heutsz" [q.v.], of "new coolies" [q.v.] or of "*pelopors* of our day and age" [q.v.] in the debate on racism. There were never references to the slave ships [q.v.], to Elimna [q.v.], Boven Digul [q.v.] or Fort Zeelandia [q.v.]. The metaphors used to warn against the dangers of present-day racism were always taken from the more recent past: "new Hitler," "new Jews," modern-day "resistance," "deportations."

The popularity of the war metaphors was not the work of the generation of the war. The comparisons were made by people who were neither "good" nor "bad" [q.v.] during the war—not because they, like most of the Dutch of that time, had just been trying to get on with their lives but because they had not been born yet. For the generation of the baby boom, which, for the most part, determines current morality, the war is the most important moral reference point.

The fact that the postwar opinion makers did not participate in the war themselves is a nasty handicap. Their actions are based on remembrances and lore, as they wrestle with the unanswered questions asked of, and by, their parents. In order to see the effect that the war has had on the expansion of taboos, we have to look at the development of the public memory of the war, that is, the memory of the murder of the only ethnically different group that has lived in the Netherlands through the ages.

THE JEWS IN THE NETHERLANDS:
INCREASING EMBARRASSMENT

For centuries, the Jews in the Netherlands have found what the Portuguese printer Athias called "an easy exile and a hospitality that was not too harsh." They formed a sort of miniature society within the Republic [q.v.]: the Jewish Nation. Life within this Nation carried restrictions with it; Jews could not be members of most of the guilds. But for the time, the position of the Jews demonstrates a rather high degree of tolerance. They were seen as free citizens who could make claim to the same protections from the government as every other Dutchman. They were never plundered or forced to wear a sign of their difference such as a Jew's patch or a Jew's hat or driven together into ghettos.

"The pragmatism of the Dutch people always won out over the feeling of aversion that is common to many with regard to strangers," said M.H. Gans in his monumental *Memorboek* on the history of Dutch Jewry. In his opinion, the relatively favorable reception of the Jews in the Netherlands was, in large part, attributable to the traditional Dutch respect for trade and to the Calvinist respect for the Old Testament. When I interviewed him in 1983, Gans emphasized that people did not belong to the Jewish Nation because of their race but because of their religious beliefs. Those who converted to Christianity were legally no longer viewed as members of the Nation and could also become members of the guilds. "The guilds were really a sort of Christian Labor Union [q.v.]. There was not even remotely any racism. That was also true of life outside the guilds: Jews could have ridden the streetcar, in a manner of speaking."[2]

In 1796 the National Assembly of the Batavian Republic [q.v.] put an end to the Jewish Nation. Jews would henceforth be ordinary Dutch citizens whose only difference from non-Jews was that they adhered to the "Israelite" faith. With the granting of civil equality to the Jews, for the first time something ambiguous crept into the relationship between the majority and minority. Jews seemed to have other things in common besides their religion. That was convincingly proven near the end of the nineteenth century, when the number of religious Jews fell, and a nevertheless clearly Jewish culture continued to exist.

The word "Jew" had always been used in Dutch without any sense of shame being attached to it. The Jews were different; everybody knew that. The Jews, in turn, spoke freely of a *Goy* (Gentile) or an *orel* (someone who has not been circumcised) when they were talking about a non-Jew. But from the nineteenth century onward a certain reserve attached to the names that were used for each other. Jew and *Goy* were now more and more often perceived as pejorative words. Non-Jews began to call Jews "Israelites." In the twentieth century double-bottomed words entered the language. *Mexicaner* [Mexican], used by Jews about a Jew, was derived from the Jiddish phrase "mag sie keiner" [no one likes him]. *Hilversummer* [someone from the city of Hilversum], used by Jews about non-Jews, was derived from 't Gooi [a homonym for *Goy*. 't Gooi is a region in Holland of which Hilversum is the center].

"After 1796, recognition of each other's differences became less and less matter-of-fact," said Gans. "Jews also began to behave more secretively about this. The non-Jewish populace did not understand this either." From time to time Gans would long for the semiapartheid of before. "A workman wore a cap and a Jew also belonged to a certain group. People recognized each other's differences. But we, with all our legislation, apparently cannot tolerate the recognition of a division, of a difference.[3]

This ambiguity did not disappear in the early twentieth century, when more and more Jews dared to take the step to the outside world. In Amsterdam—the only West-European city with an indigenous Jewish working class—socialism was usually the decisive push into the non-Jewish world. For the majority, that did not mean that they no longer wished to be Jews. To the contrary, some segments of the workers' movement "became Jewish." Under pressure of the circumstances of the 1930s, this ambiguity expressed itself in an increasing feeling of embarrassment with regard to Jews. The "feeling of nationalism" was fed by the Great Depression and unemployment and was strengthened by the streams of German-Jewish refugees that started in 1933. There was something strange about the Jews again. The people had become, as Sal Tas expressed it, "Jew-conscious."

That did not mean that antiSemitism had a grip on the Netherlands. The membership of the antiSemitic parties in the Netherlands was smaller than in other European countries.[4] In its early years, the NSB [q.v.] had many valued Jewish members. It was not until 1937, under the influence of Germany, that the movement became virulently antiSemitic. In that year's elections the party's share of all the votes cast for seats in the Second Chamber [House]—which in 1935 had been almost 8 percent of the total—dropped sharply to 4 percent.

When the Dutch Jews had to swallow their first disappointment about the stance of their fellow countrymen, it was not racism that lay at the base of it. The Jews had become a number in the complicated process of balancing the budget of national interests. Their position was viewed "pragmatically" by the government.

Initially, that was especially true for Jews not born in the Netherlands: the refugees from Germany and Austria. The Netherlands had admitted 15,000 of them since 1933, and the government found then that enough was enough. In December 1938—one month after *Kristallnacht* [q.v.], when the German Jews were practically already viewed as outlaws—the government decided that, from now on, refugees would be sent back as "undesirable foreigners." "Should there, in some individual case, be a credible fear that there was a real danger to the life of the refugee," then this could be presented to the Minister of Justice.

In 1939 some German-Jewish children could still come across the border, but not before the Dutch Jewish Refugee Committee had promised the government that it would pay all their expenses. The "Jewish portion of the Dutch people," as the government put it, had had to reimburse the government for every cent that was expended for refugees since 1933. Even the camp at Westerbork [q.v.], which was founded in 1939 to house Jewish refugees, was financed by the Dutch Jews.

Not only did this sharply restrict the age-old Dutch right of asylum, but with the requirement that Jews had to pay for Jews, the Dutch government, for the first time, had issued a regulation that discriminated against the Jews on the basis of their ethnicity. Since 1796, Jews in the Netherlands had been legally classified as "Jews," members of a church, wrote M.H. Gans in his *Memorboek*. "The refugees came not because of their religious beliefs, but as people who were being persecuted because of their race. For a government that refused to recognize racial differences, there was no defensible reason whatsoever to require the Dutch citizens who were members of the Jewish church to provide guarantees for the expenses of the refugees as a prerequisite of admittance." This deed was an act of discrimination by their own government against Dutch Jews that was not based on ideas of the superiority and inferiority of the races. What lay at its base was not racism but "pragmatism." And frugality.

A member of the resistance in the province of Drenthe who was a dour fundamentalist member of a conservative Protestant church once told me: "Our country never went so far as to push the Jews aside. Our people would never have deported them. That is the influence of Calvinism. He who lives with the Good Book, can never be an antiSemite. Look at Ezekiel 25, where the Lord threatens the Ammonites with His wrath because they clapped their hands, full of malice of heart over the suffering of the land of Israel."[5] He was right: few of the Dutch applauded when the Jews were taken away. It is just that they did not do anything else either. Just as small as the number of traitors and racists was the number of those who distinguished themselves with their deeds as "good." In between was the gray majority, who, in the words of the novelist Harry Mulisch, put up with the "reverse discrimination" that was granted them by the Germans as a fellow Germanic people.[6]

The majority included the ministers in exile in London, who never devoted a cabinet meeting to the fate of their Jewish fellow countrymen and never made a call for a boycott of the persecution of the Jews and deportation. The majority also included the municipal civil servants of Amsterdam who, in early 1941, promptly provided the German authorities with the information about Jewish households, businesses and organizations that the Germans had asked for, it included the civil servants, policemen, streetcar drivers and railroad workers, the majority of whom said nothing and helped with the deportations.

The help with the deportations that was provided by the Dutch police—the police of Amsterdam in particular—was exceptional in Western Europe. Only the French Vichy police did the same. There was an antiSemitic tradition in France and a collaborating government, that, on its own initiative, without pressure from the Germans, had already enacted and implemented anti-Jewish legislation at the beginning of the war. The Dutch civil servants did their work during the war not out of conviction or enthusiasm but out of respect for authority and a sense of duty.

"The Dutch government's administration was characterized by a thoroughness that makes one think sooner of the German than of the Belgian or French traditions," stated the historian Blom. Dutch civil servants saw to it that "the demands of the occupiers were carried out hyper-correctly and thoroughly." He quoted Eichmann's infamous statement that the transports in the Netherlands were so problem-free that it was a pleasure to see.[7] He could have also mentioned the chief of the SD, Willy Lages [q.v.], who, after the war, said that, without the help of the Dutch police, the Germans could not have rounded up even 10 percent of the Jews who were deported.

In her anthology *In Resurrection Preserved*, the writer Henriëtte Boas continues in this line. Just as the civil servants who maintained the civil registry never came up with the idea to remove the "Jewish" cards, the administration of the Jewish community never thought to destroy its membership files. That the overwhelming majority of civil servants signed the Aryan declaration in 1940 has more to do with naïveté than with malice, "just as was the case with the overwhelming majority of Jews, who complied with the *Meldungspflicht* [German: Compulsory Registration] in 1941," says Boas.

"The first call-ups for the transports were around the tenth of July 1942. You did what you were told," said Ab Caransa, who was taken to Westerbork with his family when he was 15. "We were terribly governmental. You can't just suddenly begin to doubt the authority of the government; we did not have a rabbi or a pastor who could show us the ropes, and the Jewish Council insisted that everyone strictly follow all the regulations that were enacted."[8] "There is no other country in which an organization like the Jewish Council could thrive as well as it did in the Netherlands," said Hans Knoop in an interview with Ischa Meijer. "The Dutch are super-servile. The Dutch Jews are super-Dutch."[9]

One chairman of a local Jewish Council showed what can be done when you make independent decisions. That was Sieg Menko in Enschede. As director of a big textile concern, he had a lot of non-Jewish connections, who gave him money to fund hiding out [q.v.] as many Jews as possible. When, in the fall of 1942, Menko learned that a huge raid was about to get under way, he sent out a warning everywhere to take to the underground. Of the 1,200 Jews in Enschede, more than 500 survived the war, a number that is almost twice the national percentage.[10]

Menko was an exception. The Dutch of that time did not stand out for their individualism or independence of action. Life in the Pillarized and loyal-to-the-government Netherlands turned on completely different values: the cohesion of the group, obedience, civility, conformism and perhaps also a certain amount of gullibility and naïveté—characteristics that were to be found among the overwhelming majority of the Dutch, both Jews and non-Jews alike.

LIKE THE MEN OF PUTTEN [q.v.]

"The men of Putten" is a concept from the history of the German occupation, not only because of the great cruelty with which the Germans treated this village in the province of Gelderland, by taking away the whole of the male populace as a reprisal, but also because of the fact that such a small number of these men managed to survive the German camps: fewer than 50 of the 600 returned. The psychiatrist Van Dantzig attributes this to the poor manner in which the men from Putten—coming from a strongly cohesive, Christian, agrarian social group—were equipped to survive a brutal battle for their existence by compromising and improvising.[11]

If the Dutch failed in the war, that was because, among other things, they, as a people, had something in common with the men of Putten. That is true for the complex of respect for authority and conformism discussed earlier, and also for the way in which ethnic difference was experienced in the Netherlands. For centuries, the Jews in the Netherlands had managed to get along by taking an exceptionally respectful attitude toward authority. This respect was always reciprocated by the people and by the House of Orange, "in as far as I know," said M.H. Gans in his *Memorboek*, "the only such well-placed family in Europe, that has, through the ages, generation after generation, always accorded the Jews the courtesy that befits one's fellowmen." In her exile in London, Queen Wilhelmina continued this tradition in a small way. Though she never directly called for helping Jews by hiding them, speaking via Radio Orange, she showed her indignation and distress about the "continually worsening witch-hunt" for "these fellow countrymen, who have lived together with us for centuries in our blessed Fatherland." "There is not even a word for these disgraceful practices in our language."

That is the way it was. Experience with resisting or escaping from raids and pogroms was equally as lacking. The Dutch Jews could not comprehend the existence of a murder machine run by civil servants.[12] The attitude of the non-Jewish Dutch needs to be judged against the same background. What the Nazis did was outside the comprehension of the Dutch people, who were accustomed to respecting authority and were tightly organized along philosophical and religious lines.[13]

This way of thinking came painfully and clearly to light among the members of the Workers' Central for Young People (AJC) [q.v.], the youth section of the Social-Democratic movement. The AJC was the only non-Jewish youth organization with a lot of Jewish members. Most of them, around 500, lived in Amsterdam, where some sections, such as the Transvaal district, were 90 percent Jewish. But there was no "disaster plan" for their protection. Members of the AJC made their contributions to the resistance, but they did not know how to prevent more than 350 of their Jewish friends from losing their lives.[14]

Every year, on the fourth of May, old AJC-ers get together on the Paasheuvel [Easter Hill] in the Vierhouten district, where the old clubhouse of the movement still stands. Sometimes I go there with my parents, who met in the AJC. The few speeches are short and lack pomposity. At the pillar where the names of the fallen AJC-ers are engraved in stone, a woman reads Anneke Hemrika's poem "Laplacestraat" [Laplace Street], in which she describes the departure of her friend Lotte in July 1942: *"Then I go through a Hell of hate, this image is burned into my mind: a quiet girl with a backpack on, waves good-bye as she walks down the street."*[15]

In Ab Caransa's book *Assemble on Transvaal Square*, a resident of the Transvaal district describes the departure of a neighbor's boy in the same month: "His mother told him good-bye and called to him for as long as she could see him; until he was out of the street. Why in God's name did they let him go?" It was only afterward that form could be given to this bewilderment. Neither the Jewish nor the non-Jewish AJC-ers were equipped to overstep the boundaries of the law. There was a strong emphasis on collective obedience to the law and one's duty in the AJC. Individualism was fundamentally wrong. The creed of the AJC was not that different from the way that the men of Putten viewed life.

TWO MYTHS ABOUT THE WAR

When the non-Jewish Dutch were liberated from the problems of continuing their own existence in 1945, they saw what they had let happen. Of the 140,000 Dutch Jews, more than 100,000 had been murdered. In Amsterdam—the praises of which had been sung in Jewish circles through the ages as the Gate of Heaven, Little Jerusalem, the Mother City in Israel, Amsterdam the Praiseworthy and *Mokum Olf*: "the City Above All"—only 15,000 of the 80,000 Jewish inhabitants remained. Their houses had been torn down and burned by the inhabitants of *Mokum*.

The surviving Jews were often not too warmly welcomed by those who had taken their house and worldly goods under their protection. The result was a flare of antiSemitism. "Why did my Jew have to be one of the ones to come back? was approximately the feeling of some of the custodians," explained M.H. Gans in his interview with me.[16] Another part of this postwar antiSemitism was probably an expression of the increasing reappearance of an "embarrassment" about the Jews. In his *The Fall*, Presser found it no wonder that many of the Dutch transferred the displeasure of their feeling of failure to "those, who so painfully reminded them of their shortcomings: the surviving Jews." He quotes Dr. L. de Jong, who called false condemnation the dark side of real pity: "False condemnation and pity were complementary. They both issued from the same situation and . . . were sometimes found in the same heart, shortly after the occupation."[17]

The historians Jan and Annie Romein offered a sketch of the feelings that this experience had brought about in them: "One thing is certain: that the consciousness of Jewish and non-Jewish that was imposed on us during the war, has gotten into our blood. For the non-Jews that means a nagging inhibition, and an irrational fear of giving offense, which is sometimes just plain silly, but sometimes, also, is offensive, and can, now and again, muddy up the best of friendships."[18] This is the recognition by the Romeins, who were always surrounded by Jewish colleagues and friends, that their innocence had been murdered along with the more than 100,000 Dutch Jews.

The temporary postwar solution to the increasing reappearance of embarrassment was to be silent. The silence of the non-Jewish Dutch complemented the silence in Jewish circles, where people, just as before the war, preferred not to express their feelings too openly, out of fear of *"risjes te maken"*—inciting antiSemitism. For both sides of the generation of the war this continual National Silence functioned as a sort of truce, one of the few ways that they could go on together.

Only a lone figure dared to let the bitterness shine through in public. "We Dutch let our Jews go into hiding," wrote Jaap Meijer in his book *High Hats, Low Standards*. "Except for the more than 100,000 who vanished—perhaps because they did not want to go into hiding. Perhaps for other reasons. One day a good book will come out about that." But, in general, the Dutch succeeded, in one way or another, to convince each other that, in the non-Jewish populace, the Jews had found loyal helpers and allies. In 1947 Queen Wilhelmina bestowed the motto "Valiant, Resolute, Merciful" on the city of Amsterdam for its heraldic crest. Three years later, the Jewish community of Amsterdam unveiled a monument in Weesperstraat [Weesper street], thanking the citizens of Amsterdam for the "protection" that they had given the Jewish populace during the occupation.

This myth persisted doggedly throughout the first 20 years after the war and formed the backdrop against which the postwar generation grew up. The earsplitting silence weighed heavily, especially on children born into Jewish families after the war. In the course of things, they came to understand that members of their families had not resisted being taken away and that no one had helped them. How was that possible?

Even non-Jewish children had to be satisfied with vague and evasive answers when they asked their parents questions. For the postwar generation the events of the past during the war developed into a source of unanswered questions, of "surrogate" feelings of guilt and doubt about their answer to the question, What would I have done? There remained something of the feeling in this generation that the political scientist Lucas van der Land gave word to in an interview shortly before his death: "In the end that is the only criterion against which I divide people into good and bad: would you hide me out?"[19]

In the mid-1960s the postwar generation was old enough to make its well-known assault on the holy halls of the "society run by regents [q.v.]." In doing so, they made short work of the myth of Dutch resistance. How the generation of their parents had failed was hardly a topic of discussion for the baby-boom generation. The type of failure evidenced itself in the wording of the warnings against "resurgent fascism and racism."

This is where the second Dutch myth about the war made its entrance. It concealed just as much as the first. The Dutch failures in the war were attributed to devilish ideologies. This let the real character of the behavior of the overwhelming majority remain hidden from view. This behavior was never based on contamination with Nazi ideas but on an attitude of pragmatism, accommodation and conformism. The murder of the Dutch Jews was done by the Nazis. The Dutch who stood by may well be accused of all kinds of things—indifference, naïveté, cowardice, conformism or egotism—but they were not racist murderers.

The second myth about the war broke through the silence about the fate of the Jews. The silence, the avoidance and the cautiousness were no longer applied to the memory of the war itself but to every action, regulation or statement having to do with contemporary society that could be connected with this curse. With the passage of time, the second myth about the war began to resemble a real mythological story, with the SS-ers as devils and demons and Hitler as a modern Werewolf. The remembrance was prolonged again and again, purely because of the unheard-of power of its images. Every reference to "new Jews" and "postwar resistance," in fact, contained a curse or an adjuration.

In the 1970s all kinds of action groups took over the murder of the Jews as a hat rack to hang their own opinions and demands on. Squatters spoke of "governmental racism" and "deportation-like practices" and called policemen "hunters of men." The Dock Workers' Monument [q.v.] to those who had placed their lives on the line by striking during the occupation decorated the cover of many an activist publication, which demanded "hands-off" the rights that had been achieved. The Anne Frank Association took the lead in this "hat-rack approach": in the latter half of the 1970s, it began to use the events of the war as a "didactic aid" for the timely recognition of "resurgent fascism and racism."[20] The example was followed by antifascism committees all over the Netherlands and by Amsterdam's mayor, Ed van Thijn, who, at the Auschwitz Commemoration in 1984, speaking of the relationships between the ethnic Dutch and immigrants [q.v.], said that "the signs saying 'Jews Prohibited' have appeared in Amsterdam again"; it is just that the text has been adapted to reflect the change in the composition of the populace.

Almost no one dared then to point out the risks of such an idle use of this curse taken from the war. The always fearless Henriëtte Boas was one who did dare. In an interview she stated that this sort of comparison, "in fact, trivializes the suffering of the Jews in the war." She was also afraid that ethnic minorities would "begin to feel much more discriminated against than they really were" because of it.[21]

It was not until the early 1990s that an irritation broke out in wider circles of people about the flippant use of the "hat-rack method." When the daily Trouw tried to win subscribers with an advertisement in which a Turkish girl posed as Anne Frank, it caught flak from the world of minorities itself. "Terrible things happened to the Jews earlier," said Çoskun Cörüz, chairman of the Islamic Council of the Netherlands, in HP/de Tijd. "To lump that together with the situation of the Islamic minorities in the Netherlands of today, is just like comparing apples and oranges."

AN "IRRATIONAL FEAR OF GIVING OFFENSE"

In their book *Pinkas*, D. Michman, J. Michman and H. Beem note a phenomenon that, according to them, is unique in Europe: in the Netherlands, it is usually non-Jews who take the initiative in restoring synagogues and erecting monuments, a form of public contrition that is characteristic of the Dutch remembrance of the war. The feeling of guilt can also be heard in the names that are used for the Jewish portion of the population. Beginning in the 1970s Jews were certainly not "Jews" anymore and not "Israelites" either. Thereafter, they were referred to as "Jewish people," and even that was a bit dicey. Daalder pointed out that in English one can still always speak of "Gentiles" without reservation, while in the Netherlands the best that someone can manage to get across his lips is "non-Jew."[22]

The "irrational fear of giving offense" that Jan and Annie Romein had discovered among "non-Jews," after the war remained alive and well into our time. In 1992 it was demonstrably illustrated by their son Bart Romein. A documentary was made for educational television about the pupils who had been in their first year at the Vossius high school in Amsterdam in 1945. In this class there were children of people who had been in the resistance, children of people who had been members of the NSB [q.v.], children of people who had been in the Japanese internment camps in the Dutch East Indies [now Indonesia] and Jewish children. There had always been a lot of Jewish students at Vossius . There were also Jewish teachers. When they were fired in 1940, a spontaneous student strike broke out at the school. One of the leaders of the strike was Bart Romein, who was then in his fifth year.

The makers of the documentary had wanted to say something about the Jewish tradition at Vossius in the teacher's guide to the film. But Bart Romein, in the meantime well in his 60s, threw a monkey wrench into the works. At school, according to him, Jewish classmates were never looked upon as such; that came about only during the war under pressure from the Nazis. Therefore, the book could not state that "in the years before the war, there were a lot of Jewish pupils at Vossius high school."

What caused the remembrance of the war in the Netherlands to be surrounded by so much embarrassment and reservation? Seventy-five percent of the Dutch Jewish populace was murdered by the Germans, the highest percentage of all the Western European countries, including Germany. In Belgium and Norway, 40 percent lost their lives; in France, 25 percent; in Italy, 20 percent; and in Denmark, 2 percent. The percentage of those who hid out was higher in Germany itself and in Poland than in the Netherlands. [23] Both in Belgium and in the Netherlands, 25,000 Jews managed to hide out, but at the beginning of the war, there were only 66,000 Jews in Belgium, against 140,000 in the Netherlands.[24]

The geographic and housing circumstances, which were unfavorable for the resistance and for hiding out, are often pointed to as an explanation of these differences. In the Netherlands there was also a *Zivilverwaltung* [German: civilian government], which was strongly influenced by the SS, while in other occupied countries, the *Wehrmacht* [German: Armed Forces of Nazi Germany], which was less concerned with Nazi ideology and more with military interests, was in control. In addition, the Netherlands was unique in that most of the Jews belonged to the proletariat and, therefore, did not have a lot of money to buy protection. But the cultural characteristics of the Dutch, discussed in this chapter, also reduced the chances of survival of the Dutch Jews.

In addition, Dutch society and administrative culture had a streak of morality in them. Since the end of the nineteenth century, the Netherlands had pretended to be "in the lead" on the way to a more just and peaceful world. In the colonies the Dutch were implementing "ethical policies": defending and uplifting the indigenous population—that was what it was about. Even in the personal social lives of most of the Dutch, firmly embedded in the spiritual Pillars, questions of ethics and morals played an important role. "A love of one's fellowman and a readiness to help (required, among other things, by the religious commandments) were not unfamiliar to the Dutch people," says the social demographer G.J. Kruijer, writing on the last "famine" winter [q.v.] of the war. "As a culture they showed a fairly strong Christian and humanitarian mentality."[25]

In accordance with this, the leaders of most of the Pillars had been critically outspoken on the issue of the Jews during the war. The most important Protestant denominations protested to Reich's Commissar Seyss-Inquart [q.v.] about the anti-Jewish regulations in October 1940. The Catholic Episcopate under the leadership of Archbishop Johannes de Jong [q.v.] took a courageous stand. In July 1942 a protest against the deportation of the Jews was read from the pulpit of most churches.

Still, when push came to shove, the love of fellowman and readiness to help among most of the Dutch did not reach outside their own immediate family. Not until after the liberation did it dawn on them how difficult it was to make this attitude, which was so shrilly reflected in the limited number of surviving Jews, rhyme with the civility of Dutch manners. Perhaps everybody could rationalize this contrast under the motto "Near is my shirt, but nearer my skin." But to the outside world—not only the Jews but also the members of their own communities of faith or conviction and the Pillarized Netherlands with the "spiritual characteristic" of its culture being tolerance and openheartedness—it was hard to sell this coldly logical vision of the principle of human solidarity.

Jan Bank's statement that, in the second half of the 1960s, the Netherlands was caught up in "an almost collective realization of at least passive guilt"[26] is not entirely correct. The feeling of guilt was *primarily* collective. Confronted with their own *public* yardstick of values, the Dutch people became embarrassed by the remembrance of the war. There is a train that rides through this remembrance, the train from the poem by Anneke Hemrika, on which her friend Lotte is being taken away: "*A train left here and went . . . /and rides through my memory / The train departs but never arrives / and will ride on my whole life long.*"[27]

NOTES

1. All the data are taken from the article by Maurits Schmidt in *Het Parool* of 4 March 1992.

2. Quote in Vuijsje, 1986.

3. Ibid.

4. Wout Ultee and Ruud Luijkx, "Und Alles kam wie es kommen musste, Jewish-Gentile intermarriage 1900-1940" [And Everything Came about as It Had to Come About: Jewish-Gentile Intermarriage 1900-1940], paper for SISWO Sociology Days, 11, 12 April 1996, Table 7.

5. L. Janssens, quote in Vuijsje, 1986.

6. Letter to the editor, *Haagse Post*, 17 March 1979.

7. J.C.H. Blom, "De vervolging van de joden in Nederland in internationaal vergelijkend perspectief" [The Persecution of the Jews in the Netherlands in the Perspective of International Comparison], one of the papers included in J.C.H. Blom, *Crisis, bezetting en herstel, tien studies over Nederland 1930-1950* [Crisis, Occupation and Reconstruction, Ten Studies about the Netherlands 1930-1950], Nijgh and Van Ditmar Universitair, The Hague, 1989. In his research into the attitudes of the police in The Hague during the occupation, Bart van der Boom shows that conformism—not ideological conversion—was responsible for the matter-of-factness with which the majority of police officers cooperated with the persecution of the Jews. Bart van der Boom, *Den Haag in de Tweede Wereldoorlog* [The Hague in the Second World War], Seapress, The Hague, 1995.

8. Interview in *Oost* [East], a special edition on the occasion of the 50th anniversary of the liberation of Het Woningbedrijf Amsterdam/Algemene Woningbouw Vereniging [The Housing Corporation Amsterdam/General Housing Construction Association], the Oost district, May 1995.

9. "Ischa Meijers Weekboek" [Ischa Meijer's Weekly Diary], *Haagse Post*, 14 July 1979. Ischa Meijer's father, Jaap Meijer, demonstrated the same conviction in 1969 in his book *Hoge hoeden, lage standaarden, De Nederlandse joden tussen 1933 en 1940* [High Hats, Low Standards: The Dutch Jews between 1933 and 1940], Het Wereldvenster, Baarn, 1969.

10. Willy Lindwer, *Het fatale dilemma, de Joodsche Raad voor Amsterdam 1941-1943* [The Fatal Dilemma: The Jewish Council of Amsterdam 1941-1943], Sdu, The Hague, 1995.

11. A. van Dantzig, *Normaal is niet gewoon, beschouwingen over psychiatrie en psychotherapie* [Sane Is Not Normal, Observations on Psychiatry and Psychotherapy], De Bezige Bij, Amsterdam, 1974, Chapter 2, "De tragedie der Puttenaren" [The Tragedy of the Men from Putten].

12. In *Intermediair* of 28 April 1995, Dirk-Jan van Baar points to the significant fact that a higher percentage of the Jews who fled to the Netherlands before the war survived the war than did Dutch Jews. In other countries the proportion was reversed.

13. Vuijsje, 1986, pp. 184 ff. In a presentation at a symposium entitled "De vervolging van de joden in Nederland in internationaal vergelijkend perspectief" [The Persecution of the Jews in the Netherlands in the Perspective of International Comparison] in December 1986, Blom stated that "the relatively high vulnerability of the Jewish portion of the population during the occupation, expressed in the percentage of those who died, in part, has to do with the relatively very favorable and therefore, quasi-secure position of the Jews in the Netherlands before the war." The presentation was published in *De Gids*, 150 (1987) and was included in Blom, 1989.

14. See Geertje Marianne Naarden, *Onze jeugd behoort de morgen. . . de geschiedenis van de AJC in oorlogstijd* [Our Youth Belongs to Tomorrow. . . The History of the AJC during Wartime], Stichting beheer IISG, Amsterdam, 1989.

15. Anneke Hemrika, *klein monument* [a small monument], Octavo, Bergen, 1985.

16. Quoted in Vuijsje, 1986.

17. J. Presser, *Ondergang* [The Fall], Staatsuitgeverij, The Hague, 1965, part II, pp. 518/519; L. de Jong, "Jews and Non-Jews in Nazi-Occupied Holland," in *On the Track of Tyranny*, London, 1962, pp. 153/154.

17. Jan Romein and Annie Romein, "De mens" [Man], in Jan Romein (ed.), *Jacques Presser, geschenk van vrienden bij zijn zestigste verjaardag* [To Jacques Presser: A Present from His Friends for His Sixtieth Birthday], Meulenhoff, Amsterdam, 1959, p. 13.

19. Interview with Max Pam in *NRC Handelsblad*, 18 February 1984.

20. For a good description, see Eva Rensman, *De Anne Frank Stichting en haar lessen uit de Tweede Wereldoorlog 1957-1994* [The Anne Frank Association and Its Lessons from the Second World War 1957-1994], Utrechtse Historische cahiers, 1995, no. 4, Vakgroep Geschiedenis der Universiteit Utrecht, Utrecht, 1995.

21. Quoted in Vuijsje, 1986. In his article "Herdenken in deemoed, de

toekomst van de Tweede Wereldoorlog" [Remembrance in Humility: The Future of the Second World War], *Elsevier*, 29 April 1995, H.J. Schoo pointed to the fact that as the remembrance of the war "becomes more topical," "qualification of the fate of the Jews has crept into the official remembrance." He characterized this trend as "the Netherlands' own battle of the historians."

22. H. Daalder, "Joden in een verzuilend Nederland" [Jews in a Pillarized Netherlands], *Hollands Maandblad*, October 1975.

23. Rabbi B. Drukarch in *Oost* [East], a special edition on the occasion of the 50th anniversary of the liberation of Het Woningbedrijf Amsterdam/Algemene Woningbouw Vereniging [The Housing Corporation Amsterdam/General Housing Construction Association], the Oost district, May 1995. Of the 25,000 Jews who went into hiding, 8,000 were found out, in part due to betrayal.

24. Pim Griffioen and Ron Zeller, *Achtste Jaarboek van het Rijks Instituut voor Oorlogsdocumentatie* [Eighth Yearbook of the Central Government's Institute for Documentation on the War], Amsterdam, 1997.

25. G. J. Kruijer, "De hongertochten" [The Famine Marches], *Intermediair*, 1 March 1985.

26. Jan Bank, *Oorlogsverleden in Nederland* [The Wartime Past in the Netherlands], Ambo, Baarn, 1983.

27. Anneke Hemrika, *klein monument* [a small monument], Octavo, Bergen, 1985.

CHAPTER 10

The Cohorts of the Baby Boom

The psychological relief felt at the end of the war resulted in a postwar baby boom all across the Western world. We would learn a whole lot more about these baby boomers, who were supposed to realize the new hopes of their parents. Their adventures in the 1960s have been told and retold again and again: how the generation gap was proclaimed, when their voices changed, how they locked their teachers in the coal bin a few years later, when they went to college, and how they went into "real" politics, where they immediately gave the incumbent politicians an unceremonious poke in the ribs.

When the first wave of the baby boom hit the labor market, the economic climate was in superhigh gear: employers could hardly wait for people to take jobs. In addition, the rapid de-Pillarization of society and the housecleaning that was taking place among the old leadership and the bourgeoisie were creating lots of room at the top. This is how the baby boom easily worked its way into positions of importance in society in the 1970s. The taboos in the areas of race, coercion and privacy could be strongly and "widely" propagated as a part of the trendsetting morals. Inasmuch as possible, they were institutionalized and codified.

The dogmatic approach taken to these tasks was almost religious in character. The new taboos made you think of a secular version of a Bible-thumper's mentality: people are weak, and the slightest deviation from the true path is a threat of perdition. It was precisely in those years that the arrival of the Surinamese, the Antilleans and "guest workers" provided a new touchstone. Self-appointed inquisitioners stood up, calling for excommunication in response to any deviation from the true teachings. A continuous round of soul-searching for, and confession of, concealed racist impulses was the commandment of the day. Fire-and-brimstone preachers made the rounds, flagellating themselves with the rod of everyday racism.

Evil was hiding in every breast, just as it says in Romans 7, verse 15 and following: "For I know that good does not dwell in me, that is, in my flesh . . .; For I do not do the good I want, but I do the evil I do not want." Sins of ordinary racism in spirit were put on the same level as sins in deed, just as in the Catholic confession of guilt, the Confiteor: "I confess . . . that I have sinned in my thoughts and in my words, in what I have done, and in what I have left undone; I am to blame, I am to blame, I am greatly to blame."

Could it be that, in addition to this stop-at-nothing motivation, a role was played by the personal vicissitudes of the veterans of the 1960s? Looking back, there seemed little to show for their "revolt." OK, in 1969 you let yourself be dragged out of the Maagdenhuis [q.v.] by your hair; you had defied sexually transmitted diseases and authority. But the authorities were wearing glasses and not jackboots. They reacted diffidently; they went along or stepped down instead of dragging you off to a concentration camp. Looking back, even the sexually transmitted diseases could be considered friendly enough. In the final balance, what great and compelling things had those years produced? There was not a single way in which the "revolt" could be viewed as a litmus test like the war was. The baby boomers still do not know how they would have withstood the test. In the meantime, they had children of their own. The questions could start at any minute: "What would you have done in the war, Dad?" "I don't know, son." That hurts. Maybe that is also why they were so strict and fanatical in observing the taboos that had come from the war: to overpower their own insecurity.

THE SNAKE THAT SWALLOWED A BLOCK OF WOOD

Nowhere else in Europe was the postwar baby boom as big and as long as in the Netherlands. Immediately after the war, the birth statistics shot straight up. After this peak, fertility stayed high for 20 years. At the beginning of the 1960s, the average number of children per woman of childbearing age was 3.2. That was the highest fertility rate in all of Europe, with the exception of rigidly Catholic Ireland. The high birthrate was, in part, a result of Pillarization. Up into the 1960s, the Netherlands was one of the most religious countries in Europe; in 1958 only 25 percent of the populace did not belong to a church. It was primarily the Catholics and conservative Protestants who were competing with each other in family size. But when the Pillars began to lose their power after 1965, the birthrate went into free fall. In 1985 the average number of children had dropped to 1.5: the sharpest reduction of all the European countries.

Other Western countries also saw a drop in the birthrate in the 1960s. It was the baby boomers' time to have children, but the baby boomers were the bearers par excellence of the idea of self-fulfillment, and that did not go well with having a lot of children at an early age. Potential parents want more time and opportunities for realizing their own wishes. In 1970 the average age of Dutch women giving birth to their first child was 24.3. Now it is 28.6, the highest in the world.

Most of the decrease in the fertility rate took place in the period of about ten years that followed the mid-1960s. In the words of the Dutch demographer Anton Kuijsten, the Netherlands underwent "one of the most spectacular decreases in the birthrate in the whole of the Western world."[1] The combination of a high, sustained birthrate followed by a rapid decrease in the birthrate gave the age distribution of the populace of the Netherlands a special character. "The Americans often describe their baby boom as a pig that has been swallowed by a snake," says Kuijsten. "For us, it is more like a snake that swallowed a block of wood."

Even the social and cultural environment was subject to the effects of this exceptional population distribution. The cohorts of the baby boom in the Netherlands were strong enough to considerably influence the climate of ideas.

BRABANT AND LIMBURG: AND THE FIRST SHALL BE LAST

When the baby boom caused a high tide of social and cultural change, the Catholics were the strongest wave breakers. Since the beginning of the century, the fertility rate for married women in the predominantly Catholic provinces of Brabant and Limburg was higher than in all the other provinces. Even in the postwar years, these southern provinces remained record holders in the fertility rate for married women. They did not really even have a postwar baby boom. Brabant did not show any increase at all, and Limburg had only a slight increase. The existing fertility rate was simply so high that the rest of the country could not keep up.

In his classic study *The birthrate of Dutch Roman Catholics* (1954), the sociologist Van Heek showed that Dutch Catholics differentiate themselves from their German and Belgian counterparts by their higher birthrate. He studied fertility and adherence to the faith in Catholic areas on both sides of the border. It almost always seemed that the birthrate was considerably higher on the Dutch side of the border. Important rules, like the prohibition on abortion, were followed more consistently. Van Heek concluded that the Dutch Catholics had a "front-line" mentality: a very militant understanding of the tenets of their faith, developed from being in an underdog position in competition with the Protestant majority.

Up into the 1960s, Dutch Catholicism was a "total" system. Even for the most intimate areas, Church regulations had been formulated that were so precise and finely nuanced that they could scarcely be differentiated from a legal system. The consummation of the marriage must be "complete" [q.v.]. Whosoever, "in impertinent selfishness," ignores this regulation lives in "mortal sin." That is what it said in the blue book *Marriage Instructions for Catholic Partners*, which was handed out to bridal couples in some parishes up into the 1960s. "Unnatural practices" were described in detail. This included "either intentionally ejecting the male seed outside the body of the woman or hindering it from reaching its intended goal inside the woman's body."

The only thing that the priest hearing confession would sometimes permit by the grace of God was periodic abstinence. But woe unto you if you came to confess that you had sinned by practicing the "calendar method" without permission. There was every chance that you would be "shuttered," as it was known in Brabant: the priest taking your confession would close the shutter between you, and you could forget about your absolution.[2]

These rules on sexuality and reproduction were the cornerstone and the touchstone of the totalitarian power of the Church. But they were also the Church's Achilles' heel. A number of authors in the anthology *The Brabant Solution* point to the superficial quality of the faith in Brabant. The renowned religious faith of Brabant rested "more on the externals of habit than on internal conviction." De Vet, who would later become bishop, understood that in 1960 when he said: "Going to church in Brabant was, primarily, an external, visible accentuation of the experience of religion in conformation with a social pattern. . . . The mechanism of social control worked very well in that respect."[3] At least until the last straw. The Catholics in Brabant observed the laws of the Church but were looking for loopholes.

That became clear all at once when de-Pillarization began. The birthrates in Brabant and Limburg in the 1960s were an excellent example of "the first shall be last." In 1960 they were still leading the pack, but five years later, even Limburg had dived under the national average, followed in the early 1970s by Brabant. In the early 1980s, Brabant had the next-to-the-lowest fertility rate for married women in the whole country, behind Limburg. In the 1980s, for the whole of the Netherlands, Catholic women on average expected the lowest number of children of any religious grouping.[4] This record was not achieved because many women were remaining unmarried or childless. It was not marriage that fell out of fashion with Dutch Catholics or even having children, but expressly having a lot of children. In the mid-1980s, the percentage of third and higher births in Limburg was the lowest in all of the Netherlands; for fourth and higher births Limburg followed Brabant. These figures are an echo of the huge sigh of relief with which the daughters of Catholicism put aside the blue book of *Marriage Instructions for Catholic Partners*.

In some aspects the experience of the Dutch Catholics between 1965 and 1975 recalls that of the residents of the East Bloc around 1990: the twilight of a totalitarian hierarchical system. The Dutch Catholics had become the Albanians of the world church. They held on to their passivity, isolation and respect for authority longer than anyone else. But once they broke free, they took off in a rush. In all the Western world, there is probably not another group where individualization and secularization have progressed so fast since the 1960s.

Breaking free of the straitjacket of Pillarization, which placed the Netherlands in a unique position demographically within Europe, has, in turn, placed the southern provinces in a unique position within the Netherlands. If, since 1965, the Netherlands has changed demographically from the most conservative (with the exception of Ireland) to the most progressive nation in Europe, then for the Catholic provinces of Brabant and Limburg that is true in spades. This special development inside the Catholic portion of the population also had consequences outside the Catholic Pillar. The dedication with which Catholics observed the Church's regulations regarding reproduction placed them in the vanguard of the high, postwar birthrates, and resulted in a large part of the baby-boom cohort of the 1970s that determined what the Netherlands would look like. Subsequently, they led the way in reducing the birthrate faster than any other group.

In the 1990s a more normal distribution of family size developed. Not only are Catholics forgetting their enforced reproductive zeal, but also the reaction to it—"a big family? Never!"—is dying down. The only ethnic Dutch religious groupings that remain true to the idea of a big family are the conservative Protestant churches, with an average of 4 children per family, compared to the national average of 1.6. The list of municipalities with the highest average total number of children per woman has for years been led by places like Urk, Mariekerke, Bunschoten, Staphorst, IJsselmuiden, Genemuiden and Arnemuiden. Not a one of them is Catholic.[5]

NOTES

1. Quoted in Vuijsje, 1990.

2. Marga Kerklaan, *"Zodoende was de vrouw maar een mens om kinderen te krijgen," 300 brieven over het roomse huwelijksleven* [In That Way a Woman Was Just a Human Being That Could Have Children: 300 Letters about Catholic Married Life], Ambo, Baarn, 1987.

3. Marinus Huijbrechts, "Het verloren paradijs" [Paradise Lost], in Kruis et al. (eds.), 1987, p. 27.

4. *Onderzoek Gezinsvorming* [Family Formation Study], CBS, Voorburg, 1988.

5. See also A.H. de Jong, *Provinciale vruchtbaarheidsverschillen nemen toe* [Provincial Differences in Fertility Rates Increase], *Maandstatistiek van de bevolking* [Monthly Population Statistics], 1988, nr. 10; A. H. de Jong, *Demografie van provincies, 1977-1987* [Provincial Demographics], *Maandstatistiek van de bevolking* [Monthly Population Statistics], 1989, nr. 2; A.H. de Jong and C.J.M. Prins, *Demografie van Nederland in de negentiende eeuw* [Dutch Demographics in the Nineteenth Century], *Maandstatistiek van de bevolking* [Monthly Population Statistics], 1989, nr. 4.

CHAPTER 11

The Peace of Mind of the Welfare State

"Those times will never come back," was the message from Prime Minister Den Uyl [q.v.] when the first oil crisis broke out in 1973. But the adjustment to the new economic reality was piecemeal and slow. The Netherlands warmed itself in "the peace of mind of the welfare state," as Van Stolk and Wouters called it: the inner assurance that the government will eventually take away concerns about money."[1]

Since the war, the Netherlands had only had a tailwind. In the 1950s the Netherlands was third in the West with regard to the growth of the real gross national product. Wages were not climbing equally as fast. They were being kept low by a policy of wage controls. In 1963 this led to a "wage explosion," after which purchasing power climbed to previously unknown heights. Between 1920 and 1950, the volume of consumer spending had hardly grown. Between 1950 and 1980, it grew two and a half times.

Even after the oil crisis of 1973, there was no end to the "decades of overconfidence and self-satisfaction," as the historian Bastiaan Bommeljé called them. Growth fell drastically, but that was precisely the time that the natural gas discoveries near Slochteren began to come on-line. The price for natural gas was coupled to the price for oil, which went up like a rocket in the 1970s. In 1975 the state's share of the gas profits covered almost 10 percent of all state expenditures. The government's income from natural gas profits climbed to 20 billion guilders in 1982.

The Netherlands was still stinking rich. But it was money that, in the words of the Social-Economic Council, "was being consumed rather than going into production."[2] A large part of it went into expanding the public sector and the system of social services. With the advent of the

National Assistance Act [q.v.] (1965) and the WAO [q.v.] (1967), numerous categories of citizens got much more of a chance to give up the protection of traditional ways of life and to make individual choices. This allowed women who were in the process of getting a divorce to apply for National Assistance. In addition, with a "no-fault" divorce, they could reach an agreement with their husbands that no alimony would be paid, at which time National Assistance kicked in.[3]

With this an almost complete "peace of mind of the welfare state" was possible: if necessary, the government would take over the role of breadwinner. This mentality seems to be unique in the history of the Netherlands.[4] Now one could enjoy abundance forever; prosperity and a high level of services appeared to be permanent.

Van Stolk and Wouters still found this peace of mind alive and well when doing their study at the end of the 1970s in a center for runaway women. Almost all these women were receiving National Assistance and enjoyed the feeling of inner security that the government would take on all their financial worries, while, at that time, "the economic downturn was in such an advanced stage that it was an important topic of discussion in the media daily. The public debate about the (im)possibility of continuing to finance the system of social payments over the long haul had already been going on for a long time." But none of the women interviewed connected the threat that this represented with her own personal situation. The speed with which the "peace of mind of the welfare state" was fading was, therefore, much slower than the speed of the economic recession.

BUYING OFF THE TENSIONS

There were other ways in which natural gas profits were used to soften the effects of the economic recession. Existing policy preferences could still be continued, and harmful side effects could be cloaked with love. A lot of money was spent on buying off tensions and conflicts. In the area of race relations that was very effective. The Netherlands was rich enough for it to be self-evident that immigrants could participate in the general social arrangements.

In the meantime, the generous subsidies to the business of minorities had had other effects. Where administrators and civil servants were threatened with confronting a taboo, they preferred to avoid it by throwing money at it. Mismanagement and corruption in racially based associations were often not investigated. It was better to write off the losses than to take the chance of doing something racially objectionable. The government advanced the cause of peace in the racial arena not by making requirements but by giving things away. As long as there was money, that seemed the best way to avoid any collision with the taboo on race. Not until later could the harmful side effects be seen in parts of the second generation of minorities.

Billions were also invested to keep WAO and other welfare payments at existing levels, without asking annoying questions. The privacy taboo and the taboo on coercion would not permit it. The government obviously could not go around counting toothbrushes [q.v.]. Then it was better just to dig deeper into your pockets and not to make too much commotion about the matter. Just as the first reports about petty crimes being committed by members of racial minorities were suppressed, so were the alarming reports and studies about welfare-payment fraud.

The alderman from Rotterdam, Henderson, for years—since 1989—had been keeping reports about welfare fraud to himself, which eventually cost him his job. Testifying before the commission investigating the WAO, he said that in 1989 "the time was not right" to publish the results. To which, Van der Tak, a CDA member of the commission, said that by keeping silent, the alderman had helped keep the time from changing and strengthened the taboo.

This picture had already been sketched in the eighteenth century by Hiëronymus van Alphen [q.v.]. The Dutch welfare state is like a big plum tree. All of us Joes are standing around the tree, and we all know that when the tree is so full of fruit, nobody will miss five or six plums. Just like in the poem by Van Alphen, we can be reasonably sure that neither father nor the gardener will notice anything. Father has left and lives a long way away with his new girlfriend. Because of the cutbacks, the gardener has to take care of the whole garden by himself and does not have time to keep an eye on all the Joes.

But there is one thing wrong: why is it that all the Joes of our day attack the plum trees en masse and pluck some of them clean? There is another way of dealing with abundance, the one that Joe himself chose, walking away with the words: "Should I be disobedient? No!" The fact that the riches of the Netherlands were being consumed cannot be explained by the riches themselves. We can, however, assume that the availability of money gave many administrators and decision makers an out so that they could avoid confrontation with the taboos.

NOTES

1. Bram van Stolk and Cas Wouters, *Vrouwen in tweestrijd tussen thuis en tehuis, relatieproblemen in de verzorgingsstaat, opgetekend in een crisiscentrum* [Women Torn between Home and a Shelter, Relationship Problems in the Welfare State: Notes from a Crisis Center], Van Loghum Slaterus, Deventer, 1983, pp. 74 et seq.

2. Sociaal-Economische Raad [Social-Economic Council], *Ontwerp-advies inzake het aardgasbeleid* [Draft Recommendation on Natural Gas Policy], The Hague, 1983.

3. Nowadays, the municipality automatically tries to recover the amount of the National Assistance payment from the former spouse, even if there was a "no-fault" divorce. The fact that this, in a roundabout way, reestablishes the "psychological dependence" of one spouse on the other, which the "no-fault" divorce was supposed to put an end to, is just accepted as a part of the bargain.

4. Maarten van Rossem, et al., *Een tevreden natie, Nederland van 1945 to nu* [A Satisfied Nation: The Netherlands from 1945 to Now], Tirion, Baarn, 1993, p. 98.

CHAPTER 12

The Welfare State and the Prisoner's Dilemma

In 1958 the American anthropologist E.C. Banfield wrote his standard work on cultural interaction in the south Italian village of Montegrano.[1] The inhabitants of Montegrano lived in extreme poverty, from which there was little chance of escape on one's own. The only institution that the inhabitants could count on for help was their own families. The standards of good and bad played a role only with regard to family members. Outside the family, the only consideration was how great the chance was of being caught. Each family tried to achieve as much material advantage as it could, as quickly as it could, assuming that the other families were doing the same.

Banfield calls this culture *amoral familism*. Amoral behavior is often reported in societies where extreme poverty and hopelessness predominate. The inhabitants of Montegrano had little reason to take the "general good" into consideration. Public institutions were weak and had little stature. When people had anything to do with them, it was always with an eye to gaining some personal advantage.

In the Netherlands, too, amoral dealings are more and more often being viewed as normal. During the last decades, there has also been a growing trend toward taking a calculating stance when dealing with public institutions. The difference is that it is not the interest of the family that is central in the Netherlands but the interest of the individual: *amoral individualism*.[2] It is not that we live in poverty, but in abundance. Public institutions are not weak but are especially well developed. The welfare state seems to prompt its citizens to be just as resourceful in pursuing their own interests as the weak, corrupt government of the peasants of Montegrano.

Into the 1980s the government made little effort to identify the harmful aspects of this resourcefulness and to rein them in. The great collective arrangements of the welfare state were developed for a small society of law-abiding citizens. The 1960s saw the beginnings of the change to an anonymous, large welfare state with assertive and calculating citizens. The decades in which the well-thinking Netherlands held itself in a massive *sur place* [q.v.] were also the years in which a vast, anonymous domain came into being, with all the appropriate temptations. This anonymous domain appeared to be an excellent breeding ground for totems and taboos.

SCOOTCH OVER A LITTLE

Into the 1960s the Netherlands was a small, religious, law-abiding and, in many aspects, conservative country. A long period of neutrality, a late industrialization and a strong tradition of obedience had created a certain sense of suspicion toward social and cultural change. Until 1965 the Netherlands, in the words of Hubert Smeets, had "a directed economy, a directed democracy and directed consumption."[3]

In their dealings with others, people had few individual axes to grind. If the common good made it necessary, they were willing to "scootch over a little." This attitude was typified by expressions like "a lot of docile sheep in a pen" and "herring in a barrel," which the postwar generation perhaps only uses in emergencies. The emancipation of the workers and the bourgeoisie was a question of rights, of which obligations were part and parcel. That did not count anymore in the 1970s, when the last barrier of emancipation came into sight: the emancipation of the individual. Those who "stand up for themselves" do not think about obligations and certainly not about scootching over. The modern Dutch language has a series of clear-cut epithets for people who make a display of their sense of public responsibility, where others keep to themselves. Someone who does that is an eager beaver, a la-di-da, a goody-goody, a goody-two-shoes, a milksop, or—really unforgivable—a thief from his own billfold.

Of course, those descriptions are not so readily used if people play the eager beaver for their children, their neighbors or their friends. They refer to our dealings in anonymous situations with anonymous organizations. How we behave in this anonymous domain has become a question of calculation. There is a huge temptation to put your own interest above the common good. We console ourselves with the thought that any undesirable consequences of this calculating behavior will affect only unknown victims or a distant, vague organization.

The question of "scootching over a little or not" is an example of a social dilemma. Such a dilemma comes about when someone has to make a choice of behavior that can have a personally favorable outcome or a collectively favorable outcome: everyone wants to have their share of the common good but, at the same time, wants to contribute as little as possible to it. In the present-day Netherlands, with its numerous collective and large-scale social arrangements, dilemmas like these are common. Often they take the form of the prisoner's dilemma, a classic problem from game theory. In its original form, as envisaged by the American mathematician A.W. Tucker, it relates to two players, but it can be applied to a larger numbers of players as well.

Two crooks who have committed a crime have been detained by the police. They are in separate cells, they are being questioned separately and each is confronted with the question of whether to squeal on the other. If one keeps silent, and the other one talks, the one who keeps silent gets the maximum term of imprisonment, and the one who talks will be rewarded with immediate freedom. If they both talk, then they both have to do a portion of the maximum term. If they both keep silent, then nothing can be proved, and they both go free.

Both of them keeping silent is the optimum collective outcome, but in practice, usually both of them talk, which means that they both go to jail. Why don't they both shut up? Because each of them is scared to death that the other one will talk and put all the blame on him. Each of the prisoners makes a decision that is rational from his point of view, but the result of these decisions is harmful to their mutual interests. The tragedy of the prisoners is that they are not in a position to make an agreement among themselves and to hold one another to the agreement with checks and sanctions. There is no invisible hand that can bring the individual interests of the one into balance with the interests of the other.

In a prisoner's dilemma each of them is tempted to profit at the other's expense, because it is advantageous to do so but also because of the fear that he will have to face the consequences if the other one takes advantage of his silence. By talking, each prisoner assures himself that he will not be worse off than the other. This "amoral" choice for one's direct personal interest does not have to stem from absolute deprivation or social deprivation, as is the case with the inhabitants of Montegrano.

In the last few decades, the Netherlands has developed into a good breeding ground for prisoner's dilemmas. In a small, closed society, people can easily keep a balance sheet of favors given and favors received. In an urban society where people have numerous contacts and are very mobile, the "payback" of a public-spirited act and social assistance is questionable. What does it get me? What guarantees me that another will do the same for me?

A large, urban society that is also a welfare state will be even richer in prisoner's dilemmas. A strong belief in the all-encompassing providence of the state has grown very powerful since the 1960s in the

Netherlands. The idea of personal blame and responsibility has broken down.

In the third place, prisoner's dilemmas have a chance to develop where, as in the rapidly de-Pillarized and individualized Netherlands, there are no strict standards. A decrease in social cohesion leads to people's behaving amorally and calculatingly in an anonymous domain. This tendency is increased in the Netherlands by the low chance of getting caught and the light punishments.

THE WAO: A PACT WITH THE DEVIL

The Dutch example of a large-scale prisoner's dilemma is the failure of the WAO. The most fantastic program that our welfare state ever produced—a greater contrast to Montegrano is almost inconceivable—kicked the bucket as a result of the cumulative effect of countless decisions made by employers and employees who did not care about the common good. For the individual older worker the WAO was an attractive downsizing arrangement. The individual employer was able to easily, inexpensively and pleasantly get rid of his less productive employees.

The first employer who discovered this trick thought he was getting a special advantage. After that, his counterparts started doing it, too, and soon you were "a thief from your own billfold" if you did not do it. But the more widely this trick was used, the higher the bill that would eventually have to be paid. Over the long term and seen from the point of view of the collective good, the misuse of the WAO was a pact with the devil.

There is no point in blaming individual employers and employees for being calculating. Just like everybody else, they made the most profitable use of a collective arrangement. In the public sector, supply and demand have the inclination not to keep one another in balance but to stimulate one another, that is, unless a separate organization with an independent, professional ethic steps forward as the defender of the common interests. There was no such countervailing power in the oversight of the WAO. The professional associations, the Social Security Council, the government, the Parliament, which were supposed to watch out for the soul of the welfare state, did not do anything, while, under their very noses, that soul was being sold to the devil.

In addition to the misconception that the public assistance organizations themselves were the best overseers of their own shop, various taboos played a role in the failure of the WAO. The period in which this program came into being—the end of the 1960s—coincided with the end of the time that citizens thought it was self-evident that they should give personal data to organizations. The legislation was modeled on a fairly transparent society with a population that was not too assertive, but, when it was implemented, the cultural growth spurt that would change the population of the Netherlands into one of the most assertive in the West had already started.

The actions of certifying physicians and National-Assistance inspectors were in conflict with such tenets of the modern faith as the right to privacy and self-fulfillment. Calculating citizens quickly learned how to use these noble principles to their own advantage. Before recertification began in the 1990s, almost half of those in the WAO were troubled by mental and back problems, infamous for how hard they are to test. Under the Accident Act and the Disabilities Act, the predecessors of the WAO, these complaints had been an insignificant minority of the total number of cases. Between 1985 and 1990, the number of mental cases registered with the WAO increased by 40 percent, while the number of nonmental cases increased by 10 percent.

The "gatekeepers" were not at all equipped to deal with this calculating approach to the WAO. To the contrary, while their clients "stood up for themselves" with more and more self-assurance, the insurance company doctors and inspectors became less and less sure of themselves. What had been a matter of fact for their predecessors in the 1950s—sticking your nose deep into someone else's business—was "painful" for the evaluators of the 1970s. How far could you invade someone's privacy? How distrustful could you be? Confrontation with clients is less painful the narrower your discretion, the clearer the limits, the more sure you are that your counterparts will take the same sort of action and that your boss will back you up for it. In all these areas the gatekeepers of the Sickness Benefits Act [q.v.] and the WAO were fighting an uphill battle. Their dealings with clients were much less formal, much less standoffish than before and therefore it was more difficult to be "hard."

No guidance could be expected from above. When the Accident Act was still in force, there were 20 or so medical insurance specialists at the central office of the Social Insurance Bank to prevent unfairness and uncontrolled growth in the program. For the much more complicated WAO there was one doctor with the same task at the headquarters of the Joint Medical Service of the Professional Associations. From the very beginning, doctors in the field, who were evaluating those applying for the WAO, did not have the benefit of guidance or standards from headquarters.[4]

The grace period expired in the early 1990s, and it was time to pay the piper. As always with a prisoner's dilemma, it is the collective that suffers, but as soon as push comes to shove for the collective, it begins to look for ways to shift the costs to someone else. A portion of the bill was presented to the very people for whom the welfare state was intended in the first place: those who were not so smart, those who were simple enough to be honest, the poor souls who always get it in the end, at the end of the chain of responsibility, at the end of the regulation; they are the first ones to be chewed up and spit out or abandoned.

A man who is seriously disabled at a fire in a factory no longer gets 70 percent of his income until he turns 65. Within a few years he will be at just above the level of National Assistance, even if he is 35 and had paid 15 years of social insurance premiums. "Apparently, we with our riches can no longer afford to collectively insure catastrophes that happen at work," wrote the sociologist Schuyt. "Apparently, we make such a shambles of collective solidarity, that we no longer wish to protect real cases of disability from industrial accidents. I consider that the reversal of a trend towards more civilization."[5] The notional man in the example above would have been better off in terms of the percentage of his pay that was paid out in assistance benefits under the Accident Act of 1901, the first social insurance act in the Netherlands. This law guaranteed 80 percent of wages or salary plus medical costs for life for a disability as a result of an accident at the workplace.

Things went wrong with the WAO because it was not resistant to the calculating approach of employers, employees and professional organizations. The WAO, an arrangement of great importance, was defenseless against apprehensions about privacy, fear of control and coercion, reticence to implement central instructions and the autonomy of "civil society". Anyone who sounded the alarm—like J.G. Hibbeln, a senior official with the Joint Medical Service who, in 1974, convincingly predicted the failure of the WAO—did not stand a ghost of a chance.[6] Only during the parliamentary hearings on the WAO did you hear day in and day out that the speaker had known for a long time that things would go wrong but that, unfortunately, "the time was not right" to make such assertions in public. Two journalists wrote a book about the WAO debacle under the title *A Dutch Conspiracy.*[7] But it was not a conspiracy at all. The only conspiracy that existed was a conspiracy of silence—a quagmire variant of the Mafia's omertà.

NOTES

1. E.C. Banfield, *The Moral Basis of a Backward Society*, Free Press, Glencoe, IL, 1958.

2. On the other hand, the difference with *amoral familism* becomes even more nuanced if one accepts the definition of the Dutch system of familial relations given by the Nepalese anthropologist Rajendra Pradhan: an "ego-centered kinship system." Quoted in the *NRC Handelsblad*, 16 April 1988.

3. Quoted in *Het Parool*, 25 May 1996.

4. Willem Velema in *Intermediair*, 9 April 1993.

5. *NRC Handelsblad*, 7 November 1992.

6. Reprinted in J.G. Hibbeln and Willem Velema, *Het WAO-debacle, de fatale missers van wettenmakers en uitvoerders* [The WAO Debacle: The Fatal Mistakes of the Legislators and Those Who Implemented It], Jan van Arkel, Utrecht, 1993.

7. Peter ter Horst and Wim Koehler, *Een Hollands complot, de WAO en de arbeidscultuur* [A Dutch Conspiracy: The WAO and the Ethics of Work], *NRC Handelsblad*, Rotterdam, 1991.

CHAPTER 13

Negotiating in an Arena

The faith of W. IJlst, pastor of the Christ the King Church in Rotterdam, can stand up to some rough treatment. His church was damaged by woodworm, the roof blew off in 1990 and the year after that, lightning struck the steeple, damaging it so badly that it had to be pulled down. "We can't blame Him for this," said the pastor. "To the contrary, it is a miracle that three quarters of the church is still standing."

This train of thought, so characteristic of a strongly anchored faith, could also be heard in the last few decades coming from some sociologists and criminologists from the Norbert Elias school. There are some 10 million cases of shoplifting yearly in the Netherlands. Slowly but surely, it is becoming the most common form of crime in the country. The yearly loss to shoplifting is 600 million guilders. Almost all the thefts are from self-service stores. Nevertheless, writes Paul Kapteyn, it is interesting that most people do not steal in a supermarket. "They do not abuse the trust that is placed in them, they do not give in to this 'modern temptation.' . . . They are exceptionally decent people and from their behavior . . . it appears that in this aspect morals have improved."[1]

The doctrine of growing self-coercion is the linchpin of Norbert Elias' theory of civilization. Through the advance of social differentiation, specialization and integration, an increasing number of people are becoming bound to one another through chains of dependence over an increasingly wide area and in increasingly different ways. More and more people have to take more and more other people into consideration in more and more aspects of their lives. Thereby, the balance of power becomes more complex, and differences in power are reduced. Mutual identification increases.

Elias connects the increasing integration and specialization with the processes of forming states and international integration. At the same time, these social changes also change our emotional bookkeeping. The pressure that we apply to ourselves increases. Being able to predict and count on certain behaviors becomes more and more important; therefore, so do planning and controlling emotions. Elias describes the civilization process not simply as a development toward more self-control but also as its strengthening, both in character and in breadth. People exercise control over themselves in a more balanced, uniform and continuous manner. Internalization increases: self-coercion becomes more and more matter-of-fact and more automatic. At the same time, it becomes more multifaceted and more all-encompassing: it expands into diverse situations in both our public and private lives. In modern terms it is a growth toward "integral" self-coercion.

THE WAO: A PARTY THAT BEGAN SO WELL

Cas Wouters illustrates this development with the simile of a party. The idea of a party is that people can "let themselves go"—but not too far. To prevent things from getting out of hand, it used to be that a strict etiquette and strong guidelines were considered desirable. But nowadays, the guests are expected to be able to generate the necessary self-control within themselves. It is now as if the "guidelines" were jointly applied by everyone, with the "rules" so well internalized that they are hardly thought of as such. Thereby, in addition, you have to consider that the rules are much more finely differentiated than the earlier categorical rules of behavior. We are in a position not only to exercise more self-coercion but also to fine-tune it much more precisely.[2]

In the 1960s and 1970s, states Wouters, the importance of strictly formulated "good manners" decreased, and more room was created for all sorts of alternative feelings and behaviors. According to him, this did not "change the direction" of the process of civilization. To the contrary, it continued its vigorous development, because strong shoulders were necessary to carry the luxury of this new freedom: precisely the more "informal" nature of the rules of behavior demanded an exceptionally stable, differentiated and all-encompassing self-regulation from each individual. According to the civilization theory, the matter-of-factness with which men and women nowadays can keep one another company unclothed in the sauna or on the beach is a reflection of an example of a very high level of self-control. Precisely to be able to be "freer" in their interactions with one another, people have to better regulate their spontaneous impulses and keep them inside more often. While it seems that forms of behavior have become more relaxed, the "relaxation" requires precisely new, higher forms of self-control that we are hardly aware of.[3]

The acceptability of this concept and the speed with which the change in the Netherlands took place can be illustrated on the basis of a statement from an unexpected quarter. In a radio talk show from 1949, a Catholic priest told the story about a young man who came to him. The young man often went swimming and sunbathing in a "mixed" [q.v.] group of men and women and said that this "didn't bother him at all." The priest's reply to this comment was: "My dear sir, if that 'doesn't bother you at all,' then you need to hurry to a psychiatrist and have yourself examined inside and out, because you are not normal. A young man, who can spend hours in an environment of scantily clad women and girls without it bothering him is a serious degenerate."[4]

The examples of the party and of the naked swimmers relate only to manners for face-to-face interactions. But is the internalization of self-coercion as far advanced in the domain of anonymous interactions? When we add this element to the equation, then the proposition that the breath of the civilization process is expanding seems no longer to be tenable. Higher and higher demands of self-regulation are being made on our behavior with regard to anonymous arrangements: the anonymous sector of daily life is expanding into more and more areas, while the oversight that the government exercises over it has not expanded equally. Can we get along without a master of ceremonies in these arrangements as well?

Initially, it looked as if we could. The WAO party—to name just one example—was a lot of fun when it began in 1967. The guests politely had a bite to eat and a drink; they thought that it was very exceptional that they had been invited at all. Slowly but surely, however, the whole neighborhood heard that there was a party going on with free food and drinks, and the party crashers arrived in droves. More and more, the absence of a master of ceremonies began to take its toll, and a quarter century after it had begun, the get-together had degenerated into a debauched gorge-and-guzzle party. As thanks for the pleasant diversion, the guests had messed up the carpet and had taken the furniture with them. The official invitees who arrived after 1993, only found some hors d'oeuvres with bites taken out of them and a couple of bottles of soured Chateau Migraine. The party was over, and, for the present, there were no plans for a new one.

But that is not the end of the story of the decline and fall of the WAO party. Where was the host all this time? Didn't he care that his furnishings were being ruined? The answer to this question is no: the professional organizations did not care what the WAO was degenerating into. Their dealings were based on their own institutional interests: the more the merrier, regardless of where the more came from. They had their own party, and there, too, the master of ceremonies was conspicuous by his absence. Not only is the domain of anonymous interaction a temptation for individuals to take part in less civilized behavior, but the same is also true for organizations. "Calculating organizations are much more dangerous for the welfare state than calculating citizens," said Professor Wolfson at a PvdA meeting in the WAO crisis year of 1991. Even organizations, when there is not enough supervision, can cross the line from calculation to fraud.

THE BREADTH OF THE CIVILIZATION THEORY

According to Elias, the "trend" of the civilization process is the same everywhere. Change continues to move in the direction of "more or less automatic self-censorship," whereby impulses are subordinated to less immediate goals.[5] A good example is the treatment of our own body. Goudsblom points to the fact that, in the modern industrial society, life expectancy has become so high that it is worth the effort to "invest" in a long and healthy life by carefully looking after your own body. The social prerequisites are there for an "economic" use of the limited physical capital that we have.[6] Earlier, that was not the case, as the journalist Aafke Steenhuis not long ago noted. In her youth you still had "terribly fat, deformed, ugly people, like you still see in movies from Eastern Europe. But these sorts of colorful figures have disappeared from our street scene. Nowadays everybody is getting their body in shape."[7]

Does the strengthening of the automatic self-censorship continue to apply where we are no longer talking about our own bodies or our own career but about, for example, the interests of unknown others? Will we also matter-of-factly rein in our behavior with regard to a conglomerate of strangers? The question of the breadth of the civilization theory has recently been placed on the sociology agenda.[8] Critics say that Elias' theory does not do enough justice to societies where there is no process of state formation and to processes of "decivilization," like those in the former Yugoslavia a few years ago.[9]

There is also another criticism possible that has precisely to do with the breadth of the theory in a strongly "civilized" country like the Netherlands, namely, that the civilization theory is less able to explain behavior, the more that it takes place in an anonymous space. In Wouters' terms we would, indeed, be talking about the increasing fine-tuning of the way that we deal with the rules, but there is little to be noticed of an increasing self-coercion in how much we conform to the rules.

DE SWAAN AND ACCOMMODATION BY NEGOTIATION

In 1979 A. de Swaan made his speech about the shift from accommodation by command to accommodation by negotiation. De Swaan pointed to this shift, which was gaining momentum in the Western countries, on the basis of Elias' theory. The freedom to choose your own behavior has increased, social control has decreased, but in the meantime, people have increasingly become more dependent on one another. Therefore, more and more often, they have to take one another into consideration.

Just as Elias began with the proposition that the growth of self-coercion is a general trend, De Swaan assumed that the shift to accommodation by negotiation was taking place everywhere. This development was first and most clearly seen in the modern welfare bureaucracies but was also to be found in intimate relations, in the relationship between citizens and the authorities and inside organizations. According to De Swaan, this shift was "liberating." The powers that be of old, husbands, parents, bosses, have to be more considerate of their wives, children and subordinates. De Swaan did, however, state that the shift was difficult and threatening for many people, "because accommodation by negotiation is difficult, too risky and too lonely for them."[10]

In his book *Care and the State* (1990), De Swaan stated that the welfare state "has become a strategic playing field on which people operate like contractors making calculations." But upon closer examination, the results are better than expected. Welfare arrangements cannot function without a considerable amount of "leakage," but it amounts to only 10 percent at the most. This makes social programs "wonderfully efficient," in comparison to the internal combustion engine and the incandescent lamp. If we wanted to achieve a higher efficiency, then we would come awfully close to a police state.

In 1992, in a lecture entitled "The Wrong-Doing State," De Swaan made a U-turn: with anonymous regulation, the beneficial act of negotiation that forces people to rein themselves in, is missing, and that has serious social consequences. He made it known that even in the Netherlands, cynicism and amorality are extending their grasp; welfare fraud and tax swindles have become common. Now even De Swaan is pleading for centrally enforced solutions for these sorts of social dilemmas in the form of "laws, inspections, coercion and fines."[11]

Is reality still observing the laws of the civilization process and the shift toward accommodation by negotiation? In 1994 De Swaan pointed to the increasing number of cases of "urination in public" within the city limits, which he called "an unmistakable sign of decivilization and a reversal of the process of civil refinement."[12] In 1995 he added that once individuals begin to deviate from official standards of behavior, a process is started that, to a certain degree, feeds on itself. This is why recently "the acceptance of rules of behavior for social-economic and social-cultural areas . . . has been somewhat reduced."[13]

While De Swaan did note these developments, he did not ask the question of how they were to be explained in the civilization theory. In

1995 he categorized the shift from accommodation by command to accommodation by negotiation as an "ideal." "But, taken to its extreme, it can nonetheless serve to correct the opposing stereotype that makes society out to be a chaos of monadic individuals, driven only by calculations of personal desire and advantage."

Rather than constructing such extreme oppositions, it is more fruitful to ask the question, Which aspects of that ideal have been taken to the extreme? What has changed that makes this categorization necessary? Where did this deterioration in the process of civil refinement that feeds on itself come from? The question can be easily answered on the basis of the problem of urination in public that De Swaan brought up. In a swimming pool, urination in public is the most common thing in the world. It is "anonymous:" nobody can see it happening. If everyone who urinated in the pool immediately grew a long nose, nobody would think about doing it. Because that is not the case, the owner of the pool has to take refuge in other tactics: he adds chlorine to the water to disinfect it.

Someone who urinates on the street, however, is readily identifiable as a public urinater. That is not pleasant if you are seen by people you know who live in the house that you are urinating on. If you are, on the other hand, surrounded by anonymous passersby, then it is not so bad. The increase in public urination is not to be explained by a deterioration in the process of civilization but by the expansion of the anonymous sector of daily life. This development goes hand in hand with the increase in interdependence, precisely the process that Elias views as the source of increasing civilization.

Perhaps you can say—in accordance with the civilization theory—that the behavior of the public urinater inside the city limits has become more "balanced" and controlled with the advance of an anonymous, large-scale society. More than ever, the decision depends on the time, place, company you are with and other circumstances. But this change in behavior is difficult to associate with the expansion of mutual identification that the civilization theory assumes. It is more reasonable to assume that the opposite is true. Manners specialist Inez van Eijk described the consideration leading up to the decision as: "Who knows my ass in Cologne?," apparently referring to the phenomenon of women's urinating in public. Her observation is that the choice to behave properly or not is increasingly based on a calculation of the "consequences." In a first-class train compartment, she nowadays sees a well-dressed businessman with his finger up his nose, "all the way to the first knuckle! He could care less that I think that this is a repulsive sight, because I cannot get him promoted and I am not a member of his golf club." Inez van Eijk has the impression that this consideration is further advanced in the Netherlands than in other countries.[14]

"FORGET THE RULES, WATCH THE TRAFFIC"

As a metaphor for their vision of social interaction, students of Elias like to use the behavior of drivers behind the wheel. Do people observe traffic regulations [q.v.] less often? No problem. "Forget the rules and watch the traffic," wrote Cas Wouters.[15] Even the official psychologist of the Amsterdam police, Frans Denkers, supports this point of view. On his bike, Denkers is not bothered by stoplights and takes traffic circles against the flow of traffic. In his car, when it's possible, he violates the speed limit. "Don't people using the road take each other into consideration?" According to Denkers, traffic is a perfect example of democracy, a paradise of discipline.[16]

The Dutch are, indeed, increasingly becoming their own traffic regulators. In 1991 the new Regulation on Traffic Signs and Traffic Rules came into force, which made a number of things the responsibility of drivers in traffic. The first step was taken in 1962 with the introduction of "Automatic Level Grade Crossing Half-Gates" [q.v.]. Initially, the police were there to see that no one went around them, but soon enough it was clear to everyone that the punishment was built into the violation.

In less clearly dangerous traffic situations, where "payment" for violations is not as direct, an excessive trust in other drivers' discipline can cost lives. J. Leijten gives an example in his book *The Terrible Loneliness of a Burglar*. One night in 1981, Jansen drove onto a priority road from a side street, where he should have yielded right-of-way. Another driver, Gerritsen, smashed into him. Gerritsen was, as he himself admitted, going 125 kilometers an hour in a 100-kilometer-per-hour zone. Jansen was seriously injured, but the judge said that Gerritsen was not at all to blame. A driver who enters a priority road must always "anticipate the possibility of predictable errors on the part of other drivers, which includes a violation of the speed limit," as long as these errors "remain within reasonable limits." This was the case here, opined the judge, "because it is almost common knowledge that drivers on the road often do not think of observing the legally established speed limit."

The opposite scenario—where drivers indeed anticipate an action à la Frans Denkers—can also cost lives. In 1991 there were two enormous accidents on the A16 [q.v.], involving 300 cars, in which 10 lives were lost. Both accidents happened in thick fog. In July 1992 the judge levied heavy fines on 27 of the drivers involved: they were driving too fast. Their defense was very interesting. It was not recklessness that had made them drive so fast, they said, but rather caution. They did not dare to slow down in the fog out of the fear that they would be run into from behind by someone who did not slow down. In this case, each driver found himself in a dilemma, that, in the end, caused him to take a dangerous and sometimes fatal action.

The drivers on the A16 did exactly what Frans Denkers and the judge whom Leijten wrote about recommended: they anticipated the possibility that other drivers would be speeding or the possibility that others, just as they themselves did, would anticipate speed-limit violations by others on the road. That cost a number of them their lives and the others a fine. Dilemmas like this are avoidable only if every driver can be sure that the other drivers will slow down, too. Only then can "the mutual anticipation of a violation" change into "the mutual expectation of self-control."[17]

This trust can be realized to a certain extent by the provision of information, as can be seen from the experience of the Fog Signaling System that was installed on the A16 near Breda in 1991. Sensors measure the density of the fog and send a recommended speed to electronic signs above the road. An evaluation showed that, when a recommended speed was posted, the average speed went down by eight to ten kilometers an hour. The chance of an accident is thereby reduced by 30 to 40 percent. In addition, the differences in speed are less: very high and very low speeds are less common.

Huge chain-collisions in fog in January 1997 showed that this is a long way from removing all the dangers in this situation. A greater increase in safety can be achieved only, if effective speed controls that have real sanctions are applied. Technology offers more and more opportunities to implement "mutually expected self-control." If all the cars are equipped with an automatic speed governor that keeps them from driving faster than 50 kilometers per hour in fog, there is no dilemma. You are crazy if you start tinkering with the governor, because if you drive faster, you are guaranteed to run into someone.

Accommodation by negotiation works "better" the more the participants have an understanding of their mutual interdependence and have something to offer each other. The best example is sexual intercourse between equal partners. The relationship is face-to-face, a physical entwining is paired with a very high degree of intertwined interests. The changes in sexual behavior are thought of as a liberation, but, in practice, the partners have to be even more considerate of each other and, therefore, rein themselves in more. The liberalization went together with a higher degree of mutual agreement and "a mutual expectation of self-control." This control comes about because both partners have an interest in something fun happening. A simultaneous orgasm, for example, is, according to Kapteyn, "an art form that takes a lot of talking, empathy and anticipation" and, consequently, a high level of self-control.[18]

The readiness to exercise self-coercion is really a lot less if we think about the other extreme when the other party is an anonymous organization or an accumulation of unknown individuals. Large-scale situations and arrangements are based on anonymous interdependence:

there is no personal confrontation with someone else who sets limits or demands negotiations. This, too, can be illustrated with a traffic example. In the Netherlands, annually tens of thousands of drivers hit and run. Many of these accidents happen at night on quiet roads. The chance of getting caught is small; only a small percentage of the perpetrators is tracked down. A collision at night with no witnesses is almost a laboratory test to measure the degree of self-control we have in a morally loaded, but anonymous, situation.

The number of hit-and-run cases reported to the police climbed from 12,000 in 1975, to 56,000 in 1995, an increase of 350 percent. For comparison, during that same period, the number of cars rose from 3.4 million to 5.8 million, an increase of 60 percent. The number of kilometers driven rose from 60 billion in 1979, to 76 billion in 1990, an increase of less than 30 percent. The total number of traffic accidents in the same period remained about the same.[19]

The choice of behavior that a driver is faced with, following an accident, is a good example of a social dilemma. For the collective, it is better if no one ever hit and ran, but for each individual driver, leaving the scene of an accident has a number of advantages: no responsibility for damages, no loss of the driver's no-claim insurance discount, no test for driving under the influence, no fine for reckless driving.[20] As more and more databases are interconnected, the more these advantages increase.

In a certain sense, leaving the scene of an accident takes a great deal of self-control: in a couple of seconds the driver makes a complex calculation of all sorts of variables and risks. You could say that the spontaneous impulse to stop and help has been efficiently "controlled." But, as in the example of public urinaters, it is not a case of increasing self-coercion in the sense of the civilization theory. What is missing is an increase in mutual identification and accountability. In the anonymous situation of an accident at night, it seems that for a growing number of drivers, identification with the other person is decreasing. For accountability, these days we have the Uninsured Motorist Fund, which compensates for damages caused by unknown or uninsured cars.

In a less anonymous society, where the victims and perpetrators are not strangers but neighbors or friends, leaving the scene of an accident is less common. This is glaringly illustrated by the 1991 case of a boy from the less heavily populated province of Zeeland, who, at night, not far from his place of residence, hit a pedestrian. He left the scene, and the pedestrian died. The next day, he turned himself in to the police. In the meantime, it had become clear that the victim was not a stranger. It was his mother whom he had left at the side of the road.

LIMITS ON THE CONCEPT OF NEGOTIATION

On the basis of a number of examples, I have examined the breadth of the civilization theory and the concept of accommodation by negotiation that is based on it. Now, I will try to determine its limits as carefully as possible on the basis of the social map of the Netherlands since the 1960s. Where is this concept less usable? I suggest four areas and circumstances: where social interaction is anonymous, where there are structural differences that create an inequality of power, where there are scarce resources and conflicting interests and within (semi)governmental organizations.

An increasing level of self-coercion is not self-evident among participants in a large-scale, anonymous arrangement. Without an efficient system of control, they tend to try to maximize their own benefit at the cost of the common good, and that is true not only for a select group of criminal types but also for countless citizens and organizations. In the years of "discipline and asceticism"—when the Pillars were intact—the Dutch demonstrated more "self-control" in the anonymous domain than thereafter. In the Pillarized Netherlands, "the social pressure for self-coercion" was heavy. Nowadays, many relationships are based on contacts that change or rest on the ties of an anonymous arrangement. Thereby, the ties of interdependence are so long and so differentiated that the "social pressure for self-coercion" evaporates. Instead of leading to internalized self-coercion, they result in a very well defined framework for weighing interests off one against the other, often in the form of a prisoner's dilemma.

In his speech, De Swaan described the shift toward accommodation by negotiation as a form of emancipation and power sharing. Authorities have to take citizens and subordinates more "into account" and, thereby, take on more restrictions. But not all differences in power levels are influenced by this system of accommodation by negotiation: there are a number of structural inequalities of power on which it cannot get a grip. Negotiation does not do you much good when you are too weak to achieve the protection of your life and property in the arena or are too poor to pay for it in a private arrangement. The concept of an arena or of accommodation by negotiation assumes that the parties are more or less equal, or it recognizes the inequality of their power positions and accepts it.

What should we, for example, think about the greenhouses in the west of the country, where part of the work is done in the shadow economy [q.v.] by foreigners? The arrangements between these illegal workers and their bosses are preeminently made "on their own." Can you really talk about "accommodation by negotiation" here? The distribution of power is extremely unequal: for every illegal there are ten others. These interactions make me think more of those between a cat and a mouse. As we all know, these two can come to an accommodation—let alone an accommodation by negotiation—only if you have a very smart mouse and an extremely dumb cat.

One of the policy areas where the concept of negotiation was energetically applied was zoning. In the late 1980s policy was reworked on the basis of covenants and "networked management." The National Service for Environmental Planning looked back in 1994 and came out with some straightforward criticism in its *Zoning Studies*. Due to the various "made-to-order" approaches, the program had lost its transparency. The National Service concluded that "networked management" functioned better when the parties working together recognized mutual interests and could expect some advantage. If conflicts had to be resolved, then there was the danger that the parties would be satisfied with the achievement of consensus, without sufficiently testing whether the agreement they had made had "the power to resolve the problem."

This points to a third limitation on the applicability of the concept of negotiation. Completely in line with the spirit and the possibilities of the 1960s and 1970s, it is intended for situations where all the parties can expect to benefit: those much sought-after "win-win" situations. The whole complex of decentralization, "networked management" and self-regulation seems to work well as long as there is enough for everyone. But when resources are scarce, and there are conflicting interests, negotiations are often accompanied by a lot of talking, little deciding and unclear lines of responsibility.

Beginning in 1992, in five ministries the old hierarchical lines of responsibility were replaced by "management by committee." The directorates made way for "areas of interest." The directors and the heads of services in the municipalities that went over to this model merged to form an "administrative council," which was entirely responsible for all policy implementation. Most of all, they had to spend a lot of time conferring with one another, plus dropping by the chiefs of section for a good talk.

The fruits of this "horizontal" concept of management were not all that good and justified the idea that the negotiation approach is limitedly applicable to government and semigovernmental organizations. The result of all the reorganizations was primarily that responsibilities were pushed deeper into the civil service apparatus, as far as possible out of sight. In early 1996 Twijnstra Gudde consultants reported that management by committee in the ministries seemed to be a failure. The position of the administrative councils in the departmental hierarchy was not clear. The administrative councils were dissolved in the Ministries of Justice and Social Affairs that same year and later also in other ministries.

In the last few years, the overseers of the business world—accountants—have introduced techniques related to the negotiation model: informal reporting, horizontal systems of responsibility and process-specific approaches. The traditional approach of management control and management accounting was dismissed as inflexible and centralistic. Accordingly, these new insights said that the vertical model created only "an illusion of control." Processes were controlled on paper, but in reality, the assurances were only illusory, held together with administrative tricks.[21]

In the business world, more horizontal and decentralized lines of responsibility may well stand a better chance of success. Rights and obligations to the firm will be more clearly defined and more easily measurable than in the nonprofit sector. Accommodation by negotiation can be built into a clear distribution of responsibilities. One's own interests can be so organized that they make an optimum contribution to goals of the organization. Within government and semigovernmental bureaucracies, it seems that embracing the idea of "horizontal" negotiation in the 1980s was precisely what created an "illusion of control." That was very true for the welfare bureaucracies, like the WAO organizations: through the effects of the prisoner's dilemma, the program was being hollowed out, while officially everything was under control.

ACCOMMODATION BY NEGOTIATION: A CONCEPT ANNEXED INTO A MODEL

The fact that, in the Western world and especially in the Netherlands, there is a shift under way toward accommodation by negotiation is beyond doubt. The concept is very useful for the analysis of the process of rapid change that has been taking place since the 1960s. What is of interest in the Netherlands is that this concept has also found support in policy and administrative circles, not only for describing actual developments but also as a motivation for shifts in the organization of implementation, such as deregulation, decentralization, privatization, "networked management" and management by committee.

This is how an analytic concept was annexed into a desirable "model." This negotiation model was an excellent fit with the need for informality and nonintervention that had come to the fore in the Netherlands in the last few decades. At the same time, it had a genuine seal of 1960s quality: the shift toward accommodation by negotiation was supposed to go hand in hand with power sharing and emancipation.[22] In the same period, prisoner's dilemmas became very important in the anonymous domain, without attracting much notice. There was also little attention given to the negative effects of shifting responsibility to shoulders that were often too weak to carry it. Prisoner's dilemmas can be gotten rid of only by the voluntary acceptance of government coercion, which the concept of accommodation by negotiation seemed to make unnecessary.

NOTES

1. *Het Parool*, 13 October 1990.

2. Cas Wouters, *Van minnen en sterven, informalisering van omgangsvormen rond seks en dood* [About Love and Death: The Informalization of Behaviors Having to Do with Sex and Death], Bert Bakker, Amsterdam, 1990.

3. Paul Kapteyn, *Taboe, ontwikkelingen in macht en moraal speciaal in Nederland* [Taboo: Developments in Power and Morals, Especially in the Netherlands], De Arbeiderspers, Amsterdam, 1980, pp. 267/268.

4. A. Diepenbrock , "Zomerplezieren" [Summer Pleasures], an informal talk show done for the KRO [Catholic Radio Network], included in *Actio Catholica* [Catholic Action], 1949. Quoted by Gerard van der Kroon, *In de woestijn van de moraal, een documentaire over de katholieke moraal in Nederland in de jaren 1945-1965* [In the Desert of Morals: A Documentary about Catholic Morals in the Netherlands between 1945 and 1965], Ambo, Utrecht, 1965.

5. Norbert Elias, *Het civilisatieproces, sociogenetische en psychogenetische onderzoekingen* [The Process of Civilization: Sociogenetic and Psychogenetic Studies], Het Spectrum, Utrecht/Antwerpen, 1982, vol. 2, p. 258.

6. Johan Goudsblom, *De sociologie van Norbert Elias* [The Sociology of Norbert Elias], Meulenhoff, Amsterdam, 1987, p. 209.

7. Steenhuis, 1996, p. 4.

8. See the special issue of the *Amsterdams Sociologisch Tijdschrift* [The Sociological Journal of Amsterdam]: *De civilisatietheorie herzien* [The Civilization Theory Revised], October 1995. A good overview of recent comments on the breadth of the theory can be found in the introductory article by J. Goudsblom: "De civilisatietheorie: kritiek en perspectief" [The Civilization Theory: Criticism and Perspective].

9. An example is the anthropologist Mart Bax, who did research in the Bosnian pilgrimage destination of Medjugorje. In the early 1990s there, the glorification of Mary gave way to more and more barbarian violence. At the same time, there was talk of decreasing "spontaneity" and a relative increase in the growth of "control" or "regulation" of interactive behaviors. The processes of barbarization can, therefore, be closely intertwined with the processes of "civilization." Mart Bax, "Medjugorjes kleine oorlog, barbarisering in een Bosnische bedevaartplaats" [Medjugorje's Little War: The Barbarization of a Bosnian Pilgrimage Destination], *Amsterdams Sociologisch Tijdschrift* [The Sociological Journal of Amsterdam], June 1993, pp. 22/23, Mart Bax, *Medjugorje: Religion, Politics and Violence in Rural Bosnia*, VU uitgeverij [Free University Press], Amsterdam, 1995.

10. A. de Swaan, "Uitgaansbeperking en uitgaansangst, over de verschuiving van bevelshuishouding naar onderhandelingshuishouding" [Limitations on Going Out and Fear of Going Out: On the Shift from

Accommodation by Command to Accommodation by Negotiation], *De Gids*, nr. 8, 1979.

11. A. de Swaan, "De staat van wandaad" [The Wrong-Doing State], a lecture for the Foundation Society and the Military, published in *de Volkskrant*, 14 November 1992. For a commentary on De Swaan's U-turn, see Meindert Fennema, "Morele paniek, het marktdenken en het debat over illegalen" [Moral Panic: Market Thinking and the Debate on Illegals], *de Volkskrant*, 24 December 1992.

12. A. de Swaan, "Ophouden" [Stopping], *NRC Handelsblad*, 26 November 1994.

13. A. de Swaan, "Overlegeconomie en onderhandelingshuishouding" [The Consultation Economy and Accommodation by Negotiation], summary in Maarten van Bottenburg, *"Aan den arbeid!", in de wandelgangen van de Stichting van de Arbeid 1945-1995* [To Work!: In the Corridors of the Social Economic Council 1945-1995], Bert Bakker, Amsterdam, 1995, p. 236.

14. Introduction to "Salon Utrecht" [The Utrecht Salon], 21 January 1996. This observation is all the more interesting in the light of the fact that, according to Elias, the formation of the state, integration and interdependence were coupled with an increase in feelings of shame about bodily functions.

15. Wouters, 1990, p. 99.

16. *Reflector* [Reflector], a journal for owners of driving schools, nr. 2, 1994.

17. Taken from Goudsblom, quoted by Wouters, 1990, pp. 106, 286.

18. Kapteyn, 1980, p. 134.

19. The rise is primarily caused by an increase in the number of cases exclusively of property damage. The number of injured left at the scene has climbed in the last few years to 200. The number of fatalities left at the scene varies from between two and eight per year (Traffic Accident Reporting Service, Ministry of Traffic and Waterways, Heerlen). Other sources: Cozijn, 1985, *Politiestatistiek 1980-1994* [Police Statistics], CBS, Rijswijk, 1995, *NRC Handelsblad*, 20 November 1996.

20. C. Cozijn, *Doorrijden na een ongeval, een literatuurstudie* [Hit and Run: A Study of the Literature], WODC, The Hague, 1985, pp. 4, 6, 26.

21. G. Hofstede, "The Poverty of Management Control Philosophy," in *Academy of Management Review*, 1978, pp. 450-461, J.D. Dermer and R.G. Lucas, "The Illusion of Managerial Control," in *AOS*, 1986, pp. 471-482.

22. De Swaan noted in 1994 that his speech in 1979 had "suffered somewhat from its own success. Accommodation by negotiation was simply such a handy expression that it was used for birds of all feathers." De Swaan, *Limperg Dag* [Limperg Day], 1994, p. 14.

CHAPTER 14

From Romans 13 to Post Office Box 51 [q.v.]

The government is dead. Long live the calculating citizen. That was the refrain of Pim Fortuyn's treatise *To the Dutch People* (1992). We can be happy that we can welcome the calculating citizen, because he is independent and "mouthy" and can look out for number one without any help from the government. The calculating citizen is the mover of the invisible hand: if everyone maximizes his own individual good, that is good for all of us, and the government can keep its hands to itself.

While Fortuyn welcomed the calculating citizen as savior, some politicians, primarily members of the CDA, saw citizens as pitiful sinners who had strayed from the true path. They thought that they could bring them around to responsible behavior by talking to them sternly and making an appeal to their sense of ethics and responsibility. For the people of the country, the call for an ethical revival had the feel of a reproach by The Hague. Call the citizens immoral, and then run away quickly. In fact, politicians themselves have been calculating for a long time.

Will the real calculating citizen please stand up? Calculating behavior does not have to be "immoral." An illegal asylum seeker, for example, who does everything he can to bring his family over here is acting "calculatingly" and morally. Nevertheless, the Netherlands cannot permit itself an unlimited stream of asylum seekers. It is not important if the calculating citizen is good or bad. There is only one question on the order of the day: how do we keep the calculating tendencies of citizens and organizations within socially acceptable limits?

In 1980 I wrote a biography of William Drees Sr. [q.v.]. Together with my coauthor John Jansen van Galen, I had a couple of long interviews with the main character. In the interviews we talked about the moral power that he had drawn from social-democratic thinking, and that had inspired him, among other things, to an exemplary position of resistance during the war. Where did he get his power from? Drees looked at us strangely. He thought it was a funny question. "I think that it comes from inside myself," he said finally.

What was always true for Drees is now true for the majority of the Dutch. We no longer have a solid fortress underpinning our beliefs, no Heidelberg Catechism [q.v.] or Formularies of Unity [q.v.], no organization that proclaims *nihil obstat* [q.v.] or delivers a mandate *ex cathedra* [q.v.], no Communist Manifesto [q.v.] and no assurances of the Beautiful Shiny Day [q.v.] that is to come. What has this revolution left of the moral clarity that was characteristic of our country before de-Pillarization? It generally comes down to two diagnoses. Some say that the Netherlands is "sick," consumed by the malignant tumor of "falling standards" and immorality. Others are happy precisely because individualization is expanding into the area of morals, and that diversity has now become moral diversity as well.[1] No one—not even the government—can still claim to have "the" moral truth. This concept has one thing in common with the diagnosis of falling standards: both assume that there is no longer unanimity about what is morally desirable behavior.

THE REPRESSION OF STANDARDS IN THE PUBLIC DOMAIN

In fact, the standards that regulate our behavior in the public and anonymous domains have neither fallen nor been splintered. They are still standing, recognized by everyone and generally accepted. Data from a study of cultural change in the Netherlands by the Social and Cultural Planning Bureau do not show much of a shift in public disapproval of criminal offenses.[2] The abuse of welfare payments, for example, continues to be one of the most disapproved of types of criminal behavior. Nevertheless, everyone knows that there is a lot of this kind of abuse. A study in 1989 showed that two-thirds of the residents of The Hague would be inclined to buy stolen goods if there was enough advantage in it for them, while, at the same time, two-thirds considered buying stolen goods "totally unacceptable."[3] It is, therefore, not the standards that have fallen, but rather the compliance with the standards, a process that the criminologist Jan van Dijk correctly describes as "the repression of standards."

The social psychologist Hans Boutellier offers an enlightening answer to the question of why the public domain is so vulnerable to the repression of standards. The standards have been, as he puts it, "orphaned." We have to make do with sober social contracts, the legitimacy of which we have to—just like Drees—look for "within ourselves."

Contracts like these are much more vulnerable to social dilemmas than their sacrosanct predecessors, whereby compliance with them has become much less matter-of-fact.

In a culture in which God, Nation and Society have lost their splendor as standards, all that is left, according to Boutellier, is one central moral denominator: victimization. "The degree to which someone else's suffering can be made visible, empathized with, prevented, or even relieved, becomes the decisive factor." But with sins in the anonymous domain—such as fraud, corruption, simple traffic violations, smuggling or environmental crimes—the comprehension of the idea that there are victims is, in large measure, abstract. Boutellier speaks of "virtual victims."[4]

We have always been sympathetic toward the gentleman bank robber, who goes about his work in an orderly way and without bloodshed. With the enormous expansion of large-scale, collective arrangements and the "victimization" of morals, we can all play gentleman bank robber. According to a poll done by the Dutch Institute for Public Opinion Polling in 1991, three-quarters of all the Dutch felt the need to avoid or evade taxes, compared to two-thirds in 1978. Crimes against the common good are more and more often taking on a "sporting" character. The "chance of getting caught" is the decisive factor. It becomes sort of like a game of tag. Tag! You're it! And that is when fines are handed out with coffee.

THE SPLINTERING OF STANDARDS IN THE PRIVATE DOMAIN

"Moral diversity"—whereby it is not compliance but the standards themselves that are the subject of individual choice—is found in only one area: in the sphere of personal lifestyle. Just a few dozen years ago, living arrangements for couples [q.v.], sexuality, contraception, abortion and soft-drug use [q.v.] were subject to strong, society-wide standards, primarily also to commonly accepted legal and religious limitations. In areas like this people are more and more developing their own standards. Most of the Dutch by far do not look at this as problematic, because these are purely "personal" standards: there are no victims, not even "virtual" ones.

An enlightening example is the moral teachings on self-gratification. In the sixteenth century in the Netherlands, you could be sent to the galleys *for the ghastly sin and crime of masturbation*. In the first half of our century, it was not the legal authorities but those caring for our souls who kept the fear of this sin alive. Nowadays, the thought that masturbation could have been a subject of oversight, guilt and punishment fills us with incomprehension. If anything is now a question of individual preference, then this really is it.

Even when others are involved, the fragmentation of standards in the area of personal lifestyle does not produce any "victims." Mutual consent, of course, is required. If that is missing, then it is not "good morals" that are at issue, but the standards and laws with regard to (sexual) violence or medical ethics. The imposition of penalties shifts from what is considered "morally" objectionable to what potentially victimizes others. Within a legalistic culture in which victimization is central, the legislators, according to Boutellier, can no longer consider themselves "justified in taking action as long as there is talk of behavior chosen by those involved." As an example, he points to the amendment of article 250-bis of the criminal statute book, whereby the prohibition on operating a brothel was replaced by a provision that made exploitation, violence and similar things punishable.[5]

The jurist W.G.C. Mijnssen sketched the same development for article 240 of the criminal statute book, the antipornography article. "Pornography was decriminalized in the 1960s and 1970s, because the ideas of what was sexually permissible were in flux. The moral aspect fell away as it were. But, in the meantime, a backlash has manifested itself around child porno and porno with violence. This is a shift in criterion: it is no longer sexual morals that are central, but violence against and the abuse of children and other vulnerable persons." It is, therefore, a question of "renaming," in which, in a certain sense, "old wine is placed in new legal briefs."[6]

The backlash mentioned by Mijnssen has quickly become visible in the last few years in the area of child pornography. When reports came in from the United States in the late 1980s that the Netherlands was an important link in the production and distribution of child porno, the news was laughed off nationally with a sense of deep outrage. According to American customs officials, most of the child pornography confiscated there originated in the Netherlands, but the Dutch police, the Ministry of Justice and the politicians swore in harmony that it was a marginal phenomenon. The American prudes apparently couldn't stand a few lively Dutch pictures of little naked children on a beach.

In the early 1990s the police had to admit that they could not say anything about the phenomenon, because they had no idea how widespread it was. The investigation of child pornography had a low priority; the maximum penalty for trafficking in child porno was three months' imprisonment, and investigation resources were limited. The turnaround came when videotapes with horrible child porno, part of which were purchased in a sex shop in Amsterdam, were found in the house belonging to a Swiss who was convicted of gruesome sex crimes with children. A current affairs program proved that it was possible to acquire similar things "from under the counter" without any problem. The police reacted "with bewilderment" and set up a special child porno unit.

In 1993 the Public Relations Service of the Central Criminal Investigation Division (CID) made it known that there was much more child pornography being made and sold than had previously been suspected. A presentation for the press and members of Parliament pushed political sentiment over the edge. The CID showed confiscated films in which children, often drugged, had sex with animals and were bound, raped and tortured. In February 1996 the maximum penalty for making and trafficking in child porno went up to six years, and having it in stock for sale was also made punishable. In 1999 the leader of the CDA caucus pleaded for making "life without parole" possible for serious sexual crimes. Beginning in 2000, each Public Prosecutor's Office has a prosecutor specializing in sexual crimes, and each police corps again has a specialized vice unit, seven years after these units were abolished.

"FISHERMEN FROM URK FINED"

The advancing repression of standards in the public domain brought forth pious calls and appeals from the Christian Democratic corner. In 1977 Van Agt [q.v.] started his "ethical revival," which was followed in 1986 by Brinkman's [q.v.] "caring society," later renamed "responsible society." People seemed to be counting on heavenly assistance in the form of a deus ex machina [q.v.]. It is understandable that it did not appear. Where the splintering of standards is actually taking place—in the area of private life—is where there is no problem. Moral appeals do not achieve much where it is not the standards, but the compliance with them that is becoming less matter of course: in the public and anonymous domains. As Luc Panhuysen expressed it so well in *HP/De Tijd*: "Where the government is pulling back, it is the knight-defender of morals, who covers the retreat." Or in the words of Jos van der Lans, what we are missing is not a "sense of public responsibility" but a "sense of government responsibility."[7]

Even the most law-abiding segment of the populace has not remained free of this development. When typesetting was still done by hand, every Dutch paper kept a headline already set that said "FISHERMEN FROM URK FINED." Just like clockwork, under that headline you could read a short report on the economic magistrate in Zwolle who had levied heavy fines on the fishermen from nearby Urk for violating limitations on the amount of fish they could catch, for landing fish illegally or for falsifying the identification of their boats. The fishermen from Urk are no longer filling their nets with fish but with violations. This is certainly not because the fishermen of Urk were lacking in moral fiber. You can bet that every Sunday they were sitting in a conservative Protestant church, singing a hymn about good stewardship of the Lord's creations and listening to Romans 13, verse 5: "Therefore it is necessary to submit to the authorities, not only because of possible punishment, but also because of conscience."

Even the most orthodox faith is no longer strong enough to make the words of the Good Book true. Even practicing Protestant fishermen have become calculating citizens. If we want them to comply with the law, then we do not have to bombard them with quotes from the Bible or with moral appeals but with summonses from the Inspector General's Service, or the Inspection Service of the Ministry of Agriculture, Conservation and Fisheries.[8]

Recently, even outside the Christian part of the populace, trust in moral sermons has taken off. In his song of praise for the "do-it-yourself welfare state," the Social Democrat Marcel van Dam stated, for example, that together with the annual budget, the Parliament should be presented with a communication plan. In today's society, the government can achieve a more direct relationship with its citizens only, if public communication and information get a higher priority. Communication is a much more important instrument than legislation. A communication policy ideally leads to all citizens' "making the how and why of the most essential goals of the government their own."[9]

A sympathetic starting point is that people will change their behavior if they just understand how things are put together. But it is also naive, because members of a large-scale welfare society do not have to be educated about what the government will achieve. They understand the goals very well indeed and support them ardently and simultaneously adjust their behavior so that they have the least trouble with, and most pleasure from, government policy. Informing the public does not help with prisoner's dilemmas. An information service cannot apply sanctions and, therefore, does not offer any guarantees with regard to the behavior of others.

In 1991, after a study of 70 communication campaigns, the Office of the Budget stated that, taken as a whole, "the changes in knowledge, attitude and behavior achieved are in sad contrast to the ambitiously formulated campaign goals." Hard statistics about this are lacking, because the campaign leaders almost never took the trouble to measure the effectiveness of their work.

In 1994 the researcher G. Tertoolen looked into the effectiveness of environmental campaigns and concluded that they have almost no effect on behavior. The messages are neutralized by the mechanisms of dissonance reduction (reasoning it away: what difference does my small contribution make?) and reactance (contrariness: if I'm going to be taken to the cleaners, then at least I'll get a ride out of it!).[10] With this, Tertoolen exposes a couple of interesting mechanisms for standards repression. The result, according to another study, is that environmental awareness in the Netherlands is—from an international perspective as well—high, but "the direct influence of environmental awareness on environmental behavior is almost negligible."[11]

Pleas for the government to take a role in the teaching of standards and values always make me think of Den Uyl's [q.v.] "narrow leeway." It was little more than 20 years ago that he formulated the doctrine: in a highly developed industrial society, the government has only a limited amount of elbowroom for implementing change. But, if we are of the opinion that the government is hardly in a position to bring about structural change, then why should we expect it to be an effective actor in bringing about social and cultural change? It shows a rather high degree of arrogance for a government to think that it can score with television spots where thundering, Bible-thumping preachers have to admit defeat.

It is more interesting still if we are talking about a government that lost its way in a "blind-eye" approach to problems. A government that lets such a clear gap form between theory and practice, while it is preaching a sermon on "falling morals" and moral behavior, makes you think of a chain-smoking father who wants to forbid his children's smoking. The government's opportunities to exercise a direct influence on the teaching of standards and values are already so limited. The indirect contribution that it can make, by doing what it says, is far greater. Doing your job well is also a "value." A government that consequently does what it undertakes to do contributes more to teaching values than all the information campaigns and socio-moral education packages put together.

According to the cultural sociologist Kees Paling, it is precisely the reduced capacity of the government to make good on its responsibilities that explains the popularity of information campaigns. The growth of the information budgets in the 1980s was legitimized with slogans from the 1970s—don't patronize the citizens; make them a part of the process—but served primarily to mask a lack of management by action. Paling thought up the term "Post-Office-Box-51 Leadership" for this. Even when, in the 1980s, the government was "retreating" and decentralizing, the Parliament reminded it of its responsibilities to resolve social questions. By starting a public information program, a minister can still create the impression that something is being done.[12]

AIDS: TAKE BACK YOUR OWN RESPONSIBILITY

The communication specialists in whom Marcel van Dam placed his trust used to be called advertising men. Advertising is a patented way of influencing people's decisions as they choose between attractive alternatives. Advertising is handy for increasing consumption, but it is notoriously unsuited for reducing consumption. With advertising you cannot get people to the point that they will reduce their individual freedom. It is not for nothing that the slogan that the advertising industry uses to promote itself on CNN is "Advertising . . . the Right to Choose."

When can an information campaign really achieve something? When the recommended behavior is in your own very personal interest, for example, your health. No dangerous sex, don't set off illegal fireworks—those are messages that do not appeal to one common interest or the other but to a very concrete, personal desire: to remain healthy.

When it comes down to this, citizens of the welfare state are not afraid of being accused of "putting on a display of their public responsibility," and some of them even take refuge in the old bourgeois virtue of social control. People who are bothered by smoking can dare to confront smokers in the long run, because they personally are harmed by it, and the harm is directed at a possession that is flying socially high, their health. Here the government can give them some backbone support for standing up for themselves, by running an information campaign. There are no prisoner's dilemmas where people are responsible for their own health. In protecting yourself against AIDS, for example, the idea that others might not comply with the recommended behavior is not an impetus to forget about it yourself, too. To the contrary, that idea is an extra incentive to take the advice of Post Office Box 51.

It is of secondary importance whether the national anti-AIDS television spot shows a buzzing bee, as once was the case with us, or a group of moss-covered gravestones, like the first British campaign. It is important that spots like this are aired—as a memento mori that no government can intervene against, protect you from, prevent or heal. The welfare state was always a synonym for the liberalization of behavior. The area of sexuality has seen a strong liberalization of behaviors in the last few decades. An unfettered sex life has become a basic right. If complications arise, technologists, doctors and welfare workers can be called upon to help.

The arrival of AIDS meant a confrontation with the limits of this ethos. Compared to the carefree 1970s, returning to a condom is a major surrender of "hard-won rights." It is really beyond the government's power here to protect people against the undesired consequences. It is equally powerless to force compliance with a more limited freedom of choice by applying oversight and control. Management by speech is the only real option here. With an anti-AIDS campaign the welfare state gives notice and makes it known that its providence is insufficient here. People, take back the responsibility for your own existence—that is the most important message of these campaigns.

In self-defense we will have to exercise "oversight" of ourselves. In the privacy of the bedroom we will have to take preventive measures, without there being any control over them by the government. We have to negotiate, when necessary, "lay down the law" to others, demand that they comply with our measures. After all, the chance of being caught by the government is zero. In some revolutionary groups there had earlier been talk of the "sex police." With the advent of AIDS, all of us have to be our own "sex policeman" in the seclusion of our own bedroom, unpaid and undercover.

THE FIFTH SECTOR

Conformist behavior used to be, in addition to the social control of neighbors, family and friends, advanced by specialized officials who took the lead in rituals that reinforced feelings of conscience. They continually reminded members of the parish and the community that they would one day be called to judgment. The churches provided a system of moral checks and balances, a moral ledger that was kept for everyone. On the credit side, the premium for a compliant existence was an eternal reward. On the debit side, payment for immoral behavior was not bad either: the eternal pain of Hell.

Nowadays the only seat of judgment that we have to take into account has all four of its feet on the ground. For most of the Dutch, the eternal credit balance has gone up in smoke, and the chance of getting caught in the hereafter has been reduced to zero. According to modern Catholic concepts, God loves us all so much that we are all going to Heaven. A summons is made up, as it were, for us to answer, but when push comes to shove, it is mercifully torn up. On the other side, the number of dismissals has also grown formidably. Even in the Reformed Dutch Church, the exalted God of judgment and punishment has made way for a God "who is closer to the people, who shares the people's grief and with whom people know that they will be safe."[13]

Who can reinforce a sense of conscience now that the metaphysical rod is rotting behind the door, clerics have lost their teeth and prisoner's dilemmas are gaining strongly in importance? The only way out of a prisoner's dilemma is to make agreements that people hold one another to by freely accepting oversight and coercion. You need information for that. Not the sort of no-obligation information that Van Dam would have us believe in, but the information that conformist behavior will be "rewarded" and is normal and that its opposite will be punished. Only in this way can I be assured that I am not "putting on a display of my public responsibility" or am not disadvantaging myself when I stick to the standards.

Providing this kind of information should be seen as a new stage in the provision of public services. During the buildup of the welfare state, the tasks of governmental service providers have already radically expanded. We prefer not to do the vital, but bothersome, time-consuming caretaking tasks ourselves anymore. Caring for the weak, the ill and old people has been contracted out to specialized officials and semigovernmental organizations. In the 1960s and 1970s contracting these services out created a new economic sector: "the fourth sector."

In the 1980s when the wheel of individualization completed another round, the next group of vital tasks, in which private individuals had previously played an important role, fell vacant: oversight and control. But this time the government was not in a hurry to take on these unfulfilled tasks. Oversight and control had an "infamous" reputation and a low priority.The morals of administration were strongly determined by ideas like self-regulation and nonintervention. To gain control of the problem of prisoner's dilemmas in the public and anonymous domains of a welfare state, (re)regulation is what is needed. Precisely in order to rescue its welfare functions, the government must provide hard information to its modern citizens so that they can make calculations based on it.

Today it is the sea wall that is turning the ship. While the government is busy returning some of the tasks of the fourth sector to the citizens, a "fifth sector" is growing up: a permanent public relations effort in the form of oversight and control.

NOTES

1. See, for example, J.C.J. Boutellier, "Criminaliteit als moreel vraagstuk: vijf jaar justitieel preventiebeleid" [Criminality as a Moral Question: Five Years of Ministry-of-Justice Prevention Policy], in P.B. Cliteur et al. (eds.), *Burgerschap, levensbeschouwing en criminaliteit, humanistische, katholieke en protestantse visies op de kwaliteit van de huidige samenleving* [Citizenship, Weltanschauung and Criminality, Humanistic, Catholic and Protestant Views on the Quality of Today's Society], De Horstink, Amersfoort/Leuven, 1991, pp. 230/231.

2. Cora Maas-de Waal, "Verhardt de publieke opinie over misdaad en straf?" [Is Public Opinion Hardening Concerning Crime and Punishment?], in Dekker and Konings-Van der Snoek (eds.), 1992.

3. The Municipal Police of The Hague, Policy Affairs and Research Service, *Een onderzoek naar de kennis van en de houding tegenover heling* [A Study of the Knowledge of and Attitude toward the Fencing of Stolen Property], The Hague, Instituut voor Psychologisch Marktonderzoek [Institute for Psychological Market Research], 1989.

4. Hans Boutellier, "De moraal van de kwetsbaarheid" [The Moral of Vulnerability], in *Filosofie Magazine* [Journal of Philosophy], June 1995. A more expanded version is in Hans Boutellier, *Solidariteit en slachtofferschap, de morele betekenis van criminaliteit in een postmoderne cultuur* [Solidarity and Victimization: The Moral Significance of Criminality in a Postmodern Culture], Sun, Nijmegen, 1993. For more, see Chapter 9.

5. Boutellier, 1995.

6. Interview in *NRC Handelsblad*, 19 February 1994. See also W.G.C. Mijnssen, "Discriminatie en strafrecht, de relevantie van de bedoeling en de

betekenis van religie in zaken van discriminatie wegens ras" [Discrimination and Criminal Law: The Relevance of Intention and the Significance of Religion in Cases of Race Discrimination], *Nederlands Juristenblad* [Dutch Lawyers Papers], 26 September 1987. In this article, Mijnssen calls the shift that was mentioned a "displacement of taboos" in which "pornography is called discrimination in a number of cases."

7. Van der Lans, 1995, p. 36: "The public morality is . . . not a virtue descended in individuals, as is implicitly assumed in all that worrying moralizing about the calculating citizen, but rather the result of an interaction between citizens and organizations or officials who represent the public interest." See also Jos van der Lans, "De cultuur van afzijdigheid" [The Culture of Disengagement], *Socialisme & Democratie* [Socialism and Democracy], November 1996.

8. In the last few years the number of convictions of fishermen has clearly been reduced. In addition to a more focused intervention by the Inspector General's Service, this can also be attributed to the effect of the "Biesheuvel groups." This refers to a system of quotas and fishing days that was recommended by the Biesheuvel Commission, combined with self-imposed controls within groups of fishermen. Opinions on whether this approach will result in long-term adherence to the standards by the fishermen are varied. See, for example, Ellen Hoefnagel, "Kettingreakties in het visserijbeleid" [Chain Reactions in Fishing Policy], *Facta* [Facts], 1993, nr. 4; August Gijswijt, "Noordzee-vissers gevangen in prisoner's dilemma?" [Are North Sea Fishermen Caught in a Prisoner's Dilemma?], *Facta*, 1993, nr. 5.

9. Van Dam, 1994, pp. 169/170.

10. G. Tertoolen, *Uit eigen beweging. . .?!, een veldexperiment over beïnvloedingspogingen van het autogebruik en de daardoor opgeroepen psychologische weerstanden* [Of Your Own Initiative. . .?!: A Field Experiment on Attempts to Influence Automobile Use and the Psychological Resistance It Engendered], University of Utrecht Press, Utrecht, 1994.

11. P. Ester, *Cultuur van de verzorgingsstaat* [Culture of the Welfare State], Tilburg University Press, Tilburg, 1994.

12. Kees M. Paling, "Heeft de overheidsvoorlichting nog toekomst?" [Is There a Future for the Government's Public Relations Service?], in Dekker and Konings-Van der Snoek (eds.), 1992.

13. Dekker, 1992, pp. 138/139.

CHAPTER 15

The Short and the Long Wave

At the beginning of this book I compared Dutch sociocultural developments of the last few decades to a *sur place* [q.v.] in a bicycle race. It is only when one of the riders makes a move that all of them start a sprint. In a number of areas this sprint got under way in the 1990s. It is not surprising that ideas and institutions lag behind rapid economic and social change. It often takes a while before our patterns of thought adapt to new circumstances. The sociologist W.F. Ogburn developed a term for this concept: "cultural lag."[1] The cultural lag that the Netherlands underwent in a number of areas in the last few decades was exceptionally long. Despite the economic reversal of the 1970s and despite its harmful side effects, the politically correct Netherlands continued to hold on tightly to its totems and taboos.

The length of the cultural lag varied strongly by area. In the area of "antiauthoritarian education" it took only a few years before the reins were tightened. The ideology of nonintervention in social psychiatry held out for 10 years before the human and social damage called forth a correction. With the WAO, it took 25 years before the sea wall turned the ship. Apparently, the spread of new ideas does not follow the same pattern everywhere. In order to get a better understanding of these patterns, I tested the actual course of change in the Netherlands with a few general models of sociocultural change.

THE TRICKLE-DOWN EFFECT

In the nineteenth century, new patterns of thought spread most easily along the big rivers, said the sociologist J.W. Becker in the *NRC Handelsblad*, "because that is where the sailors were who carried the ideas."

Later, paved roads also played a role. As late as 1955, researchers from the agricultural university in Wageningen, working in the Achterhoek [literally: the outback] region in the east of the Netherlands, measured a level of adoption for new agricultural technology that was clearly lower the farther the farm was from the paved road.[2] When "the distance to the paved road" became less important, cultural change could spread more rapidly. Even social barriers quickly lost their importance. Pillars, ranks and classes function less and less as a filter and linkage.

In 1978 the *Haagse Post* brought the LAT-relationship [Living Apart Together] to the Netherlands, the newest thing for the demanding young single. A few years later, inside the Amsterdam Beltway of Canals [q.v.] use of the term only caused raised eyebrows, while in the *Algemeen Dagblad* and *Telegraaf* [popular newspapers], one 65-plusser after the other was suggesting "a LAT-relationship first" to see if "things would work out." In his Alexander Hegius Lecture (1992), Ben Knapen expressed his amazement at the speed with which the male ponytail was sweeping the Netherlands. "New York's Madison Avenue had hardly just gotten used to it, the barber in Houston, Texas, had never seen one himself, before the snackbar owner in the Achterhoek was shaking his ponytail at the local disco on Saturday night."

Despite the sharp increase in the speed with which sociocultural change spreads, a number of patterns have become clear in the last few decades. In both ideas and behaviors the avant-garde is made up of young, areligious, well-educated urbanites, and the rear guard is made up of religious ruralites. A cultural change in the Netherlands has run its course when, in his remote farmstead, the most conservative, most secluded, Bible-thumping, poorly educated graybeard gives "in" (and when the last, elderly, poorly educated, orthodox Muslim surrenders). Slowly but surely, down to the last stable door, that is the scenario for the trickle-down effect.

This theory is one of the few available aids for examining how cultural change spreads, but it is certainly not valid in every case. Becker pointed out that a model like this is valid for the spread of new behaviors and technologies—like divorce, a decline in religion and birth control—but is not applicable to the spread of new ideas. The ideas of all the Dutch on such subjects as crime, income inequity and minorities change at the same speed. With regard to sex, urban growth, religious persuasion et cetera, the initial differences in progressiveness remain. If you ask the Dutch for their opinion, they are like a polonaise: the Beltway of Canals leading, the Bible-thumpers at the end; there he goes, but the order of march has not changed.[3]

THE PROOF OF THE PUDDING

The theory of the trickle-down effect is a variant of the diffusion theory, the idea that came from anthropology that says that cultural change spreads over areas, groups and individuals in a certain order. In the metaphor of the trickle-down effect, society is presented as a sort of peat bog, where change is likened to precipitation that sinks slowly into the peat. In an equally "wet," but less muddy, comparison, society is likened to a pond into which rocks are being thrown. Cultural change spreads like the expanding pattern of ripples in the water.

The regularity of the spread can, however, run into strictures. Sometimes the economic situation changes so fast that the expanding pattern of ripples quickly levels out, as if the rock had been thrown into a bowl of pea soup [q.v.] instead of into water. An example of this is the ideal of unbridled self-fulfillment. The idea that everyone had the right to a "creative" job with lots of freedom was a typical product of the 1960s, but its spread ran into the economic recession of the 1970s and 1980s.

The spread of sociocultural change is not only influenced by economic factors (and demographic factors, like the division of the populace into age cohorts), but has its own dynamics. For every new set of ideas the question inevitably comes up, But will it work? If a change does not deliver what was expected of it, there will not be any talk of its spreading. In this case, the stone falls into a pudding, hardly causing a ripple at all.

This was the way in which the fate of antiauthoritarian upbringing came full circle. This doctrine had hardly become fashionable before it was refuted by empirical experience. Within a few years, antiauthoritarian upbringing got stuck in a viscous pedagogical liquid, and parents were pulling out their hair because of the beastly children, who were growing up headed for prison. Inasfar as they could, they shifted into a lower gear—too bad for the ideology but good for the peace of mind of mom and pop. Paul Kapteyn describes an experiment in a kindergarten in the Noord [North] district of Amsterdam in 1974-1975 in which a number of antiauthoritarian parents decided to break through the taboo on violence and to allow their children to play with toy weapons and to take other aggressive toys to school. Who knows? Maybe the little ones will learn "to deal with their own aggressiveness" in this way and thereby be better able to control it when they are older. Within a few months "a real arms race was under way. . . . There were not any real fatalities, but, for the children, it was real enough." Long after the parents and teachers had intervened, the fighting continued to flare up for years.[4]

The antiauthoritarian approach was also popular in the institutional Netherlands during the 1970s, especially in the area of the legal system and social psychiatry. Even though shortcomings jumped out at you, the correction here took longer than in the bosom of the family. The proof of the pudding could be implemented here only after decades of discussion and policy preparation. In addition, this was not a case of parents versus their children but of organizations and officials versus anonymous clients. What can happen spontaneously in a family had to be fought out to a strictly official and ideological consensus.

Earlier, I called one of the ways in which ideas develop through the years "paradoxical continuity." Various changes that came out of the ideas of the 1960s outwardly continued to spread during the cultural lag but, thereby, gradually changed their substance. In some cases, the results they produced were the opposite of the original intention.

Values such as "mouthiness" and assertiveness, for example, were anchored in the liberating ideas of the 1960s, but in the 1970s and 1980s they underwent a mutation whereby they were adapted to the unencumbered pursuit of self-interest (see Chapter 1). The liberating, 1960s idea of respect for personal privacy and autonomy expanded in the following decades into a broad taboo on intervention that was easily used as a front for individual interests (see Chapter 3). Embracing decentralization, self-regulation and privatization was also partly traceable to the ideas on democratization and participation from the 1960s. When they were implemented in the 1980s, these totems turned out to be a handy way to push through economy moves and shove responsibility off onto others, on the one hand, while, on the other, they were a way to pursue private interests unhindered.

The Short and the Long Wave

A last way to look at sociocultural change is the dialectic method. In his book *New Rules*, the American sociologist Daniel Yankelovich describes the development of the ethos of self-fulfillment in the United States from this perspective. In the 1960s some people—Yankelovich calls them *strongformers*—embraced this new cultural property so strongly that they later had to retreat. But that does not mean, he emphasized, that the development did not continue in a more moderate form, breaking a path for itself to "the basis of our society."

The differentiation between the "short" and the "long" wave is very enlightening for looking at Dutch trends. Even after the downfall of antiauthoritarian upbringing, the liberalization of children's education continued, but at a more moderate rate. Even now that the government is taking a harder position on such areas as oversight and coercion, the "socialization" of guilt and responsibility is continuing as a long-term process. In the late 1960s and early 1970s this long-term trend gained momentum and resulted in radical forms of expression, which, in Yankelovich's terms, make the Netherlands stand out among other countries as a *strongformer*. That was also to be seen in the area of self-fulfillment. In the Netherlands the idea that everyone had the right to a "creative" and professional job was quickly accepted, for example, in a great number of advanced professional schools.[5] After a while, this radical approach proved infeasible and was adjusted. But that does not mean a "turnaround" or a "restoration": over the long run, these developments continue spreading at a more gradual pace.

Even the expansion and subsequent contraction of politically correct totems and taboos were this kind of short-wave phenomenon, whereby it was primarily the breadth of the phenomenon that fluctuated. The power of the totems and taboos continues unbroken. The Dutch continue to be horrified about racism and the police state; individual autonomy and privacy continue to have high esteem. The idea that leadership needs to be exercised as close to the citizens as possible, will—even after its turnaround from overly hasty and thoughtless decentralization and self-regulation—continue to set the tone.

That the Dutch government so obediently conformed to the broadly expanded totems and taboos, can be equally well seen as an expression of the shortcomings of the insight into this confluence of short- and long-wave movements. An example is the panicked reaction of the authorities to the protest about the census in the 1970s, which resulted in the census being completely canceled (see Chapter 3). The protest was the high point of the "short wave," but the trend watchers at the Central Statistical Bureau thought that it was the long wave.

The course of this dialectic development can be clearly illustrated by the history of the Dutch fence. This story was told to me by Frans Ruigrok, the founder of Heras Fencing in Oirschot. When he went into fencing in 1952, fences were heavy, threatening constructions, with big spikes. Beginning in the 1960s his fences became lighter and lighter, and the spikes smaller and smaller. After a while, the spikes disappeared altogether. Those who wanted spikes had to pay extra. "We wanted to move toward a tolerant society," said Ruigrok, "but now tolerance has clearly been transformed into a fall in standards. We are now putting fences around people's gardens, because folks won't let the cauliflowers alone!"

The spike came back, too. Standard fences are once again delivered with a row of spikes like a comb. If Heras satisfied every request from its clients, the whole of the Netherlands would be full of fences topped with rolling rows of spikes and razor wire. But it won't get that far. Under Ruigrok's leadership, Heras has embraced an interesting market principle: *the best fence is no fence*. If there has to be a fence there, then, in any event, try to keep it from looking like an unsympathetic fence. That is how Ruigrok began producing colored fences in the early 1980s, fences that do not dominate their surroundings. Natural green, for example, makes a fence almost disappear in the landscape. This brought the ideal of the Dutch fence maker in sight: the "invisible fence." Thanks, in part, to the pioneering role of Heras, the Netherlands has developed into the European leader in the development of more "humane" fences.

"My father did that based on his ideology," says Peter Ruigrok, who followed him as director. "Those were standards and values that came up out of his toes, and with which he managed to permeate the whole company." It later also proved to be a commercial success: nondominating fences fit well into modern ideas about security. Proudly he showed me pictures of the truly "invisible" fence that Heras now delivers to football stadiums. It is 2.5 meters high, does not have any spikes and consists of dividing walls made from lexan, an artificial resin that looks like glass.

The fate of the Dutch fence shows a clearly "dialectic" development. The reaction to the earlier authoritarian fences in the Netherlands was very strong: in the 1960s and 1970s spikes came to be thought of as "infamous" and were discarded. A synthesis comes into view with the "invisible fence." Now the spike is back, but compared to earlier generations, it is a nice spike. Floor Biel, an industrial designer at Heras, has trouble drawing spikes. "Spikes simply give an aggressive impression, a spike is an aggressive shape. It is not easy to make a spike look pleasant."

Fences are a typical form of external control. When this control is reduced by removing the spikes, for example, then more trust is placed in the public's self-control. The arrival of the "nicer" fences of the 1960s agrees with Elias' civilization theory, which assumes an expansion of self-control. The return to more sturdy fences in the 1980s suggests, however, that the level of trust had been set too high. External control has returned, but in a more subtle form than before.

NOTES

1. W.F. Ogburn, *Social Change with Respect to Culture and Original Nature*, New York, 1950, W.F. Ogburn, "Cultural Lag as Theory," *Sociology and Social Research*, 41 (157), p. 167-174. In the term *cultural lag* Ogburn tried to capture the gap between cultural change and technological developments. I use the term in the broader sense of the gap between social and economic developments and the transformation of ideas and institutions.

2. B. Benvenuti, *Farming in Cultural Change*, Van Gorcum, Assen, 1961, pp. 376-382.

3. *NRC Handelsblad*, 15 October 1994. One group changed at such a rapid rate that it overran Becker's difference. Dutch Catholics dragged themselves from behind to take the lead in the polonaise and became trendsetters on the rebound, not just in terms of behaviors but also in terms of ideas. In their ideas on such topics as "Pillar-loyalty," religious orthodoxy, abortion and divorce, they "passed" the Dutch Reformed Church on the left (see De Loor and Peters, in Stouthard and Van Tillo [eds.], 1985, pp. 152-154, Sociaal en Cultureel Planbureau [Social and Cultural Planning Bureau], *Sociaal en Cultureel Rapport 1994* [Social

and Cultural Report], pp. 538-541, De Fijter, 1991). This development was confirmed by a comparative study on changing values in 15 European and North American countries by Ester et al. In 1990 Dutch Catholics were more "permissive" than Protestants. In other countries with a religiously mixed populace, this difference was missing or much smaller (Ester, Halman and De Moor, 1993, p. 59). This jump in permissiveness is all the more striking when you consider that the de-churchification among Catholics is also progressing the fastest. You can, therefore, assume that a selection is taking place among them whereby the "flexible" moderates leave, and the diehards stay in the church. Nevertheless, it remains true that those who remain Catholic are, as Becker expresses it, "liberalizing and modernizing full steam ahead." See also Chapter 10.

4. Kapteyn, 1980, pp. 177 et seq.

5. H.J. Schoo, Flip Vuijsje and Herman Vuijsje, "De gesel van de creativiteit" [The Scourge of Creativity], *Haagse Post*, 20 December 1980.

CHAPTER 16

The Trendsetters Forbid Contradiction

Thus far I have presented four factors that can explain why taboos and totems influenced Dutch thinking so strongly and for so long: the memory of the war, the baby boom, our continuing prosperity and the rapid expansion of the anonymous domain. One last factor requires in-depth exploration. That is the role of the elite members of society, the trendsetting intellectuals, the ones who take the lead in critical reflection and social change.

In the early 1990s it was not the intellectuals but politicians, like Hirsch Ballin [q.v.], Brinkman [q.v.] and Bolkestein [q.v.], who began throwing stones into the standing waters of the pond of noninterventionist thinking. In 1992 Brinkman said that if he saw a boy with a knife, he would intervene with a fatherly word: "What are you doing with that knife, son?" Hirsch Ballin said that if he saw that someone was being threatened by a youth gang on the streetcar, "as a true Amsterdamer, he would give the kids an admonition."[1] They were attacked across the full spectrum of the press from the progressive *Vrij Nederland,* to the conservative *NRC Handelsblad.* Frank Kuitenbrouwer, the commentator for the *NRC Handelsblad,* sounded the alarm bell for this "fatal" development: "Morals are threatening to become a subject of government policy and control in modern criminal prevention."

That politicians have no business discussing moral values was also the opinion of Jaap van Heerden in a debate on "Public Dissatisfaction." They always have some interest and are thinking—in connection with the upcoming elections—of the effect that their words will have, while "the first requirement for any innovative debate is for disinterested parties." Following this line of thought, you would therefore expect that independent intellectuals would give strong leadership to the moral debate. In reality, for 15 years an important part of the trendsetting intellectuals declared any "incorrect" statement out of order. One does not trouble about certain things, neither as a citizen nor as the government, neither on the street nor in an intellectual debate.

Before, the standards dictated that in certain areas you bothered about others and intervened in their affairs. Standards were anchored in the conformism of the Pillars. After de-Pillarization, the conformism remained, but internally it has undergone a Copernican transformation. Nowadays, conformism in the public sector leads to disengagement. Social control has become "asocial control." The Netherlands used to be vicar-country but has become anti-vicar-country. What remained was the fear of openly being a dissident.

Never on a Sunday and not wearing a priest's collar or robes, the anti-vicars, however, also stood ready to expound ex cathedra [q.v.] on the way that things should be. Whosoever dared to ignore their mandates was subjected to an auto-da-fé [q.v.], whereby great inquisitors like Hugo Brandt Corstius [q.v.] first pronounced the horrible curse of the war on the heretic, personally held the torch to the bonfire and then mightily stirred things up by throwing the victim's writings in the flames.

In the 1990s, the climate changed. A wave of senseless violence swept the nightlife centers, in which innocent people were killed while bystanders looked the other way. This put an end to the glorification of nonintervention. In Amsterdam a young man named Joes Kloppenburg was beaten to death when he stepped in to intervene in a fight. He did exactly what Brinkman and Hirsch Ballin had pleaded for, but there was no derision this time. In 1998 a member of the VVD caucus in Parliament described Joes Kloppenburg as a "resistance hero" of our times. Nobody objected to his statement. He was right.

"When the boat tends to the left, I move to the right, and when the boat tends to the right, I move to the left." This was Thomas Mann's description of the task of an intellectual. In the last 20 years, a strong tendency has sprung up among Dutch intellectuals to do exactly the opposite: they placed themselves firmly on whichever side that the whole of the trendsetting Netherlands is already occupying, so that the ship would have certainly capsized if the sea wall had not changed its course.

Intellectuals as inquisitors who do not lead the debate but forbid it have, in the last few decades, protected us from many an undesirable exchange of ideas on topics such as heredity, medical screening, the forced commitment of schizophrenics, the abuse of public assistance, ethnicity and immigration, privacy, criminality and government control. Thereby the progressive Netherlands has been caught empty-handed, now that the sea wall is turning the ship, public assistance is being cut down to the bone, asylum seekers are being sent back to murderous countries and personal data are being linked without much to-do.

In the meantime, no apologies have been made. Not to Professor Buikhuisen, who wanted to do research to determine if, in addition to social factors, biological factors also played a role in criminal behavior and who was dispatched to the other world nationally by the murderous pen of Brandt Corstius in *Vrij Nederland*. No apologies. To the contrary: in 1995 Brandt Corstius was given the opportunity by the *NRC Handelsblad* to level another solid kick at "that silly Buikhuisen" 20 years after he "had silenced him."[2]

Equally few apologies for Tineke van den Klinkenberg, who, as the director of a center for asylum seekers in the late 1980s, got to deal with theft, extortion and violence by asylum seekers. She could not find an ear for her story anywhere in the political Netherlands. "It was thought that if you just keep quiet about it, ordinary people won't see it. But it is on their doorstep. They can see that stolen property is being sold, that sixteen people are living in an apartment instead of three; that there are drug dealers there." Finally, Van den Klinkenberg broke the omertà with a confidential letter to the PvdA Parliamentary caucus. The letter leaked out, and Van den Klinkenberg had to resign. She was led out of the building like a criminal and was made out everywhere to be a racist. "And there was no one who objected, not even the people who should have known better; Mayor Ed van Thijn, for example."[3] That was in 1990. Van den Klinkenberg is still waiting for an apology.

PHENOMENA OF SELF-CENSORSHIP

In 1990 Philomena Essed was granted a Ph.D. for a thesis entitled "Understanding Everyday Racism." The empirical material consisted of interviews with 28 black women in the Netherlands, who had been selected by the researcher herself, about their experiences with racism. These experiences were compared with those of 27 black women in the United States. The conclusions were considerably broader than the empirical basis: Dutch society, outwardly tolerant, was permeated with a subtle, but malicious, form of everyday racism.[4]

Vladimir Bina, who reviewed Essed's book in *Intermediair*, compared Essed with Cyrano de Bergerac. Cyrano thought that others had nothing better to do than to secretly make fun of his big nose. The word "handkerchief" was enough for him to challenge the speaker to a duel. "For Essed a pat on the back is already sufficient evidence of a racist attitude."[5] Bina was one of the few who were critical of the book. Despite the combination of selective data collection and generalized conclusions, most reviewers were enthusiastic.

Two years later Jerôme Inen interviewed a number of the reviewers in his paper "Phenomena of Self-censorship" and demonstrated that the reaction that many of them had, was avoidance or fear: they sought refuge in positive discrimination and self-censorship. Jan Blokker, who in a speech, also in 1992, examined the role of taboos in journalism, apparently found self-censorship "too big a word." He preferred to speak of "self-regulation, self-correction and self-limitation."[6]

The Essed reviewers interviewed by Inen did not beat around the bush themselves. "Afterward, when it turned out that the thesis and the way that she had graduated was a mess, I was sorry," said Aldert Schipper of *Trouw*. "I had fallen into a trap of my own making. . . . I started the interview with her on the wrong foot. I thought: she is a representative of a minority group, so she is probably right." Even *de Volkskrant* refrained from a critical review. Within the paper, just the thought of Essed's book would send editors "to the toilet to throw up," said the head of the department in question, but the readers had to decide for themselves what Essed's conclusions were worth.

In the *NRC Handelsblad* Hans Moll broke the taboo and strongly criticized her scientific approach.[7] He was rewarded with a stream of letters in which he was accused of contempt for the work of a black researcher. Two years later, Moll said that he had really wanted to stay far away from this thesis, but his colleagues thought that, as an Indo [q.v.], he should be the one to review the book. As white journalists, they did not want to burn their fingers on it. "When they read what I had written, they commented that my ideas coincided with theirs. I have never written another piece that got such a positive reaction within the NRC."[8]

Inen's paper is especially interesting because of the readiness with which a number of reviewers admitted that the praise given the work originated from fear and social pressure. The difference is between 1990 and 1992—just two years—but these were the years in which the "consensus" on ethnic taboos turned around. That is how fast one established opinion can make way for another in the Netherlands.

Not only journalism but also science had forbidden changes during the 1970s and 1980s. "Sensitive" data, for example, on ethnic topics, were quickly seen as "reprehensible entities" (see Chapter 3). If someone succeeded in doing some research in such unwelcoming territory, then the results were often hidden from sight. Examples of this are the first report on the activities of Moroccan youth gangs in downtown Amsterdam (see Chapter 2) and a number of studies on the abuse of public assistance.

Intellectual conformity is not a Dutch specialty. Kuhn, who studies the philosophy of science, has shown that scientific researchers are, as a rule, careful not to be too far out of step. If need be, they adjust their findings when that is necessary to protect their position in "quotable society" and with sources of funding. The French trendsetting coterie is proverbially "correct." In and of itself, it is not exceptional that intellectual taboos in the Netherlands were at a premium. What was remarkable, were the tenacity with which the taboos were defended and, second, the speed with which the intellectual elite "turned around," once things began to move. The latter is illustrated by the superfast U-turn of the Essed reviewers named earlier. Frits Bolkestein has thought up a good term for intellectuals who are thus estranged from their calling: *Lumpen intellectuals.*[9]

An attempted explanation was delivered by the previously named researcher from Surinam, Ruben Gowricharn. He observed, to his surprise, that, in the Netherlands, the culture of the group under study could not be viewed as a contributing factor for the group's deprivation. Gowricharn found it frankly irritating that he also encountered this taboo among social sciences researchers. In the Netherlands, the government is the largest contractor for, and user of, socioscientific research; it wants results that are "relevant to policy." Even though, formally, they are independent, research organizations speak the language of those who feed them: the policymakers in the civil service. Researchers are hardly interested in "the truth" anymore, states Gowricharn. They contribute to the version of reality "constructed by officialdom." The research industry in the Netherlands is, therefore, strongly influenced by the "official mania of the day."

THE OFFICE OF THE ADVOCATE FOR FUTURE GENERATIONS

With the expansion of taboos, the area that is screened off from doubt, scepticism and contradiction was widened. This process was slow and more or less unnoticed. Nonetheless, it is not difficult to identify these sorts of processes in a timely way and to analyze them. They are, after all, not the consequence of incomprehensible natural forces but of social developments, the cultivation of myths, the pursuit of interests and the forging of coalitions.

In the *Social and Cultural Report 1992,* casual mention was made of the desirability of policy evaluation ex ante: the best possible advance determination of the effectiveness of proposed regulations and measures. Existing organizations such as the Parliament and the Office of the Budget should really be doing this, but they are already busy enough. This recommendation deserves extra attention in the light of the conformist tendencies that we have noted in the Dutch intellectual climate. The intellectual correctness of the last few decades, amplified by the position of power that the government holds as contractor for socioscientific research, has protected the prevailing image of reality from painful questions. Under the circumstances, it would do no harm to provide our system of policy research with a few extra checks and balances.

Spain has a kind of ombudsman, who is known as *defensor del pueblo.* In the Netherlands we should set up an Office of the Advocate for Future Generations, manned by professional troublemakers who bombard the accepted articles of faith in the area of science and policy with politically incorrect questions about their long-term effects. Give them the independence and the express task of not giving a fat lot for established ideologies and political expediency. In the battle against intellectual conformism and terrorism, the defense could well use some backbone support.

NOTES

1. *Vrij Nederland*, 5 September 1992.

2. *NRC Handelsblad*, 23 December 1995.

3. The quotes were taken from an interview with Tineke van den Klinkenberg by Pauline Sinnema in *Het Parool*, 28 October 1995.

4. Philomena Essed, "Understanding Everyday Racism: An Interdisciplinary Theory and Analysis of the Experiences of Black Women," 1990.

5. Vladimir Bina, "Zwarte Cyrano" [Black Cyrano], *Intermediair*, 25 January 1991.

6. Jan Blokker, "De kroon en de mestvork, enige opmerkingen over de pers en haar vrijheden" [The Crown and the Manure Fork: Some Observations on the Press and Its Freedoms], inaugural speech, De Harmonie, Amsterdam, 1992.

7. Hans Moll, "Het onvermogen van de anti-racistische wetenschap" [The Insolvency of Antiracist Science], *NRC Handelsblad*, 4 May 1991.

8. Jerôme W. Inen, "Verschijnselen van zelfcensuur" [Phenomena of Self-Censorship], paper, School of Journalism, Utrecht, 1992.

9. Frits Bolkestein, "Hans Daudt en de gênante stencilcultuur" [Hans Daudt and the Embarrassing Culture of Mimeos], *Het Parool*, 13 September 1996.

CHAPTER 17

The Other Side of Consensus

After the years between 1940 and 1945, the 1960s are undoubtedly the best-documented period in Dutch history. Especially between 1965 and 1970, the Dutch made unprecedented leaps in thought and deed; the five following years also had a high rate of change. That the changes in the Netherlands were more serious and took place faster than elsewhere is demonstrable in areas like church membership and sexual permissiveness. It is generally accepted that this is also valid for other areas. A number of authors have gone out in search of an explanation for these exceptional and exceptionally rapid changes. Most of these descriptions stop in the 1970s. In his *Objections to the Fall of the Netherlands* (1995), Herman Wigbold continues a number of interesting lines into the 1990s, but his work is more polemic than analytic.

Hans Righart makes a detailed report of the events during the magic decade of the 1960s in his *The Endless Sixties* (1995). He sees a generation crisis in both the prewar and the postwar generations as characteristic of the decade. This "double generation crisis" acted as a catalyst for the rapid process of societal change. Righart describes this process as an earthquake, with its epicenter at the fault line between the generations. Righart assumes that the aftershocks could be felt until deep in the 1970s "in broad social layers or in more distant social sectors," but he does not provide a description or an analysis of them.

Even James Kennedy, in his book *The New Babylon under Construction* (1995), limits himself to the period up to 1975. In his closing chapter, he warns that there are no guarantees that the attitude of the elite will "produce the same positive results in less friendly times" as in the 1960s, but testing this premise was outside the scope of Kennedy's work.

Do the explanations given for the exceptional character of the Dutch "sixties" remain valid in the light of the period after that? Below In the following I look at the prevalent opinions to see if they can also offer an insight into the changes in the 1970s and 1980s.

THE POSTMATERIALISTIC NETHERLANDS?

The fact that most authors limit themselves to the period between 1965 and 1975 has an influence on the nature of their explanations. Their attention is primarily directed at the personal, "liberating" aspects of the Dutch mental legacy of the 1960s. The magical years stand primarily for changes in the private domain: less narrow-mindedness in the area of sexuality and relationships, more room for one's own lifestyle and more opportunity for self-fulfillment.

After 1975, these developments in the area of people's private lives consolidated their position and continued their advance. In 1990 of 15 European and North American countries, the Netherlands had the highest level of permissiveness. Areas in which the Dutch demonstrated exceptional permissiveness were homosexuality, prostitution, abortion and minors having sex.[1] The Netherlands can, therefore, boast of an impressive list of "soft" records. Of all the Western countries, the Dutch are the most tolerant of minors having sex.[2] The Netherlands has the world's lowest record of unwanted pregnancies and abortions among teenagers. Information on the morning-after pill can be requested via the Advice Line for Children. The Netherlands is the only country in the world that has a seal of approval for "relaxation firms": Erotikeur [Erotic-quality].[3] Only in the Netherlands is there an Association of the Customers of Whores: KLEP. The Netherlands is the only country in the world with an interest group for homosexuals in the Armed Forces that is subsidized by the Ministry of Defense. Further, the Netherlands is the only country in the world where the handicapped can get a driver's license for motorcycles. The Netherlands has the largest Euthanasia Association in the world: the Dutch Association for Voluntary Euthanasia, which has 84,000 members.

These are the sorts of developments that, since the 1960s, have kept the Netherlands on international front pages. Social scientists have contributed to creating this image by providing the Netherlands with labels such as "permissive," "postmaterialistic" and "feminine." The social psychologist Geert Hofstede found that among 40 "modern" nations, the Netherlands scores extremely high in individualism, "femininity" and "caring" mentalities. According to him, the Netherlands is a "feminine" and caring society where helping the weak is more highly thought of than the spirit of competition.[4]

According to the political scientist Ronald Inglehart, no country in the world has more "postmaterialists" than the Netherlands.[5] This means that the Netherlands has taken the lead in this area, because, according to Inglehart, all societies are developing, in the long run along the lines of less hierarchy and more individual choice. Postmaterialist ideas, according to him, touch not only on private lifestyles but also stretch to the public domain. Postmaterialists, therefore, score low on such items as "maintaining order," "maintaining a stable economy" and "fighting crime."

The postmaterialist orientation was given a strong boost by the baby boom, which grew up in material security and, therefore, places less importance on discipline and obedience. Inglehart assumes that people remain faithful to the values that they acquire in their youth for the rest of their lives, therefore, once a postmaterialist, always a postmaterialist. Only in times of economic recession can people fall back into patterns of materialistic thinking, but that is a short-term effect, which disappears when the economy improves again.

Even Hofstede thought that the Netherlands' "feminine" characteristics would remain stable with the course of time. With the passing of the years and the ebbing of the idea of anything goes, the baby boom generation, however, indeed seems to be losing its postmaterialistic spots. Of the limited interest in "combating crime," which, according to Inglehart, is characteristic of postmaterialists, little remains. "The high level of crime has increased the preference for maintaining order," says the *Social and Cultural Report 1994*. "The desires for reduced government expenditures, lower social assistance payments and greater socio-economic inequality are an equally poor fit in the postmaterialist picture."[6]

Models such as Inglehart's and Hofstede's primarily help to understand change in people's private lives. They seem less useful for explaining sociocultural changes in the public and anonymous domains. Neither policymakers nor researchers have devoted a lot of attention to the unique character of the latter. In the 1970s, "the personal" [q.v.] was thought to be "political" as well; this caused differentiating between these two sectors of people's lives to go out of fashion. In addition, in the anonymous domain ideas and behavior did not change the way that they did in people's private lives, with a bang between 1965 and 1975. The changes in the anonymous domain only gradually became visible afterward.

THE CALVINIST NETHERLANDS?

One thing is immediately noticeable when reading the books written about the 1960s in the Netherlands: most of the authors explain the exceptional character of the changes based on Dutch traditions that took shape in the distant past. In his book *Regents, Rebels and Reformers*, Ernest Zahn looks for the answer in our latently religious philosophy of life: the Dutch, even if they are no longer members of the church, are still zealous and principled. The major changes of the 1960s reflected a "turnaround of religious attitudes in the direction of salvation 'on earth.'"

Even Von der Dunk explains the ease with which the "leftist" concept of progress gained entry to the Netherlands, in part, on the basis of centuries-old cultural traits. Calvinism and the antifeudal and antimonarchical Republic [q.v.] contributed to our "exceptionally deep-seated anti-hierarchical sentiment" and our ethos of equality and justice.[7] Becker and Nauta likewise attach great significance to the "historically anchored Calvinist philosophy of life." This is, according to them, why the changes have continued to make themselves felt for so long: once the Dutch have accepted a point of view, they continue to hold fast to it with a sort of secularized religious zeal.[8]

Kennedy, too, attributes the Dutch 1960s to our Calvinist heritage. The Dutch elite did not try to hold back the arrival of the anarchically inspired "New Babylon" but decided "to make the best out of a bad situation" and to cooperate in its construction. Just like their predecessors from the Republic, the "regents" [q.v.] of the postwar period had an aversion to conflict and violence and tried to reach consensus and achieve a compromise. Kennedy explains this pragmatic belief in the inevitability of change with, among other things, the continuing effects of Calvinism. "The Calvinists had a vision of God's hand in history; every human effort to arrest this divine course of action was senseless, because history was the unfolding of God's plan."

The preceding illustrates the fragility of this sort of cultural-historic explanation. Kennedy attributes an effect to Calvinistic tradition that is exactly the opposite of the one attributed to it by Zahn. According to the latter, it is the idealistic zeal of the protest generation that can be explained by the heritage of Calvinism. According to Kennedy, it is the pragmatic inclination to adaptation of the old elite.

In addition to this, there was little to be seen of any great influence of Calvinist tradition in the period immediately before and immediately after the 1960s. During the German occupation, the overwhelming majority of the Dutch gave little indication of antihierarchical sentiments and a strongly developed ethos of equality. There was absolutely no talk at all of Calvinist stubbornness: by and large, in those years, it was precisely an indication of an inclination "to accommodation" that emanated from the Dutch. In the 1990s, there was equally little Calvinistic obstinacy to be seen. The politically correct Netherlands is shifting easily from "puritanical" 1960s principles to a new realism.

CONSENSUSLAND—THE NETHERLANDS?

Some authors trace the changes of the 1960s back to an even more remote past. They look for answers in the sopping peat bogs and rising water from which the Dutch national character bubbled up in the Middle Ages. They make note of the early origins of democratic consultation and administrative cooperation necessitated by the need for flood control; they point to the importance of trade and middle-class culture and to the absence of absolute monarchs. A small country full of minorities, condemned to rowing together on this small piece of ground and having to keep it above water too. A deed of darring-do that has been pulled off for centuries by a culture of give-and-take.

This tradition of good consultation forms the foundation of our secret national pride: trying to achieve consensus is democratic, fair and sensible, and just look at what a fine little country it has given us. That began early on with the success story of our Republic as a "society of many temperaments." According to Wilbert van Vree, a specialist on meetings, the Netherlands has given birth to "the first let's-have-a-meeting caste in Europe." "This has placed a strong stamp on society. For centuries, the Netherlands has had a headstart in the area of meetings—a headstart that has prevented a lot of bloodshed."[9]

Even politicians happily point to the consultation model of the Golden Age. The Republic gave proof of everything in which a small country can be great; the comparison almost forms a justification in and of itself. This was how minister Sorgdrager [q.v.] traced the Dutch policy of "turning a blind eye" back to the "proverbial Dutch tolerance" of the seventeenth century.[10] The minister conveniently forgot that our forefathers had not been especially "tolerantly" inclined towards vandals, thieves and burglars. Even the amount of room for eccentricities in one's private life was not too great. The—relative—tolerance of the regents was primarily with regard to religion and democratic freedoms.

This traditional preference for consensus and compromise plays an important role in a number of explanations for the exceptional character of the Dutch 1960s. Kennedy does "not find it difficult to observe a continuing line of forbearance in Dutch history, from the legendary tolerance of the regents in the Dutch Republic to the conciliatoriness of mayor Samkalden" [q.v.] (with regard to the rebellious, young soft-drugs users). According to Kennedy, the Dutch elite showed itself in the 1960s to be not only flexible, but also sensible and "far-sighted," whereby "future problems" could be avoided. This assertion was not substantiated, because Kennedy did not devote a lot of attention to the long-term consequences of the changes of the 1960s.

The tradition of consensus was tied not only to the Golden Age. The model of the Pillars was also based on it: another success story from the point of view of conflict management. The power of the Pillars lay in their special combination of consultation and conformity. Through reasonable negotiation at the top and obligingness at the base, all interests could be dealt with properly, so that the government did not have to play the feared Mr. Busybody. In the society of that time, which was so conveniently arranged that it was easy to comprehend, the motto of "freedom through bondage" worked very well. Now that group cohesion and loyalty have been fragmented, and every citizen and organization is calculating its individual interests, this conformist inclination has been robbed of its cadres. Even conformity has become "calculating." In taking a position, certainly one on a "sensitive" issue, we no longer look to the Pillar and its leaders but to the established opinions of the reference group that is important for us at that moment. In setting a course, we use "radar, not the gyroscope," as Bolkestein [q.v.] described Lubbers' [q.v.] assortment of navigation instruments.[11]

This calculating conformity distinguishes itself from conformity during the period of the Pillars in yet another aspect: it is not applicable to all behaviors. The Dutch arrange their private lives exactly as they want them. In their living rooms, nurseries and bedrooms the actions they take are based on their own convictions and preferences. But in the public domain, a compliant attitude toward the prevailing patterns of thought is sensible.

Even during the occupation, the conformity of most of the Dutch took on a "calculating" appearance. Compliance and accommodation were widespread. Only one police inspector from Amsterdam, J. van de Oever, refused to cooperate with the roundup of the Jews. Only one of the 12,000 non-Jewish civil servants in The Hague refused to sign the Arian Declaration, the inspector for the Service for Urban Development and Housing, Ms. A. Kuipers. One Dutch mayor protested against the deportation of gypsies to the concentration camps, the mayor of Zwollerkerspel. Only one of the career sailors of the Dutch Navy refused to sign a declaration not to do anything to the detriment of Germany.[12] There is no J. van de Oever Street in Amsterdam, and there is no A. Kuipers Square in The Hague, but they are precisely the ones who deserve to be commemorated and honored by having streets named after them. They not only defied the occupiers but also dared to reject the conformity that was so matter-of-fact for their colleagues.

James Kennedy does not devote much attention to the attitude of the Dutch elite during the war. He mentions Colijn's [q.v.] pamphlet *On the Border between Two Worlds* (1940) in passing as an example of the "almost comic reactions" to which the Dutch sensitivity to the inevitable can lead in crisis situations. This pamphlet was not comical at all and was equally unconvincing evidence of the characteristics that Kennedy ascribed to the elite of the 1960s: a sensible approach and a farsighted vision with which "future problems" could be avoided. Colijn gave an ideological justification for the compliant attitude that the overwhelming majority of the Dutch would put into practice with regard to the occupiers. He helped smooth the way for a calculating conformity that would later present huge problems during the war for the Dutch Jews and after the war for broad groups of the Dutch, in the form of a long-lasting feeling of guilt.

If Kennedy's compliments for the Dutch elite are justified, then that is only for the period 1965 to 1975. They are not applicable to the position of the Dutch elite either during the war, or in the 1970s and 1980s. In these two periods, the Dutch consensus model was not clad in the gold brocade cloak of the Republic but in an unobtrusive, off-the-rack cloth coat.

It has often been reported that there is a conformist streak in Dutch public life. "The Dutch people are not unimpassioned," stated the criminologist Peter Hoefnagels in 1992, for example. "They are burdened down by mass hysteria and mass taboos."[13] Even member of Parliament Hans Hillen says that we do everything en masse. "Views to the contrary are not tolerated. In the fifties, middle-class morality was stronger here than anywhere else . . . The Netherlands forms the tail of the procession, that always continues swinging longer in one direction. That is why our tolerance also goes further than in other countries. In the end, we will—very uniformly—all also swing the other way."[14]

But it is primarily foreign Holland-watchers who have held the mirror of this conformity in front of our noses. The American sociologist Derek Phillips did that 15 years ago in his book *The Naked Dutchman*. In 1993 in his *Histoire des Pays-Bas* [French: History of the Netherlands], the French historian Christophe de Voogd concluded that the Dutch have a very strong herd mentality. The conformity that goes with that brings along with it an aversion to expressing another opinion within a group. Discussions are avoided—a sign of intolerance. "If I had to typify the Dutch national character, then it would be 'obedient,'" said Yaël Pinto, a Moroccan-Dutch minorities specialist, in an interview. "This obedience, in turn, comes from wanting to avoid problems, from wanting first of all to keep things calm."[15]

In his book *Despite Knowing Better*, Ruben Gowricharn, who comes from Surinam, worked out a "hypothetical set of standards" for the behavior of the Dutch in the job market and at work, based on his experiences and on what foreign observers have written about the Dutch. His standard prescribes the following: always go along with the group; show initiative but do not stand out too much; do not speak your mind; do not take risks; do not admit mistakes but have an "explanation" ready if you did not live up to expectations. An important element of this set of standards is its constant encouragement to conform.

These statements provide descriptions but no explanations. If we forget about national character analysis and geopsychological speculation, how could we then explain this Dutch conformity? For the period of Pillars, this is immediately clear: conformity was the cornerstone of the system. The fact that during the occupation an attitude of calculating conformity manifested itself had to do with the heavy pressure that people were exposed to. But in the 1970s and 1980s, there was no one who compelled obedience. The politically correct Netherlands was censoring itself.

Psychologists have primarily encountered group censorship processes under extreme circumstances. I.L. Janis, who studies group dynamics, described these sorts of processes in situations where decisions have to be made under heavy time pressure. At times like these, group cohesion and consensus are primary values. Divergent information is systematically repressed, because this could lead to "forbidden policy alternatives." Afterward, those who have taken part in a process like this have a feeling of having awakened from a dream in which they went down paths that they are no longer able to explain to themselves.[16]

But what were the extreme circumstances in the Netherlands following the 1960s that led to group censorship and conformity? A plausible explanation is offered by Von der Dunk. The rapid breakdown of the ideological Pillars, which had created clear boundaries, has, according to him, left the Dutch in a state of inner uncertainty, which developed into a "fear of conflict." The Dutch see themselves as forced "to keep their powder dry, with an eye on their careers," and express themselves profusely in a "lifeless jargon of pacification that is . . . as transparent as vanilla pudding."[17]

SUMMARY OF THE CAUSES

With the insight of Von der Dunk, we have found the last contribution to the answer to the question that I asked in this book. Now a comprehensive picture can be sketched. Why could certain ideas from the 1960s get so far and continue for so long in the Netherlands, even when harmful side effects showed up? In answering this question, I have looked for explanations, for which we do not have to go back three centuries but, at most, a few dozen years. Before tying recent developments to some national character or the other or to our roots in the Middle Ages or Golden Age, it seemed more sensible to me to look for explanations in the recent past. This search produced five factors:

- the strong "public" feeling of guilt about the large number of Jews who were deported in the war
- the huge scope and long duration of the baby boom
- the Netherlands' continuing prosperity (i.e., from natural gas)
- the rapid expansion of the anonymous domain
- the strong conformity with which the trendsetting elite held fast to totems and taboos

These five factors presented themselves gradually, "meshed together" and reinforced one another. Can they be reduced to a common denominator? Three factors show a commonality. The passivity of the Dutch during the war had to do with the conformity that was matter-of-fact in a small-scale, Pillarized society. After the war, the feeling of guilt was great, because this very same passivity was painfully in conflict with the inner, ethical spiritual hallmark of the Pillarized Netherlands. Even the scope of the baby boom cannot be viewed separately from Pillarization. With a last eruption of faithfulness to their Pillar, the Dutch—primarily the Catholics and conservative Protestants—competed with one another in having large families. A third factor, the strong conformity with which the elite held fast to totems and taboos, can be explained by de-Pillarization, which left the Dutch at a loss when it came to determining public attitudes.

A number of the factors I presented were already active in the 1960s, and have been named by others as such. This was often combined with other explanations for the exceptional character of the Dutch 1960s, such as the importance of Calvinism and postmaterialism. In the light of the 1970s and 1980s, these explanations do not seem to hold water. More comfort is offered by the dialectic approach in which the conformity of the period of Pillarization, the sudden de-Pillarization that followed it and the rapid turn toward an anonymous welfare state are important driving forces.

Even the trendsetting elite's determination of its attitude can be well described in dialectic terms. The most extreme example is provided by the leaders of the 1960s, who declared afterward that everything had been much too far to the left. Some of them immediately threw the whole of the mental legacy of the left wing overboard and declared that "the Right was right." Wasn't there still something called solidarity? Wasn't there a threat of the heaviest burden being placed on people with weak shoulders? Not for these heroes of the retreat.

In the period that I described in this book, the 1970s and 1980s, it is hard to say that the politically correct avant-garde was "too far to the left." More likely the opposite is true. Being left-wing is talking back. It forbid talking back. Being left-wing is caring for the weak. It kept alarming reports about the weak hidden under the table. After that, they ducked out, leaving behind a welfare state that had been plucked clean. In addition to that, a large number of the heroes of the retreat are refusing, by casting the mental legacy of the Left onto the dung heap of history, to analyze their own mistakes.

NOTES

1. P. Ester, L. Halman and R. de Moor, *The Individualizing Society, Value Change in Europe and North America*, Tilburg University Press, Tilburg, 1993, pp. 57/58, 114.

2. Ibid. p. 114.

3. Erotic-quality guarantees clients hygienic, safe and drug-free service and that prostitutes are not forced into unsafe sex. At registered sadomasochistic clubs the guarantee is that yelling, "Mercy!" will terminate the love play and that there is a chain cutter for cutting loose handcuffs.

4. Geert Hofstede, *Allemaal andersdenkenden, omgaan met cultuurverschillen* [They All Think Differently: Dealing with Cultural Differences], Contact, Amsterdam, 1991.

5. Ronald Inglehart, *Culture Shift in Advanced Industrial Society*, Princeton University Press, Princeton, 1990.

6. A study in 1992, aided by the items that Inglehart used, produced much lower postmaterialistic scores than would be expected, based on Inglehart's 1987 results. According to Inglehart, 25 percent of the populace of the Netherlands between the ages of 16 and 74 was postmaterialistically oriented in 1987. In 1992, on the basis of Inglehart's items, the populace should have had only 10 percent postmaterialists. Because of methodological differences, the comparability of these studies is, however, relative. See Social and Cultural Plan Bureau, *Sociaal en Cultureel Rapport* [Social and Cultural Report 1994], pp. 505, 560, 561 (note).

7. H.W. von der Dunk, *Twee buren, twee culturen, opstellen over Nederland en Duitsland* [Two Neighbors, Two Cultures: Essays on the Netherlands and Germany], Prometheus, Amsterdam, 1994, p. 36.

8. Jos Becker and Aat Nauta, "Hoe zijn de veranderingen van de jaren zestig in Nederland te verklaren?" [How Can the Changes of the Sixties in the Netherlands Be Explained?], in Paul Dekker and Marjanne Konings-van der Snoek (eds.), *Sociale en culturele kennis* [Social and Cultural Knowledge], VUGA / Social and Cultural Plan Bureau, The Hague/Rijswijk, 1992, p. 86.

9. Wilbert van Vree, "Niet vechten maar liever vergaderen" [Don't Fight, but Have a Meeting instead], *Intermediair*, 22 March 1996.

10. W. Sorgdrager, "Nederlands gedoogbeleid, pragmatisch en effectief" [The Dutch Policy of Turning a Blind Eye, Pragmatic and Effective], in *Justitiële verkenningen* [Legal Studies], October/November 1995, pp. 9/10.

11. Frits Bolkestein, "Ruud Lubbers, radar, geen gyroscoop" [Ruud Lubbers, Radar, Not a Gyroscope], in Frits Bolkestein, *Het heft in handen* [Hand on the Helm], Prometheus, Amsterdam, 1995. Bolkestein borrowed the concept of "radar" and "gyroscope" from David Riesman, who introduced it in his description of the "inner-directed personality."

12. Data taken from Guus Meershoek, *Het Parool*, 15 February 1992, Van der Boom, 1995, p. 36, B.A. Sijes, *Vervolging van zigeuners in Nederland 1940-1945* [Persecution of the Gypsies in the Netherlands], Nijhoff, The Hague, 1979, p. 88, C.M. Schulten, *Verpletterd wordt het juk, verzet in Nederland 1940-1945* [The Crushing of the Yoke, the Resistance in the Netherlands], Sdu, The Hague, 1995.

13. *Het Parool*, 24 October 1992.

14. Janny Groen, "God noch gebod" [Nothing's Sacred], *de Volkskrant*, 3 July 1993.

15. *HP/De Tijd*, 17 June 1994.

16. I.L. Janis, *Groupthink, Psychological Studies of Policy Decisions and*

Fiascoes, Houghton Mifflin, Boston, 1982, Elisabeth ter Borg, "Is stedelijke vernieuwing de Tom Poes van de postmoderne stadsbestuurder?" [Is Urban Renewal the Dick Whittington's Cat of the Postmodern Urban Administrator?], in Dekker and Konings-Van der Snoek, 1992.

17. H. W. von der Dunk, "Nederland wordt een fluwelen regelstaat" [The Netherlands Will Be a Velvet State of Rules], speech on the occasion of the opening of the academic year 1993-1994 at the Free University, Published in Von der Dunk, 1994.

Annotations

These annotations are intended to provide the non-Dutch reader with a brief summary of what every Dutch(wo)man subconsciously "knows" and could, therefore, be left out by the author when writing for that audience. The annotations are arranged alphabetically. The political affiliation of twentieth-century politicians follows their birth-death year. Each of the party abbreviations is expanded in a separate entry.

1795. In 1795, when the French Revolution overflowed into the Netherlands, creating the Batavian Republic, Stadholder William V (1748-1806) fled to England. The States-General repealed the Stadholdership and declared the Batavian Republic on 26 January 1796. The new political leadership bent over backward to appease the French to keep them from annexing the northern Netherlands the way they had already done with the Austrian Netherlands (present-day Belgium).

1848. In 1848, when a more violent type of revolution was sweeping through many European countries, the Netherlands peacefully became a democratic, constitutional monarchy. After the February Revolution in France, King William II decided, quite literally overnight, that it was time for constitutional reform. The new liberal constitution gave more power to the middle class and made the government's ministers responsible to the Parliament instead of to the king.

A16. The Dutch road-numbering system designates high-speed highways with the prefix "A." The A16 is the highway from Breda to Rotterdam.

Allochtoon. There are two words in Dutch for alien: *buitenlander* and *allochtoon*. The dictionary treats them both equally, but in practice, *allochtoon* is most often used for aliens of color and *buitenlander* for aliens who are white. The *allochtoon* population consists of Moroccans, Turks and those from the northern Mediterranean countries (Greece, Italy, Portugal, Spain and the former Yugoslavia), Surinam, the Cape Verde Islands and the Netherlands Antilles. Even though those of Indonesian descent would seem to qualify to be called *allochtoon* because of their skin color, they are not. They were the first wave of postcolonial emigration, and they assimilated completely into Dutch society. They are, therefore, better accepted than the other ethnic minorities and are not generally referred to as *allochtoons*, but as Indonesians [q.v.].

AJC: *Arbeiders Jeugd Centrale* [Workers' Central for Young People]. The AJC was a Social Democratic youth organization formed in the 1920s with the support of the SDAP (*Sociaal Democratische Arbeiders Partij* [Social Democratic Workers' Party])—the predecessor party to the PvdA [Labor Party—q.v.]—and NVV (*Nederlands Verbond van Vakverenigingen* [Dutch League of Trade Unions]). The AJC dissolved itself during the war. Reconstituted after the war, it never regained its old esprit and dissolved again in 1958.

Auto-da-fé. This Portuguese term comes from the Inquisition. An *auto-da-fé* was a public trial against persons accused of heresy. The court consisted of inquisitors and prominent persons. If found guilty, which was normally the case, the heretic was sentenced to death, typically by burning at the stake.

"Automatic Level Grade Crossing Half-Gates." Before the installation of Automatic Level Grade Crossing Half-Gates (AHOB) at railroad crossings, the gates blocked the whole street in front of the tracks, and the gates were manned. The presence of a person at the gate added an element of social control that is missing with the new automatic installations. The biggest cause of accidents at railroad crossings is a lack of traffic discipline, says Dutch Rail (9 January 1996, *Eindhovens Dagblad*). People do not want to wait for the train to pass and think that they can get across the tracks in front of it.

To deal with the problem of people who think that they are an exception to the prohibition on crossing the tracks that AHOBs represent (see also traffic regulations), *Railinfrabeheer*—the new postprivatization organization for rail infrastructure—is testing a new automatic barrier for rail crossings: the ADOB, *automatische dubbele halve overwegbomen* [Automatic Level Grade Crossing Double-Gates]. The new system completely closes off the crossing, but it does it in two steps. First, the gate on one side of the street lowers, and five seconds later, the other. This prevents cars from becoming trapped between the gates on the rails. When the second gate is down, the ADOB completely closes off the crossing so that people can no longer slalom across the tracks as they could with an AHOB.

In responding to complaints about delays in bringing out its report to the minister on safety at level grade crossings, the spokesperson for the railroads said: "Before [privatization] it was only Dutch Rail that was responsible for safety. Now there are more parties involved. We are still trying to determine exactly who has which competencies" (15 July 1998, *Dagblad de Limburger*).

"B" Diploma. The requirements for the "B" *Zwemdiploma* [Swimming Diploma] are to dive into the water fully clothed and swim 75 meters using the breaststroke and then an additional 25 meters using the backstroke; to dive into the pool in a swimsuit and swim 125 meters using the breaststroke, the first 7 meters of which have to be underwater, and then swim 75 meters using the backstroke; to tread water for one minute with the hands held out of the water.

Batavian Republic. In 1795, when the French Revolution overflowed into the Netherlands, creating the Batavian Republic, the last Stadholder, William V, fled to England. The Parliament repealed the Stadholdership and declared the Batavian Republic on 26 January 1796. In May 1806, the Batavian Republic was replaced by the Kingdom of Holland. Napoleon thought that a monarchy that was dependent on him would be more reliable in his struggle with England, so he appointed his brother Louis king, a practice he followed in other countries as well. When King Louis renounced the throne in 1810, as a result of the conflict with his brother, Napoleon annexed the Netherlands. Shortly after Napoleon was defeated in the "Battle of the Nations" near Leipzig (1813), the Netherlands was liberated, and William V's son was declared King William I.

Black Peter (*Zwarte Piet*). Sint Nicolaas—the Dutch predecessor of the American Santa Claus—arrives in the Netherlands late in November by steamboat from Spain and hands out presents on his birthday, 5 December. He is accompanied by a host of Black Peters, whose role is fulfilled by the elves in America. Black Peters are, as the name implies, black, and they had traditionally been played by ethnic Dutch in blackface. Their role is that of clown and servant, which was the main point of racial contention about *Zwarte Piet*.

Bopz: *Wet bijzondere opnemingen in psychiatrische ziekenhuizen*: Special Admittance to Mental Hospitals Act.

Beautiful Shiny Day. This promise of the Communist Revolution, which kept the Soviet people waiting for a great, big beautiful tomorrow that never came, was also keenly felt by the Socialists in the Netherlands. In the Netherlands, it was in the refrain of a well-known song of the Socialist movement. It was the day that the workers would be freed from oppression.

Beltway of Canals (*Grachtengordel*). A ring of canals that defines the city of Amsterdam, in much the same way that the Beltway defines Washington, D.C. Inside the Beltway is where the trendsetters are. What is outside the Beltway is considered provincial and reactionary.

Bolkestein, Frederik "Frits" (1933-) VVD. In 1978 Bolkestein went into politics to—as he expressed it—save the country from the damage that had been done to it since the 1970s, when the Den Uyl [q.v.] government was at its nadir. He took a seat in Parliament, where he remained until 1982, when he took the position of State Secretary for Foreign Trade. He stayed in that position until 1986, when he became the deputy leader of the VVD [q.v.] parliamentary caucus. In 1988 he left that position to take up the portfolio of Minister of Defense, which he held into 1989. In 1990 he became the leader of the VVD parliamentary caucus. In 1994 he refused a seat in the "purple" [q.v.] coalition government, preferring instead to remain in Parliament, where he felt that he could exert a greater influence on the course of events. In 1999 he accepted nomination as the European commissioner responsible for internal markets, financial services, customs and taxation.

Boven Digul. Between 1926 and 1947, the Dutch had an internment camp at Boven Digul in Indonesia (formerly the Dutch East Indies). Mohammad Hatta, one of the first leaders of postcolonial Indonesia, was detained there. The camp is named for its location on the *boven* (upper) Digul River in the southern part of Irian Barat (formerly Dutch New Guinea).

Brandt Corstius, Hugo (1953-). Brandt Corstius writes under a number of pseudonyms: Victor Baarn (with Ferdinandusse and Blokker), Gerard Balthasar, Battus, Drs. G. van Buren, Raoul Chapkis, Dolf Cohen, Jan Eter, Jan Eter Jr., Piet Grijs, G. Prijs, Stoker, Juha Tanttu. His attacks on political and scientific leaders are often the topic of public debate and legal action. In 1985 the Minister of Welfare, Health and Culture, Brinkman [q.v.], refused to award him the P.C. Hooft Prize for Literature, because of the smear tactics he uses.

Brinkman, Leendert Cornelis (1948-) CDA. Studied political science at the Free University of Amsterdam, graduating in 1972. He then took a law degree from there as well, completing that in 1974. From 1975 to

1979, he was the head of the office of the Secretary-General at the Ministry of Domestic Affairs. In 1979-1980, he took over as acting Secretary-General. From 1980 to 1982, he was the Director General of Administration at the Ministry. In 1982 he became the Minister of Welfare, Health and Culture in the Lubbers [q.v.] government, a post he held until 1989. In 1989 he became the leader of the CDA parliamentary caucus.

CBS: *Centraal Bureau voor de Statistiek*: Central Statistical Bureau.

CDA: *Christen-Democratisch Appel*: Christian Democratic Appeal coalition. The CDA, which favors democratic government and a middle-of-the-road social policy, was originally three separate religious parties, one Catholic and two Protestant: the KVP (*Katholieke Volkspartij* [Catholic People's Party]), the CHU (*Christelijk-Historische Unie* [Christian Historical Union]) and the ARP (*Anti-Revolutionaire Partij* [Anti-Revolutionary Party]). In 1977 they joined together to form the CDA in order to challenge the lead that the PvdA [q.v.] gained after its victory in the 1972 elections. In the 1977 elections, the PvdA won more seats than the CDA but was unable to form a government. This allowed a Christian Democratic coalition to form a minority government.

The Christian Democratic coalition under Prime Minister Ruud Lubbers [q.v.] remained in power until 1994, when it was replaced by the "purple" government [q.v.]. The CDA supports free enterprise and holds to the principle that government activity should not replace private sector action but supplement it. Politically, the CDA stands between the individualism of the VVD and the governmentalism of the PvdA.

Cheesehead. The sobriquet for the Dutch, which refers to the enormous amounts of cheese that the Dutch produce and consume. Over half of all the milk produced in the Netherlands is turned into cheese. The Netherlands is the world's largest exporter of cheese, butter and powdered milk. Dutch exports of milk and dairy products are about 2.5 percent of all exports. The total production of cheese for 1997 was 690,000 tons.

Christian Labor Union: *Christelijk Nationaal Vakverbond* (CNV). The Christian National Labor Union was formed in 1909. See also Pillars.

COC: *Cultuur en Ontspanningscentrum*: Culture and Relaxation Center. The Dutch Association of Homosexuals. COC maintains this abbreviation as a part of its name as a remembrance of the association's origins before it came out of the closet. From 1946 to 1949 it was called the Shakespeare Club, and from 1949 to 1971, the COC. In 1971 the association came out of the closet and took its present name.

Coffee. Coffee is the oil of social interaction in the Netherlands. The first thing that a host or hostess says when a visitor stops by is not "Hello," but "Would you like a cup of coffee?" A friend, who speaks no Dutch, once went to visit in the Netherlands and came back beaming with pride that he had learned the Dutch word for "Hello!" "Koffie?" he said with almost no accent. That was the first thing people said to him when he went to visit.

Colijn, Hendrik (1869-1944) ARP (see CDA). In 1929 he became the leader of the party parliamentary caucus. Following the elections of 1933, he formed a compromise, minority government. His was the government that had to deal with the effects of the Great Depression. In 1939, on the eve of World War II, Colijn stepped down. He returned to the editorship of the party newspaper and took a seat in the Upper House of Parliament.

His formulation of the situation regarding German occupation in his pamphlet, *Op de grens van twee werelden* (On the Border between Two Worlds, 1940), was not well received. His description of the situation was "that a German defeat no longer seems within the boundaries of the possible." A statement like this from "the strong man" of the elections of 1937 could not but weaken the Dutch will to resist. Colijn himself did not give up the fight and was taken prisoner by the Germans in 1941. He died in German captivity in a camp near Ilmenau.

Colonial Past. During the seventeenth century, Dutch seafarers, searching for new trade routes, gave the small republic an empire 60 times its own size. The activities—and profits—of the colonies were, in large part, responsible for the prosperity that made the Golden Age of Holland possible. "New Amsterdam" (present-day New York), Surinam (Dutch Guiana), Brazil, the Netherlands Antillies (the ABC Islands [Aruba, Bonaire and Curaçao] and the SSS Islands [Saint Martin, Saint Eustatius and Saba]), South Africa (the Cape Colony) and Indonesia (the Dutch East Indies) were all Dutch colonies.

Complete. "The consummation of the marriage must be 'complete'" is an admonition against coitus interruptus as a form of birth control.

Coolie. The Dutch defining dictionary explains *koelie* as "a hired, colored worker for the factories, plantations and mines of the East and West Indies." The Dutch referred to their colonies as the Indies. The specification of East or West refers to which hemisphere the colonies were in. See Colonial Past.

Communist Manifesto. *Das Kommunistische Manifest* (German) is the political program prepared by Karl Marx and Friedrich Engels in 1848 that found its ultimate expression in the policies of the Union of Soviet Socialist Republics (USSR) and its satellite states.

Confessional Education. Between 1806 and 1917 the issue of public versus private schools was a defining issue on the Dutch political scene. Public schools were areligious. Private schools were confessional. Because a permit was required to open a school, the state used its power to create a virtual monopoly for the public schools. Dutch Liberals of the mid-nineteenth century were not populists, but intellectuals. They wanted diverse secular schools in which students of all faiths were taught in the same classroom. They wanted the schools to provide each individual with the intellectual tools to make up his or her own mind about religion without having religion imposed on them by the school.

The Protestants and the Catholics wanted their children to be educated in the spirit of the faith of their parents and instilled with their moral values. They considered the right to choose the type of education that their children received to be a basic human right. In the end, it took a constitutional amendment to resolve the issue. Article 23 of the Dutch Constitution, which defines state policy on education, is in the first chapter, which is entitled "Basic Rights."

Today the Dutch state is responsible for funding the education of all children, regardless of the type of school they attend. The state sets standards for facilities, class size, subjects taught and teacher certification. All regulations, however, must take the religious beliefs of "private" schools into account. The state can say that you have to be able to read and write Dutch, but not what textbook you have to use to learn how. Prayer in school is a matter of school, not state, policy.

Since the state funds all schools, both public and private, parents can send their children to any school they wish. This brings the mechanisms of the marketplace to public education. Schools that cannot attract the minimum number of pupils to stay open lose their funding and are closed.

Couzy. Lieutenant General H.A. Couzy was the Commander Dutch Ground Forces at the time that Srebrenica fell to Bosnian-Serb forces in July 1995, while the safe area was under the protection of Dutch troops detached to the United Nations for peacekeeping duty.

D66: *Democraten 66* : Democrats of (19)66. D66 grew out of an increasing wave of discontent with the other major political parties and the erosion of party and Pillar discipline in the mid-1960s. Its political fortunes have varied widely since it was founded in 1966. The 1994 election brought it 24 seats in the Second Chamber (house), twice the party's average over the last 20 years. In the 1998 elections, the number of seats that the party won in the Second Chamber again dropped to 14. Politically, D66 is a center-left party, somewhere between the CDA [q.v.] and the PvdA [q.v.]. It comes closest to being a "liberal" party in the American sense of the word. Its strongest support is from young, urban professionals.

Democracy by Consultation. Consensus is the Dutch answer to diversity. It stems from the time that the first inhabitants got together to build dikes that would keep the collective heads above water, because the alternative to getting together was, to paraphrase Benjamin Franklin, drowning separately. They had to come to an agreement that was acceptable to all for the common good. The tradition of consensus and compromise plays a major role in Dutch culture. The Pillars [q.v.] were based on this, as is Kok's [q.v.] "Polder Model." The success of the Pillars is based on a combination of consensus between the Pillars and cohesion within the Pillars. The goal of both was to avoid conflict.

Den Uyl, Johannes "Joop" Marten (1919-1987) PvdA. Den Uyl was trained as an economist at the University of Amsterdam. He was prime minister (1973-1977) of the PvdA-D66-PPR cabinet. During his premiership, Den Uyl was faced with the OPEC-induced oil crisis, the Lockheed bribery scandal surrounding Prince Bernhard (Queen Beatrix's father) and the hostage incident in which South Moluccan terrorists took over a school and a train. Even though his party won a plurality of the vote in 1977, he was unable to form a government, and the CDA [q.v.] under Van Agt [q.v.] took over the political leadership of the country with a minority government. When he withdrew from political life, he was succeeded as party leader by Wim Kok [q.v.].

Deus ex Machina. This Latin expression comes from the classical theater. It refers to a clichéd theatrical device for extracting the characters from the difficult situation that they had gotten into and producing a happy ending to the play. A god (*deus*) unexpectedly appears onstage to resolve the problem for them.

The Dock Workers' Monument. The Dock Workers' Monument in the old Jewish area of Amsterdam on Jonas Daniël Meijer Square was erected to commemorate the "February Strike" against anti-Jewish actions being taken by the Germans and NSB [q.v.] in 1941. The detention and deportation of 425 Jews on 22 and 23 February as a reprisal for Jewish resistance to WA [q.v.] attacks on Jews and Jewish property were the immediate cause of the strike. It began in Amsterdam and spread to the Zaanstreek, Haarlem, Weesp, Hilversum, Velsen, Utrecht en Muiden, but it collapsed under German pressure, having lasted only two days: 25 and 26 February. The

Germans declared martial law and a curfew, fired on the strikers and made a number of arrests.

Drees, Willem, Sr. (1886-1988) PvdA. Drees Sr. is the personification of Dutch politics in the 1950s. He was prime minister from 1948 to 1958, when the basis of the welfare state was laid. Drees was an old-style Social Democrat with a Calvinist upbringing. He did not drink. He did not smoke. He biked to work. He was very scrupulous. He is often characterized as a strict, but just, father figure. The party leader of the PvdA, he became the prime minister of the great postwar Catholic-Socialist coalition of the PvdA [q.v.] and the KVP (see CDA). A pragmatic idealist, Drees built up the basis for the Dutch welfare state piece by piece, striving for a solid system of social security for everyone, based on full employment. He realized that it was impossible to do everything at once and worked slowly toward his goal.

Drees is perhaps most famous as the father of the Dutch social security system of old age pensions. The system began in 1947 with the *Noodwet-Drees* (Drees Emergency Act). In 1957 it evolved into the *Algemene Ouderdomswet* (AOW) (General Old Age Pensions Act) under J.G. Suurhoff (1905-1967; PvdA), the Minister of Health and Social Affairs. While young people today have written off the AOW as a dying social program and are looking to finance their own old age, for the generation of the Great Depression and the war, the introduction of the AOW was a monumental change in social policy. It became the cornerstone of the welfare state.

DS'70: *Democratisch Socialisten 1970*: Democratic Socialists of 1970. DS'70 was a splinter party that broke off from the PvdA [q.v.] in 1970, because they thought that the policies of party leader Den Uyl [q.v.] had moved too far to the left. The new party was headed by Willem Drees Jr. (1922-), the son of the postwar prime minister. It won eight seats in the 1971 elections, and Drees became the Minister of Transportation and Waterways in the new Biesheuvel (1920-) cabinet. By the 1977 elections, however, the party had been reduced to only one seat. In the 1981 elections, the party did not win any seats and was subsequently dissolved. Since then, however, most of its political goals have been realized by other political parties.

DutchBat. The 13th Battalion of the Dutch Airmobile Brigade was on peacekeeping duty under the United Nations flag in July 1995, when Srebrenica fell to Bosnian-Serb forces. The commander was Lieutenant Colonel Th.J.P. Karremans and his deputy was Major Rob Franken.

Dutch-Indonesians. See Indonesians.

EC: *Europese Commissie*: European Commission.

Elimna. The slave castle at Elimna in Ghana was built by the Portuguese in 1482. It was later taken over by the Dutch, who continued to use it as a slave depot.

Ex Cathedra. A pronouncement by the pope as the head of the church to clarify a point of faith or morals, which is binding for all the faithful.

Famine Winter. In the summer of 1944, the Allies landed on the beaches of Normandy on 6 June. By September the first areas in the south of the Netherlands had been liberated. In support of the Allied advance, the Dutch government-in-exile requested Dutch railways to go on strike in September. The strike paralyzed the rail system, and the Germans had to rely on their own personnel and equipment for transportation. Unfortunately, the strike also meant that the Dutch in the occupied areas suffered, too. Supplies of food and fuel for them had to be moved by train, but the trains were not running in the occupied Netherlands. The Allied push stalled when operation Market Garden failed to take the strategic bridge over the Rhine at Arnhem, the story of which is told in *One Bridge Too Far*. For the people living to the north of the Rhine, liberation had to wait until May 1945. The intervening winter is now infamous as the *hongerwinter* (famine winter).

Foreigner's Service. The Dutch Foreigner's Service is roughly equivalent to the Immigration and Naturalization Service in the United States.

Formularies of Unity. There are three formularies of unity in the Protestant Church: (1) the Dutch Confession of Faith (or article 37), (2) the Heidelberg Catechism [q.v.] and (3) the Dordrecht Teachings (or article 5 against the Remonstrants). Abraham Kuyper (1837-1920), the leader of the Protestant Anti-Revolutionary Party (see CDA) wrote a book on them: *De Drie Formulieren van Eenigheid* (The Three Formularies of Unity), Amsterdam: J.H. Kruyt, 1883.

Fort Zeelandia. Fort Zeelandia was the first Dutch stronghold in Paramaribo, Surinam. It was the place where the slaves were disembarked for this Dutch colony. More recently, Fort Zeelandia reaffirmed its evil reputation. In 1982 it was the scene of the "December Murders," where then-military dictator Desi Bouterse killed 15 Surinam intellectuals.

Fun Things. Fun things for the people (*leuke dingen voor de mensen*) is immediately recognizable to the Dutch as a reference to a social program under Prime Minister (1973-1977) Den Uyl [q.v.]. By fun things Den Uyl meant the social extras that make life fun to live. This is a recognition that the minimum guaranteed income of the welfare state is only just adequate for existence, but existence does not necessarily permit one to have a life. There is a "Fun Things" welfare supplement that covers the actual cost of cultural, educational and recreational activities, such as joining a music or theater group or a choir, joining a sports club or a hobby association, taking a course, paying the membership fees for a library or buying a year's museum pass, going to a play, subscribing to a magazine, and so on.

Gas Chamber. The Third Reich's "ultimate solution" to the "problem" of Jews, Gypsies, homosexuals and other "undesirables." The primary tool of the Holocaust.

GMD: *Gemeenschappelijke Medische Dienst*: Public Health Service.

Good and Bad. During World War II, collaborators were "*bad*" (*fout* = literally: wrong) and everybody else was "*good*." The issue has not been entirely laid to rest in the Netherlands. The Dutch are still writing books and producing movies today that explore this issue. When the World War II generation began to retire, there was a huge debate on whether those who had been *fout* during the war should get state pensions. Of late, the debate has shifted to the question of whether those who did not actively resist the Germans are really entitled to the epithet "good." See also Hiding.

Green Heart. The Green Heart is a rural area of green at the center of the horse-shoe-shaped Randstad conurbation [q.v.]. It is full of farms and outdoor recreation areas. Urban sprawl is the greatest threat to its existence.

Groen Links (Green Left Alliance). The Green Left Alliance is the largest left-wing party. It is a combination of the *Communistische Partij Nederland* (CPN [Communist Party of the Netherlands]), the *Evangelische Volkspartij* (EVP [Evangelical People's Party]), the *Politieke Partij Radikalen* (PPR [Radical Party]) and the *Pacifistisch Socialistische Partij* (PSP [Pacifist Socialist Party]). Since the PvdA [q.v.] holds a middle-of-the road political position, *Groen Links* is winning more and more voters away from the PvdA.

"Guest Workers". "Guest workers" began arriving in the Netherlands in the 1940s and 1950s, when industries in Western Europe were having trouble finding enough workers. They were recruited from Southern Europe, primarily from Italy, the former Yugoslavia, Spain and Portugal, which had high unemployment. These guest workers were meant to be just that: guests. It was never expected that they would remain in the Netherlands, and no thought was given to their assimilation into society.

In the 1960s the European economy improved. Competition for guest workers increased among the Western European countries, and the employment situation improved in the home countries of the original guest workers. The Netherlands found itself forced to recruit guest workers from further afield. In 1964 the Netherlands concluded an official agreement on recruiting guest workers with Turkey. An agreement with Morocco followed in 1969. The expectation was still that these workers would return home. The official view was that the heavily overpopulated Netherlands could not afford to become a host country for immigrants.

Guest worker recruitment hit its high point in 1970 and 1971. It continued after that, despite climbing unemployment among ethnic Dutch, brought on by the economic downturn marked by the oil crisis of 1973. The Dutch may have been out of work, but not enough of them were willing to do the heavy, dirty jobs that the guest workers took.

In the 1970s and 1980s more and more guest workers decided to stay in the Netherlands rather than return to their home country. As they stayed longer, they brought their families to the Netherlands to join them. It was not until the early 1980s, however, that the Dutch government finally recognized the fact that the guest workers had turned into immigrants.

Heidelberg Catechism. The *Heidelberg Catechism* is a summary of the teachings of Calvin (1509-1564), prepared by two professors at the University of Heidelberg in 1563 at the behest of Frederick III (1620-1688). It became the obligatory standard of Protestantism throughout Frederick's domains. The first Dutch translation was published in Emden in 1563. The Synod of Dordrecht (1618-1619) approved the catechism as conforming to the Holy Scriptures and dictated that it be used in all theological education.

Heutsz, Johannes Benedictus van (1851-1924). Military commander and colonial official. During the course of his career, he served tour after tour in the Dutch East Indies, in increasingly senior positions, ending as the civilian and military governor of Atjeh, in North Sumatra. In this position, he introduced a new military policy that finally led to pacification of the countryside in 1904. He returned to the Netherlands in that year, only to be reassigned to the Dutch East Indies a few months later as governor-general. He is generally seen as the personification of the Dutch colonial past.

Hiding. In the context of those in hiding during the war, who were betrayed to the Germans, Anne Frank (1925-1945) is the example that will immediately come to mind for a Dutch reader. Anne Frank and her family hid from the Germans in a concealed room behind a bookcase in a house on the Prinsengracht in Amsterdam. The family was found and deported to the concentration camp in Bergen-Belsen in 1944. The question of who betrayed Anne Frank was still playing in Dutch papers in 1999.

Hiëronymus van Alphen (1746-1803). Hiëronymus van Alphen is famous for his book of didactic poems for children: *Kleine gedichten voor kinderen* (Small Poems for Children), which was first published in 1778. They are still well known enough so that every Dutch(wo)man will recognize the reference to:

De pruimeboom	The Plum Tree
Eene vertelling?	A Story?
Jantje zag eens pruimen hangen,	Joe saw some plums a'hanging,
O! als eijeren zo groot.	Oh! they're big as eggs.
't Scheen, dat Jantje wou gaan plukken,	It seemed that Joe would go pick some,
Schoon zijn vader 't hem verbood.	Though his father had forbidden him to.
Hier is, zei hij, noch mijn vader,	Here, he said, neither my father,
Noch de tuinman, die het ziet:	Nor the gardener will see it:
Aan een boom, zo vol geladen,	On a tree so fully ladened,
mist men vijf zes pruimen niet.	Nobody will miss five or six plums.
Maar ik wil gehoorzaam wezen,	But I want to be obedient,
En niet plukken: ik loop heen.	And not pick them: I'll walk away.
Zou ik, om een hand vol pruimen,	Should I be disobedient,
Ongehoorzaam wezen? Neen.	For a handful of plums? No.
Voord ging Jantje: maar zijn vader,	Joe left: but his father,
Die hem stil beluisterd had,	Who had overheard him,
Kwam hem in het loopen tegen,	Chanced into him on his walk,
Voor aan op het middelpad.	At the beginning of the middle path.
Kom mijn Jantje! zei de vader,	Come, my Joe, said the father,
Kom mijn kleine hartedief!	Come, small thief of my heart!
Nu zal ik u pruimen plukken;	Now I'll pick some plums for you;
Nu heeft vader Jantje lief.	Now Joe's father loves him.
Daarop ging Papa aan 't schudden	Then father began to shake [the tree].
Jantje raapte schielijk op;	Joe gathered up a lot;
Jantje kreeg zijn hoed vol pruimen,	Joe got a hat-full of plums,
En liep heen op een galop.	And ran away at a gallop.

Hirsch Ballin, E.M.H. (1950-) CDA. He took a basic law degree from the University of Amsterdam in 1974, following it with a Ph.D. in law in 1979. He worked at the Ministry of Justice from 1977 to 1981, when he took a professorship in law at the University of Nijmegen. He held this position until 1989, when he became the Minister of Justice. He remained in that position until 1994, when the "purple" coalition [q.v.] came to power, and he became a member of Parliament.

He is a legal specialist instead of a career politician. The effect of his lack of political savvy was evident in his less than successful term as minister. Even his own party was not always an enthusiastic supporter, when problems arose like the shortage of prison cells, or open arguments broke out between the ministry and the police. He is a zealous supporter of law and order. His activism was a clear contrast to the passive spirit that had become characteristic of the Dutch police force and Ministry of Justice since the 1960s.

"Hollanditis." Pacifism, antimilitarism and neutrality have long been a part of Dutch history. The changes of the 1960s and 1970s started with questions of the economy and domestic politics, and as those things changed, the foreign policy elite also found themselves dealing with public opinion. The questions of Vietnam, membership in NATO and the stationing of nuclear weapons on Dutch soil were subjected to public debate that dominated the front pages of the Dutch and international press. Between 1979 and 1985, the debate took to the streets, and the American commentator Walter Laqueur (1921-) coined a name for it: Hollanditis.

Immigrants. See Minority Problems.

Indo. The word for a Dutch(wo)man of mixed Dutch-Indonesian origin. See the following entry.

Indonesians. The integration of the immigrants from Indonesia into Dutch society is often recounted as a "success story," because the Eurasians who were "repatriated" to the Netherlands after Indonesian independence in 1949 understood that the Dutch expected them to assimilate completely into Dutch society and that they would be accepted by the ethnic Dutch only if they acted as Dutch as the Dutch, and that is what they did. While cultural differences between the ethnic Dutch and the Eurasians still occasionally lead to misunderstandings on both sides, most Eurasians are hardly considered minorities by the ethnic Dutch, nor does the government classify them as such. The Ministry of Internal Affairs lists the ethnic minorities in the Netherlands as Turks, Moroccans and other North Africans, Cape Verde Islanders, Southern Europeans, Surinamese, Antilleans and Arubans, Moluccans, refugees and asylum seekers.

Jong, Johannes de (1885-1955). He served as the archbishop of Utrecht from 1936 to 1951. He was made a cardinal in 1946. During World War II he gained wide renown both in and outside Catholic circles by his openly anti-German position.

Kok, Wim (1938-) PvdA. He studied at the prestigious Nijenrode Business School but, after a short career in the private sector, went into trade union work. He entered Parliament in 1985 and remained there until 1989, when he became Minister of Finance. He remained Minister of Finance until he became prime minister in 1994, as the leader of the "purple" coalition [q.v.]. He is considered the father of the "Polder Model" of cooperation between labor and capital (see also Democracy by Consultation).

Kristallnacht (German: The Night of the Broken Glass). *Kristallnacht*—the night of 9-10 November 1938—was a night of organized anti-Jewish riots in Germany and Austria led by the SA [q.v]. It marked a major turning point in the Nazi campaign against the Jews. Rioters burned hundreds of synagogues and ransacked over 7,000 Jewish businesses and homes. At least 91 Jews lost their lives in the riots. More than 20,000 Jews were detained, and about 10,000 of them were sent to the concentration camp at Buchenwald. The name *Kristallnacht* comes from the fact that the SA and their accomplices broke so many windows in Jewish homes and businesses that the streets were strewn with glass.

Lages, Willy. During World War II, Lages was the German in charge of the *Aussendienststelle der Sicherheitspolizei und Sicherheitsdienst* (SD) (German: Field Office of the Security Police and Security Service). He was responsible for the deportation of 70,000 Jewish residents of Amsterdam.

Live Together. See below.

Living Arrangements for Couples. The Dutch have long accepted couples who live together without the benefit of marriage. There is no stigma to this living arrangement, and couples who can demonstrate a stable, continuing relationship receive the same benefits as married couples. The phenomenon has been going on for so long that in Dutch there is a widely accepted counterpart to the word "spouse" (*echtgenoot*), that is used for unmarried couples: "*partner.*" It appears on any number of official forms. Unmarried couples are so common that they have become a part of the Dutch television landscape: Gert-Jan and Teuntje were long a part of the popular Dutch sitcom *Zeg 'ns AAA. . .* (Say Ah, Please . . .), before they were replaced by Wiep and Doctor John, also unmarried.

Lubbers, Rudolphus "Ruud" Franciscus Maria (1939-) CDA. He is a graduate (1962) of the Dutch School of Higher Economics in Rotterdam. He worked in the private sector from graduation until 1973. After that, he worked in the Ministry of the Economy until 1977. In 1977 he took a seat in the Lower House of Parliament, becoming leader of the CDA parliamentary caucus in 1978. He left Parliament in 1982 to become prime minister, a position he held until 1994, when the "purple" coalition [q.v.] came to power. He was the first prime minister to balance the budget and led the fight to cure the Dutch of "Hollanditis" [q.v.].

Lucebert. Lucebert is a pseudonym for Lubertus Jacobus Swaanswijk (1924-). He is viewed as the most revolutionary of the experimental poets. His revolutionary zeal was directed against every institution of power: the church, the state, philosophy, science and the arts themselves. He was awarded the Constantijn Huygens Prize in 1965, the P.C. Hooft Prize in 1967 and the Grand Prize of Dutch Letters in 1983.

Maagdenhuis. The occupation of the Maagdenhuis—the administrative center of the University of Amsterdam—was a watershed event in the struggle of university students for more say in the running of the universities. Police cleared the building on 21 May 1969. The victory that the students won there gave them more influence in the university system. In the 1980s, however, the process reversed, and student power was systematically reduced.

Man-made Landscape. See Polders.

Manure Surpluses. Phosphate pollution from all the manure produced by domestic livestock is a major environmental problem in the Netherlands. This problem is only just beginning to be recognized in the United States, while the Dutch have been wrestling with it since the 1980s. The Dutch have not found a solution yet. It is a politically sensitive issue that is being dealt with in typical Dutch fashion: a seemingly endless series of regulations requiring permits and paperwork.

Mauthausen. The Mauthausen Concentration Camp Memorial is located in the Austrian state (Bundesland) of Oberösterreich. Mauthausen operated as a concentration camp from 1938 to 1945.

Minority Problems. The Netherlands' present minority problems are the result of immigration. The first wave of immigration was postcolonial. When Indonesia was finally declared independent in 1949, roughly 300,000 Eurasians were "repatriated" to a country that many of them had never seen before: the Netherlands. (See also Indonesia.) After that, the flow of immigrants was more like a trickle than a wave. Highly skilled and well-educated immigrants came from the remaining colonies looking for a better life. At the same time, unskilled "guest workers" [q.v.], who were not really seen as immigrants but were envisioned to be "temporary" workers, added to the numbers of foreigners. The most recent wave followed the end of colonial rule in Surinam. When Surinam became independent in 1975, almost a third of its population emigrated to the Netherlands.

The problem is further exacerbated by the Netherlands' generous treatment of asylum seekers, providing them with free housing and living allowances. This is coupled with weak enforcement of extradition orders for those whose cases have been adjudicated. These two factors, together with the Netherlands' reputation for tolerance, have made the Netherlands the destination of choice for great numbers of economic refugees, most of whom, to the great dismay of many of the Dutch, are *allochtoons*.

The proverbial Dutch hospitality for the oppressed is being stretched to its limits. Like the WAO [q.v.], Dutch asylum policy was set up for a small target populace: those seeking asylum for reasons of conscience. It was simply not intended to handle the arrival of large numbers of economic refugees, whom their Dutch hosts are beginning to look on as "party crashers."

Indications of widespread fraud in claims for "family reunification" by those with official refugee status are triggering the same reaction as the initial reports of welfare fraud: a feeling of having been wronged. This feeling is amplified by incidents like the murder, in 1999, of Marianne Vaatstra (age 16) near a camp for asylum seekers in Friesland. The suspected perpetrators are Iraqis from the Asylum Seekers Center Kollum. Initially, the press was reticent to report the ethnic origin of the suspects, and the Ministry of Justice, the police and municipal officials held press conferences to suppress rumors that the perpetrators were from the Asylum Seekers Center. Nine weeks after the murder, when the police issued a warrant for one of the Iraqis, residents of the town near the camp were up in arms. The police posted extra security around the center to protect the asylum seekers from possible retribution.

In late December 1998, rather than let the municipality use a former institute for the blind to house asylum seekers, the residents of a wealthy neighborhood in Vught (in the province of Brabant) pooled their resources to buy the complex. Predictably, there was an immediate outcry in the politically correct Netherlands against this action. Seven of the nine participants in the syndicate that bought the property had anticipated this reaction and had preferred to remain silent (i.e., unknown) partners of the syndicate rather than face this reaction. A poll by the Centerdata Institute at the Catholic University of Brabant showed that the extremes of public opinion were almost in balance. Ten percent of those sampled thought that this was a good way to keep asylum seekers out. Eight percent of those polled thought that the purchase was improper. Thirty percent felt that there was nothing wrong with the purchase since it was completely legal. Forty percent objected to the purchase on the grounds that the rich should not be able to get their way in such a sensitive social area simply because they are rich (28 January 1999, *Brabants Dagblad*).

"Mistake." Troelstra's [q.v.] coup attempt in 1918.

"Mixed." In the 1950s, in the Netherlands, segregated pools for men and women were still reasonably common.

Murdered Girls. See "Violent Incidents in The Nightlife Areas."

National Assistance Act: *Algemene Bijstandswet* (ABW). The ABW is the most important social program in the Dutch welfare state. It was introduced in 1965. Everyone in the Netherlands who does not have enough money to cover their own cost of living is entitled to an ABW benefit. For couples it is 100 percent of the minimum wage. For heads of household it is 70 percent. For singles it is 50 percent.

NEI: *Nederlands Economisch Instituut*: Dutch Economic Institute.

Nihil Obstat. This Latin formulation (literally: there is no objection) is used by the Catholic Church authorities to grant permission for the publication of a book.

NSB: *Nationaal Socialistische Beweging*: National Socialist Movement. The Dutch counterpart of the German Nazi Party was founded in 1931 by A.A. Mussert and C. van Geelkerken. The movement reached its zenith in the 1935 elections, when it captured 8 percent of the vote. In the 1939 elections, however, the movement's strength had fallen to only 4.2 percent of the vote as a result of actions taken against the NSB by the political parties, trade unions and the church. When the Germans occupied the Netherlands, the NSB became the only official political party. After the war, party members were interned, and some of the party's leaders, including Mussert, were condemned to death.

NVHP: *Nederlandse Vereniging van Hemofiliepatiënten*: Dutch Association of Hemophiliacs.

NVVE: *Nederlandse Vereniging voor Vrijwillige Euthanasie*: Dutch Association for Voluntary Euthanasia.

Opening a Can of Policemen. "Opening a can of policemen" was the epithet that the Left applied to the idea of putting more policemen on the street to combat rising crime in the 1970s and 1980s. They dismissed this idea as treating the symptoms and not the causes of the problem.

Pea Soup. Pea soup is at the top of almost every list of what is considered typical Dutch cuisine. There is a World Championship Pea-Soup Cook-Off held in the Netherlands every year. No entrants ever come from outside the Netherlands. Typical Dutch pea soup is normally almost thick enough for the spoon to stand up straight in it. It is a favorite winter dish, which can be bought canned or fresh at the greengrocer's.

Pelopors. In the wake of World War II, the Dutch East Indies (now Indonesia) declared its independence. The Dutch did not want to lose control of the colony and sent an expeditionary force to restore colonial rule. *Pelopors* was the name that Dutch troops gave to the enemy. The emotional connotation is much the same as that for the sobriquet that American troops gave to the enemy in Vietnam: "gooks."

"The Personal." "*Het persoonlijke is politiek*" [The personal is political] was a slogan popular in radical circles in the 1960s in the Netherlands. It was a call for political activism to expand individual freedoms by changing the system. An abortion, for example, may at first appear to be an individual decision, but on closer examination, it is a political decision as well that requires legislative changes.

Pillars/Pillarization. Pillarization (a sort of social apartheid) used to be the primary force that shaped and constrained Dutch politics. The Protestant and Catholic Pillars (*zuilen*) date to the sixteenth and seventeenth centuries, the time of the revolt against Spain. When the Protestants displaced the Catholics as the ruling power in society, the Catholics formed a closed "Pillar" within Dutch society to preserve their own Catholic identity. The Dutch sense of tolerance, which allowed them to do so, was an unusual concept in this time of religious wars. The front-line, "them-or-us" mentality of this religious power struggle reinforced group cohesion and made adherence to group values extremely important for the group's members. This produced a bipolar society, with clearly defined political fault lines. At the height of Pillarization, almost all social activities were voluntarily segregated on the basis of religious or philosophical views. There were separate sports clubs, newspapers, schools, insurance companies, labor unions, agricultural associations and political parties for each Pillar.

Inthe nineteenth century, liberalism became increasingly popular in the Netherlands. The Liberals displaced the Protestants as the leading power in society, and the Protestants and Catholics closed ranks in their individual Pillars, as economic and political power shifted to the liberal, secular elements of society. In the 1960s, under the influence of television and other factors, the Pillars began to break down.

Polder. Holland literally means "land in a hollow." About 27 percent of the country is below sea level, and that is where about 60 percent of the population lives. The average elevation is only 11 meters/37 feet above sea level. What is now dry land in the Netherlands has not always been so. The Frisians, who settled in the northern part of present-day Netherlands over 2,000 years ago, built huge earth mounds called "terpen" to protect them and their livestock from high tides and floods. Eventually, some of these mounds were connected by earthwork walls for additional protection. These were the first dikes. Diking in shallows to recover land from under the water has allowed the Dutch to expand the surface area of the country without having to take land from someone else, as other nations have at times done. The saying goes: God made the earth, but the Dutch made the Netherlands.

The Dutch call land reclaimed from under the water a polder. The largest, and best-known polders are in the former Zuiderzee (*zuider* = south; *zee* = sea). The four Zuiderzee polders form the newest province, named Flevoland, which officially became the 12th province in 1986.

Post Office Box 51. Post Office Box 51 is the address of the government's public information service. It provides the public with free brochures, containing information on a variety of topics. It also runs television spots with information the government wants everyone to be aware of. In 1999, for example, tax authorities were paying close attention to the value of improvements that homeowners make to their homes, and Post-Office-Box-51 television spots encouraged homeowners to be sure that they had declared all of them on their tax returns.

Provo: *Provocerende anarchisten*: Confrontational Anarchists. Provo was a short-lived (1965-1967) protest movement centered in Amsterdam. It was an eclectic combination of groups and initiatives that were connected as much by what they were against as by what they were for. The common thread to the things Provo opposed was the Establishment; capitalism, communism, fascism, militarism, bureaucracy, professionalism, snobbism and commercialism were their targets. Their only common ideology was playful confrontation. Provo was constantly in the press and seemed to seek confrontation for the sheer enjoyment of it.

PSP: *Pacifistisch Socialistische Partij*: Pacifist Socialist Party. See *Groen Links*.

"Purple" Cabinet. The "purple" cabinet is a coalition of Social Democrats and Liberals: PvdA [q.v.], D66 [q.v.] and VVD [q.v.]. It is called "purple" because that is the color that results when you combine blue and red: the colors of the VVD and the PvdA. The "purple" government came to power in 1994, displacing the Christian Democrats, who had been in power since 1977. Together the coalition partners won 92 of the 150 seats (61 percent) in Parliament.

Putten. Putten is a village in the province of Gelderland. As a reprisal for an attack on a German vehicle in which a German officer was killed, on 1 October 1944, the Germans rounded up and deported all the men in the village between the ages of 16 and 50: 660 of them.

PvdA: *Partij van de Arbeid*: Labor Party. The PvdA is a European Social Democratic party (left of center). It was established in 1946, when its policy concerns were the postwar reconstruction of Dutch society and, in particular, the establishment of the welfare state. It now follows mainly national interests instead of strictly socialist ones. It was the successor to the SDAP (*Sociaal Democratische Arbeiders Partij* [Social Democratic Workers Party] see Troelstra), which was founded in 1894 in Amsterdam, the longtime center of the workers movement in the Netherlands.

Randstad. The most heavily populated area in the Netherlands is the Randstad (*rand* = edge; *stad* = city) conurbation. This name describes the urban agglomeration in the west of the country that encompasses the cities of Dordrecht, Rotterdam, Delft, The Hague, Leiden, Haarlem, Amsterdam and Utrecht. These heavily populated urban areas form a horseshoe-shaped area that opens to the southeast. The less-heavily populated and less-urbanized area in the center of the horseshoe is known as the "Green Heart" [q.v.].

Refugee Status. See Minorities.

Regents. The regents were the burgomasters and members of the city council in the Dutch Republic[q.v.]. In the seventeenth and eighteenth centuries, the gap between the regents and the populace widened until the regents formed a closed caste, which controlled all the important positions of power. The protest movement of the 1960s used the same word as an epithet for the postwar ruling elite that they were attacking, much the same way as the protest generation in America attacked "the Establishment."

Republic. The Dutch Republic came into being at the end of the Eighty Years' War of Independence, which was fought against Spain. The war was concluded in 1648 by the Treaty of Westphalia. From that point on, the Republic of the Seven United Provinces (roughly the present-day Netherlands) was recognized as an independent state, where previously it had been a part of the Spanish empire.

RIAGG: *Regionaal instituut voor de ambulante geestelijke gezondheidszorg*: Regional Institute for Outpatient Mental Health Care.

Saint Peter's Mountain. Saint Peter's Mountain is located near Maastricht, in the eastern province of Limburg, in the only part of the country that has anything that can, by any stretch of the imagination, be called mountains. The average elevation in the Netherlands is only 11 meters/37 feet above sea level. The elevation rises as you move from west to east. The highest point is in the southeast corner of Limburg. It is the Vaalserberg, which is 321 meters/1,053 feet above sea level.

Samkalden, Ivo (1912-1995) PvdA. From 1967 to 1977, he was the mayor of Amsterdam. His term in office as mayor was a turbulent one. It covered the problems with the construction of the Metro in Amsterdam and the occupation of the Maagdenhuis [q.v.], the administrative center of the University of Amsterdam. In 1971 Samkalden made the pages of the world press, when the Soviet News Agency TASS attacked him for a speech he made at a reception for a Soviet delegation, in which he called on the Soviet Union to allow Jews to emigrate.

Schiphol. Schiphol Airport in Amsterdam is the fourth largest handler of airfreight in Western Europe. The airport's location is typically Dutch. It is located 13 feet below sea level in a polder that was drained in the nineteenth century. Its name literally means "ship's hollow." Schiphol is the third best connected airport in the world after London (Heathrow) and Paris (Charles de Gaulle). There are flights from Schiphol to 227 destinations in 97 countries.

SDAP: *Sociaal Democratische Arbeiders Partij*: Social Democratic Workers Party. See PvdA.

Seyss-Inquart, Arthur (1891-1946). The Austrian Arthur Seyss-Inquart, a trusted friend of Hitler's (1889-1945), was appointed the Reich's Commissioner for the occupied Netherlands. He was the highest civilian authority in the Netherlands during the occupation. Seyss-Inquart was tried at Nuremberg for crimes against peace and humanity. He was found guilty and hanged.

Shadow Economy. The shadow economy is that part of the economy where taxes and social insurance premiums are not paid. In Dutch, working on the shadow economy is known as working "black." Those who work in the shadow economy do not pay social security or income taxes and are, therefore, cheaper to employ, but the loss of income to the state is a drag on the finances of a welfare state. Workers in the shadow economy place another drain on state finances as well. Many of them continue to draw assistance payments while working "black."

Sickness Benefits Act: *Ziektewet* (ZW). The Sickness Benefits Act was introduced in 1967, at the height of the government windfall from the natural gas fields in the north of the country. It made generous payments to those who were too ill to work or were disabled. Benefits were set at 70 percent of the last salary/wage that the disabled worker had earned, but not less than the minimum wage. On 1 March 1997, in an economy move, the government shifted ZW payments—except in cases of pregnancy and maternity—to employers under the *Wet Uitbreiding Loondoorbetaling bij Ziekte* (Act on Expanding Continuing Salary Payments during Illness) (WULBZ). Now employers have to pay sick or disabled workers 70 percent of the last salary/wage that they earned for a maximum of one year. (Some politicians are discussing making it three years.) At the end of the year, if the worker cannot return to work, he or she qualifies for the WAO [q.v.].

    The unforeseen side effect of the shift of responsibility from the government to the employer has been a tendency for employers not to hire people with health problems. The shift has also prompted a huge political debate over the proposal from the *Stichting van de Arbeid* (Association of Labor) to give priority health care to those who are employed. In this case, time really is money, while an employee is waiting for medical treatment that will return him or her to work.

    The Dutch health care system does not operate on free market principles but is a planned system. The result is that there are waiting lists for certain services. Under WULBZ, the employer has to continue to pay the employee's salary while the employee waits for treatment. The employers' view of the proposal is economic. They want to control the costs imposed upon them by the WULBZ. Public reaction to the proposal has been devastating. The public does not seem to mind waiting for medical services as long as the decision of who gets treated first is a medical one, not a political or economic one.

Slave Trade. The Dutch were actively involved in the slave trade only from about 1630 to 1795. During the peak of Dutch activity, they carried approximately 10 percent of the total volume of slaves. All told, the number of slaves landed by the Dutch was 460,000, only about 5 percent of the total. England, Portugal (together with Brazil) and France accounted for 90 percent of the slaves landed, or about 8.6 million. The Netherlands abolished the trade in slaves in 1808 but was one of the last countries to abolish slavery in its colonies. The slaves were freed in Surinam and the Caribbean island colonies in 1863. They had been freed in neighboring French Guiana several years before, in 1848. The British passed the Slave Emancipation Act, which freed all the slaves throughout the British empire in 1834.

Social Rejuvenation. In the late 1980s "Social Rejuvenation" was the name for the Social Democratic program that was initiated in response to Liberals' policy of decentralization, which was known as "Administrative Rejuvenation." One of the program's key components was a public works program to put the long-term unemployed to work in security patrols, graffiti cleanup and ticket checking on public transportation.

Soft Drugs. Dutch drug policy treats the issue as a health problem rather than as a moral one, stressing prevention and treatment. The Dutch approach is best characterized as "harm reduction" or "damage control." The Dutch categorizations for different types of drugs reflect this approach. "Hard" drugs (XTC, heroin and cocaine) are those presenting an unacceptable health risk, and "soft" drugs (hashish, marijuana) present a lesser health hazard. The Dutch policy on "soft drugs" is to turn a "blind eye" to their open sale in so-called "coffee shops." The Dutch view this policy as compartmentalizing "hard-drug" addicts and "soft-drug" users from each other to prevent "soft-drug" users from "stepping up" to "hard" drugs.

This "blind-eye" policy on "soft" drugs is in conflict with the policies of total prohibition that exist in other countries such as the United States and Sweden. While, de jure, the possession of user quantities of both "hard" and "soft" drugs is illegal in the Netherlands, it is only a misdemeanor—not a felony as it is in many other countries—and is seldom prosecuted. The Dutch prefer treatment to imprisonment for addicts.

Dutch drug policy is under pressure both internationally and domestically. People in the Netherlands are becoming tired of drug-related crimes against property (theft) by "hard-drug" addicts and of their antisocial behavior. In some neighborhoods, the fabled Dutch consensus and tolerance, which are the foundation of Dutch drug policy, have broken down, and the inhabitants of the neighborhood have formed vigilante groups to run the "hard-drug" addicts out of the neighborhood.

Sorgdrager, Winnifred "Winnie" (1948-) D66. The Minister of Justice from 1994 to 1998. She holds a law degree (1971) from the University of Groningen. In 1991 she became the youngest Attorney General in Dutch history. A relative unknown when appointed minister, she is a technical specialist instead of a political insider, chosen for her extensive experience in the legal system. While she is a supporter of more police on the street, she says that this does not make sense until the rest of the legal system (courts/prisons) has been expanded. She was forced to step down in 1998 when an undercover police drugs operation went wrong.

Squatters. The first squatters' actions in Amsterdam began in the mid-1960s. The original motivation for squatters' actions was the scarcity of, and the long waiting times for, public sector housing. This was coupled with an aversion to the profits being made in the private housing sector, which made private apartments targets as well. In 1971 a Supreme Court decision declared that squatting an empty apartment was not a violation of the law on trespassing (article 138), and the number of squatters' actions rose considerably.

The squatters' movement reached its high-water mark on 30 April 1980: the coronation of Queen Beatrix. Up until that time, the movement had had some popular support, but the fights and disturbances that day turned public opinion against it. The last major clash between the squatters and the authorities was in 1985, when the Staatsliedenbuurt (Statesmen's neighborhood) in Amsterdam was cleared.

STE: *Stichting Toezicht Effectenverkeer*: Association for Securities Exchange Oversight.

Sur Place. *Sur place* is a French term used in bicycle racing, which is very popular in the Netherlands. The term refers to a tactic in bicycle racing. The participants balance on their bikes, standing still, waiting to see who will take the lead. The lead cyclist in the race has to work harder than the rest, breaking the air for those behind. There is, therefore, some tactical advantage to not taking the lead early in the race.

Tickets. Dutch movie theaters do not have open seating as is the custom in the United States. The prices of the seats vary by the distance from the screen. The entertainment tax on the tickets is a percentage of their price, and the controller's job was to make sure that no one was evading the entertainment tax by paying for a cheap seat but sitting in an expensive one.

Toothbrushes. "Counting toothbrushes" is a widely recognized metaphor in the Netherlands for the government's sticking its nose into people's lives and investigating the living arrangements of someone who gets a public assistance benefit. The level of many benefits is dependent on the type of household in which the recipient lives. If the recipient is married or living together with a steady partner, the total benefit could be less than if the couple were living separately. There is, therefore, a temptation for the couple to report that they are living apart so that they can get a larger benefit. To combat this tendency, welfare workers on a home visit to the recipient may unexpectedly visit the bathroom to count toothbrushes. If there is more than one toothbrush in the bathroom, then the recipient is obviously living with someone and not alone and, thus, not entitled to the higher benefit. An example of how intrusive this kind of lifestyle investigation is can be seen in the movie *Green Card* (1990) with Gérard Depardieu and Andie MacDowell.

Traffic Regulations. When a Dutch(wo)man encounters a new rule, the tendency is to exclaim: *"Het zou toch moeten kunnen!"* (This should really be possible!). They all know that there is an exception to every rule. You only have to look at traffic signs as you go about the city to see how rampant it is. "NO ENTRY! (EXCEPT FOR BICYCLISTS)" says one. "NO PARKING! (EXCEPT FOR PERMIT HOLDERS)" says another.

In the Netherlands, the ultimate explicit statement that there is no exception to a rule is a physical barrier to make it impossible to do whatever it is that the rule prohibits. If you really are not supposed to drive up a small country lane for any reason, there is a post in the middle of it that blocks your way and a sign below the NO ENTRY! sign, warning you that there is a POST IN THE ROAD. If you really should not park here for any reason, there are barriers along the curb half a car-length apart and only one lane of traffic. If you are really not supposed to walk on this wall, the top is built on a sixty-degree angle. If you are really not supposed to sit on this railing, the top is a row of very uncomfortable spikes. If you are really not supposed to run this red light or speed on this street, there is a robot-camera that takes your picture if you do. Your citation for speeding or running the red light arrives, essentially untouched by human hands. These types of barriers and automatic enforcement are nonconfrontational. If the individual wants to argue about the rule, he or she can do so with the barrier or the machine, and the person who made the rule avoids a confrontation.

Troelstra, Pieter Jelles (1860-1930). Troelstra was one of the founders of the SDAP (see PvdA). He served in the Second Chamber (House) from 1897 to 1925 with only a short break. He was very active in the international Socialist movement as well.

In the wake of World War I and the Russian Revolution (1917), political tensions were running high, and mainstream Dutch politicians were afraid of the possibility of a Socialist revolution in the Netherlands. The mayor of Rotterdam, A.R. Zimmerman, was so disturbed by the situation that he contacted the SDAP to begin the turnover of power in the city. Troelstra, who was the leader of the SDAP at the time, overreacted and in a speech in the Second Chamber on 11 November 1918 called on the working classes to seize power in the Netherlands. The "Revolution" was a complete failure. Troelstra later admitted that he had misjudged the situation and that the "Revolution" had been a "mistake."

The "Revolution" did result in political concessions to the Socialists by the mainstream parties in such areas as housing, the eight-hour workday, improved old age legislation and women's suffrage.

Truants Bus. Truants buses were a product of the extreme tolerance of the 1970s and 1980s; taking a hard line with children could damage their psyche. Instead of picking up truants and carting them off to school, the truants bus served up coffee [q.v.] with a cheery word of encouragement. In the mid-1990s the tide turned and now truants buses do pick kids up off the street and cart them off to school.

Van Agt, Andreas "Dries" Antonius Maria (1931-) CDA. Van Agt was trained as a lawyer at the Catholic University in Nijmegen. He was a longtime political opponent of Den Uyl [q.v.], but served as the vice prime minister and the Minister of Justice in Den Uyl's cabinet (1973-1977). He was prime minister in the CDA-VVD cabinet (1977-1981) and the short-lived CDA-PvdA-D66 cabinet (September 1981- May 1982), which fell over the issue of employment. In the CDA-D66 cabinet that followed, he was the Foreign Minister. When the CDA-D66 coalition fell as well (1982), Van Agt withdrew from national politics, to be succeeded by Ruud Lubbers [q.v.] as party leader and prime minister. Van Agt later became the European Union ambassador to Japan (1987) and the United States (1990-1995). He was ahead of his time in calling for an ethical revival and one of the first politicians to attack the negative aspects of rapid individualization.

Violent Incidents in the Nightlife Areas. The Dutch media are awash with reports of what they are terming "senseless violence," as if some other kinds of unspecified violence make sense. The most prominent such incident in 1999 was the walk-by shooting of two teenage girls in Gorinchem. On 9 January 1999 Froukje Schuitmaker (age 17) and Marianne Roza (age 18) were killed when shots were fired through the door of the nightclub that they were visiting. The girls were innocent bystanders. The shots were fired blindly through the door of the club, apparently in an act of revenge against the club's bouncers. When it was discovered that the alleged perpetrators were Turks, the media did not know how to react. Most reports said nothing about the ethnic origins of the perpetrators. Froukje's parents went out of their way to extend the hand of peace to the Turkish community. They broke bread with a Turkish imam in the nightclub where Froukje had been killed and then went to Froukje's school to pass out the "bread of peace" with two Turkish boys.

VVD: *Volkspartij voor Vrijheid en Democratie*: People's Party for Freedom and Democracy. The VVD is a Liberal party in the European, rather than in the American, sense of the word. It advocates free enterprise, separation of church and state and individual liberties. The liberal tendencies of the VVD trace their roots to the constitutional reform of 1848 [q.v], which laid the groundwork for parliamentary democracy in the Netherlands. It used to be the most conservative of the political parties, but since Bolkestein [q.v.], it has begun criticizing the "laissez-faire" philosophy of the CDA [q.v.] and has voted with the PvdA [q.v.] in the "purple" [q.v.] government for the restoration of government responsibility.

WA: *Weerbaarheidsafdeling*: Protection Section. Just as the Nazi Party in Germany had the SA (*Sturmabteilung*: the "Brown Shirts"; German: literally the "Assault Section"), the NSB [q.v.] also had a uniformed strong-arm section, which was known as the WA. The name more resembles that of the Nazi SS (*Schutzstaffel*: Protection Unit), than the SA.

WAO: *Wet op de ArbeidsOngeschiktheid*: Disability Benefits Act. The Disability Benefits Act was introduced in 1967, at the height of the government windfall from the natural gas fields in the north of the country. It makes payments to workers who become disabled and are unable to work for more than a year. When the program was first introduced, it was predicted that the number of persons receiving benefits under WAO would rise only to between 150,000 and 200,000. Within four years the number of recipients was above 200,000 and still growing. By 1976 the number of WAO recipients climbed to 500,000. By 1988 it was over 800,000 and still climbing. One reason behind this was that the WAO was being used as an early retirement program to get rid of older workers. It was a way out of the unemployment crisis, which hit its peak in the Netherlands in the 1980s.

There was little resistance to this for a number of reasons. The workers who were being let go were supported by the Dutch welfare safety net, which made it possible for older workers to stop working with little or no impact on their standard of living. These workers were also the generation of the postwar reconstruction era, which felt itself responsible for the economic success of the Netherlands. The offer of early retirement was viewed as a reward for their hard work. Early retirement was also presented as a way to give younger workers a chance to keep working, because if the older workers did not go, then younger workers would, and the prospects were that they would be unemployed for a very long time. Cooperation and compromise have long been a hallmark of Dutch society, and this approach was a typical Dutch consensus solution.

In the mid-1990s the government and employers finally realized how much the program actually cost. It had been very effective in doing what they wanted. Only about 25 percent of those over age 55 work in the Netherlands, one of the lowest percentages in the world. To put this in perspective, in France about 33 percent of those over 55 work. In the United States and the U.K., it is about 50 percent. In Sweden and Japan, it is 66 percent.

WCPV: *Wet collectieve preventie volksgezondheid*: Act on the Collective Protection of the Public Health.

Westerbork. Camp Westerbork, located in the province of Drenthe, was the central refugee camp for Jewish refugees from Germany before the war. During the German occupation of the Netherlands during World War II, it became a transit camp for Jews on their way to the death camps.

WVG: *Wet voorzieningen gehandicapten*: Handicapped Programs Act.

'Yoos'. The use of the word 'yoos' here points to a "verbal class distinction" as Henry Higgins called it in *My Fair Lady*. "It's "Aoooow" and "Garn" that keep her in her place. Not her wretched clothes and dirty face."

The "poor upkeep of the stairwell" refers to another cultural distinction. The Dutch are fastidiously clean and are appalled by *allochtoons* who do not keep common areas in apartment buildings—stairwells and the sidewalk in front of the building—as clean as common Dutch civility calls for.

Bibliography

The bibliography is in Dutch style. It is an exact copy of the one in the original. The vast majority of the sources are only available in Dutch, and are of no interest to those who cannot read Dutch. Dutch bibliographic style was, therefore, maintained for the specialist reader. Titles are not translated in the bibliography. Titles are, however, translated in the notes so that the reader can better match the notes to the text, where the titles appear only in translation.

Aben, Frédérique, *Heeft de Nederlandse Filmkeuring recht van bestaan?* Doctoraalscriptie, RU Leiden, juli 1992.

Algemene Rekenkamer, rapport Voorlichtingscampagnes bij het Rijk. Tweede Kamer, 1990-1991, 22 152, nrs. 1 en 2.

Algemene Rekenkamer, rapport Convenanten van het Rijk met bedrijven en instellingen, Den Haag, 1995.

Banfield, E.C., *The Moral Basis of a Backward Society,* Free Press, Glencoe, IL, 1958.

Bank, Jan, *Oorlogsverleden in Nederland,* Ambo, Baarn, 1983.

Bax, Mart, *Medjugorje: Religion, Politics and Violence in Rural Bosnia,* VU uitgeverij, Amsterdam, 1995.

Becker, J.W., en R. Vink, *Secularisatie in Nederland, 1966-1991, de verandering van opvattingen en enkele gedragingen,* Sociaal en Cultureel Planbureau/VUGA, Rijswijk/Den Haag, 1994.

Benvenuti, B., *Farming in Cultural Change,* Van Gorcum, Assen, 1961.

Berdowski, Z., en E. van Schooten, onderzoek 'Waar een wil is en geen weg', Bureau O + S van de gemeente Amsterdam/SCO-Kohnstamm Instituut, Universiteit van Amsterdam, 1995.

218   The Politically Correct Netherlands

Berg, J.Th.J. van den, en H.A.A. Molleman, *Crisis in de Nederlandse politiek*, Samsom, Alphen aan den Rijn, 1974.

Bleich, Anet, Peter Schumacher e.a., *Nederlands racisme*, Van Gennep, Amsterdam, 1984.

Blokker, Jan, *De kroon en de mestvork, enige opmerkingen over de pers en haar vrijheden*, intreerede, De Harmonie, Amsterdam, 1992.

Blom, J.C.H., *Crisis, bezetting en herstel, tien studies over Nederland 1930-1950*, Nijgh & Van Ditmar Universitair, Den Haag, 1989.

Boas, Henriëtte, *Herlevend Bewaard, aren lezen in joods Amsterdam*, Keesing, Amsterdam, 1987.

Bolkestein, Frits, *Het heft in handen*, Prometheus, Amsterdam, 1995.

Boom, Bart van der, *Den Haag in de Tweede Wereldoorlog*, Seapress, Den Haag, 1995.

Boutellier, Hans, *Solidariteit en slachtofferschap, de morele betekenis van criminaliteit in een postmoderne cultuur*, Sun, Nijmegen, 1993.

Boutellier, J.C.J., 'Criminaliteit als moreel vraagstuk: vijf jaar justitieel preventiebeleid'. In: Cliteur e.a. (red.), *Burgerschap, levensbeschouwing en criminaliteit, humanistische, katholieke en protestantse visies op de kwaliteit van de huidige samenleving*, De Horstink, Amersfoort/Leuven, 1991.

Bovenkerk, Frank (red.), *Omdat zij anders zijn, patronen van rasdiscriminatie in Nederland*, Boom, Meppel, 1978.

Bovenkerk, F., K. Bruin, L. Brunt en H. Wouters, *Vreemd volk, gemengde gevoelens, etnische verhoudingen in een grote stad*, Boom, Meppel/Amsterdam, 1985.

Bunt, H.G. van de, *Organisatiecriminaliteit*, Gouda Quint, Arnhem, 1992.

Burg, J. van der, en J.H.J. van den Heuvel, *Film en overheidsbeleid, van censuur naar zelfregulering*, Sdu, Den Haag, 1991.

Caransa, Ab, *Verzamelen op het Transvaalplein, Ter nagedachtnis van het Joodse proletariaat van Amsterdam*, Bosch & Keuning, Baarn, 1984.

Centrale Commissie voor de Statistiek, Jaarverslagen 1978, 1979 en 1980, Voorburg, 1978, 1979 en 1980.

Cozijn, C., *Doorrijden na een ongeval, een literatuurstudie*, WODC, Den Haag, 1985.

Daalder, H., *Van oude en nieuwe regenten, of: Politiek als beroep*. Rede uitgesproken t.g.v. zijn afscheid als hoogleraar in de wetenschap der politiek aan de Rijksuniversiteit te Leiden op 2 april 1993, Leiden, 1993.

Daams, Maja, 'Naast wie zal ik nu eens gaan zitten?' In: Frank Bovenkerk (red.), *Omdat zij anders zijn, patronen van rasdiscriminatie in Nederland*, Boom, Meppel, 1978.

Dam, Marcel van, *De opmars der dingen*, Balans, Amsterdam, 1994.

Dantzig, A. van, *Normaal is niet gewoon, beschouwingen over psychiatrie en psychotherapie*, De Bezige Bij, Amsterdam, 1974.

Dasberg, Lea, 'Meelopers en dwarsliggers', lezing t.g.v. het vijftigjarig jubileum van *Trouw*, aangevuld met de reacties daarop uit het onderwijsveld, *Trouw*, Amsterdam, 1993.

De Voogd, Christophe, *Histoire des Pays-Bas*, Hatier, Paris, 1992.

Dekker, G., *De stille revolutie, de ontwikkeling van de Gereformeerde Kerken in Nederland tussen 1950 en 1990*, Kok, Kampen, 1992.

Dekker, Paul, en Marjanne Konings-van der Snoek (red.), *Sociale en culturele kennis*, VUGA/Sociaal en Cultureel Planbureau, Den Haag/Rijswijk, 1992.

Drees, W., *Openbare uitgaven*, 1994, nr 2.

Duijn, Roel van, *Provo, de geschiedenis van de provotarische beweging 1965-1967*, Meulenhoff, Amsterdam, 1985.

Elias, Norbert, *Het civilisatieproces, sociogenetische en psychogenetische onderzoekingen*, Het Spectrum, Utrecht/Antwerpen, 1982.

Essed, Philomena, *Inzicht in alledaags racisme*, Het Spectrum, Utrecht, 1991.

Ester, P., *Cultuur van de verzorgingsstaat*, Tilburg University Press, Tilburg, 1994.

Ester, P., L. Halman en R. de Moor, *The Individualizing Society, Value Change in Europe and North America*, Tilburg University Press, Tilburg, 1993.

Feijter, Henk de, *Voorlopers bij demografische veranderingen*, NIDI, rapport 22, Den Haag, 1991.

Fortuyn, Wilhelmus S.P., *Aan het volk van Nederland: de contract-maatschappij, een politiek-economische zedenschets*, Contact, Amsterdam, 1992.

Gans, M.H., *Memorboek*, Bosch & Keuning, Baarn, 1971.

Geertz, Clifford, *Agricultural Involution, the Process of Ecological Change in Indonesia*, University of California Press, Berkeley/Los Angeles, 1963.

Ginneken, Paul van, 'Een zodanig gevaar', NcGv-reeks 93-21, Utrecht, oktober 1993.

Goldenweiser, A., 'Loose Ends of a Theory on the Individual Pattern and Involution in Primitive Society'. In R. Lowie (ed.), *Essays in Anthropology, Presented to A.L. Kroeber*, University of California Press, Berkeley, 1936.

Goudsblom, Johan, *De sociologie van Norbert Elias*, Meulenhoff, Amsterdam, 1987.

Gowricharn, Ruben, *Tegen beter weten in, een essay over de economie en sociologie van de 'onderklasse'*, Garant, Leuven/Apeldoorn, 1992.

Gras, M., e.a. *Een schijn van kans, twee empirische onderzoekingen naar discriminatie op grond van handicap en etnische afkomst*, Gouda Quint, Arnhem, 1996.

Griffioen, Pim, en Ron Zeller, Achtste Jaarboek van het Rijks Instituut voor Oorlogsdocumentatie, Amsterdam, 1997.

Hemrika, Anneke, *klein monument*, Octavo, Bergen, 1985.

Hibbeln, J.G., en Willem Velema, *Het WAO-debacle, de fatale missers van wettenmakers en uitvoerders*, Jan van Arkel, Utrecht, 1993.

Hirsch Ballin, E.M.H., *In Ernst, oriëntaties voor beleid*, Sdu Juridische & Fiscale Uitgeverij, Den Haag, 1994.

Hofstede, Geert, *Allemaal andersdenkenden, omgaan met cultuurverschillen*, Contact, Amsterdam, 1991.

Inen, Jerôme W., *Verschijnselen van zelfcensuur*, scriptie, School voor Journalistiek, Utrecht, 1992.

Inglehart, Ronald, *Culture Shift in Advanced Industrial Society*, Princeton University Press, Princeton, 1990.

Janis, I.L., *Groupthink, Psychological Studies of Policy Decisions and Fiascoes*, Houghton Mifflin, Boston, 1982.

Jansen van Galen, John, en Herman Vuijsje, *Drees, wethouder van Nederland*, Sijthoff, Alphen aan den Rijn, 1980.

Jong, L. de, 'Jews and Non-Jews in Nazi-Occupied Holland'. In *On the Track of Tyranny*, London, 1962, pp. 153/154.

Kapteyn, Paul, *Taboe, macht en moraal in Nederland*, De Arbeiderspers, Amsterdam, 1980.

Kapteyn, Paul, *In de speeltuin Nederland*, De Arbeiderspers, Amsterdam, 1985.

Kennedy, James C., *Nieuw Babylon in aanbouw, Nederland in de jaren zestig*, Boom, Amsterdam, 1995.

Kerklaan, Marga, *'Zodoende was de vrouw maar een mens om kinderen te krijgen', 300 brieven over het roomse huwelijksleven*, Ambo, Baarn, 1987.

Kroon, Gerard van der, *In de woestijn van de moraal, een documentaire over de katholieke moraal in Nederland in de jaren 1945-1965*, Ambo, Utrecht, 1965.

Kruis, Gerrit, e.a. (red.), *De oplossing van Brabant, essays en interviews t.g.v. het veertigjarig bestaan van het Provinciaal Opbouworgaan Noord-Brabant (1947-1987)*, PON, Tilburg, 1987.

Kuypers, Paul, 'Een hotelbrand'. Inleiding bij: Vuijsje, m.m.v. Bestebreurtje, 1996.

Kuypers, Paul, en Jos van der Lans, *Naar een modern paternalisme*, De Balie, Amsterdam, 1994.

Lans, Jos van der, *De onzichtbare samenleving, beschouwingen over publieke moraal*, NIZW, Utrecht, 1995.

Leijten, J.C.M., *De verschrikkelijke eenzaamheid van de inbreker*, Balans, Amsterdam, 1992.

Lindwer, Willy, *Het fatale dilemma, de Joodsche Raad voor Amsterdam, 1941-1943*, Sdu, Den Haag, 1995.

Loef, Kees, *Marokkaanse bendes in de Amsterdamse binnenstad*, gemeente Amsterdam, 1988.

Meijer, Jaap, *Hoge hoeden, lage standaarden, de Nederlandse joden tussen 1933 en 1940*, Het Wereldvenster, Baarn, 1969.

Merton, Robert K., *Social Theory and Social Structure*, Free Press, Glencoe/New York/London, 1949, 1957, 1968.

Michman, D., e.a., *Pinkas, geschiedenis van de joodse gemeenschap in Nederland*, Kluwer, Amsterdam, 1992.

Mijnssen, W.G.C., 'Discriminatie en strafrecht, de relevantie van de bedoeling en de betekenis van religie in zaken van discriminatie wegens ras', *Nederlands Juristenblad*, 26 september 1987.

Mutsaers, M., en L. Boendermaker, *Criminaliteitspreventie in het onderwijs, eerste deelexperiment: spijbelcontrole*, WODC, Ministerie van Justitie, Den Haag, 1990.

Naarden, Geertje Marianne, *Onze jeugd behoort de morgen. . . de geschiedenis van de AJC in oorlogstijd*, Stichting beheer IISG, Amsterdam, 1989.

Nationale ombudsman, De, Openbaar rapport nr 95/271, 18 juli 1995.

Ogburn, W.F., "Cultural Lag as Theory," *Sociology and Social Research*, 41 (1957): pp. 167-174.

Overkleeft-Verburg, G. *De Wet persoonsregistraties, norm, toepassing en evaluatie*, Tjeenk Willink, Zwolle, 1995.

Peper, Bram, *Vorming van welzijnsbeleid, evolutie en evaluatie van het opbouwwerk*, Boom, Meppel, 1972.

Peppel, R. van de, *Naleving van milieurecht, toepassing van beleidsinstrumenten op de Nederlandse verfindustrie*, Kluwer, Amsterdam, 1995.

Phillips, Derek, *De naakte Nederlander, kritische overpeinzingen*, Bert Bakker, Amsterdam, 1985.

Pleij, Herman, *Het Nederlandse onbehagen*, Prometheus, Amsterdam, 1991.

Presser, J., *Ondergang*, Staatsuitgeverij, Den Haag, 1965.

Raad voor de ruimtelijke ordening, *Het Groene Hart*, advies nr 206, aangeboden aan de minister van VROM, Sdu, Den Haag, 1996.

Rensman, Eva, *De Anne Frank Stichting en haar lessen uit de Tweede Wereldoorlog 1957-1994*, Utrechtse Historische cahiers, 1995, nr 4, Vakgroep Geschiedenis der Universiteit Utrecht, Utrecht, 1995.

Righart, Hans, *De eindeloze jaren zestig, geschiedenis van een generatieconflict*, De Arbeiderspers, Amsterdam, 1995.

Rijksplanologische Dienst, *Ruimtelijke Verkenningen 1994/Balans van de Vierde nota over de ruimtelijke ordening (extra)*, Den Haag, 1994.

Romein, Jan en Annie, 'De mens'. In: Romein, Jan, e.a., (red.), *Jacques Presser, geschenk van vrienden bij zijn zestigste verjaardag*, Meulenhoff, Amsterdam, 1959.

RoRo-Projectteam, *Evaluatie Interprovinciale Verstedelijkingsvisie op de Randstad*, Haarlem, 1995.

Rossem, Maarten van, e.a., *Een tevreden natie, Nederland van 1945 tot nu*, Tirion, Baarn, 1993.

Rozendaal, Simon, *Blus de brand, gesprekken over de Nederlandse aidsbestrijding*, Stichting Aids Fonds/Uitgeverij Jan Mets, Amsterdam, 1996.

Schoo, H.J., 'Wie zijn wij?'. In: jubileumuitgave *Elsevier 50 jaar*, Amsterdam, 1995.

Schröder, Peter, *Data-infrastructuur*, Utrecht, 1990.

Schuyt, C.J.M., *Ongeregeld heden, naar een theorie van wetgeving in de verzorgingsstaat*, rede uitgesproken bij de aanvaarding van het ambt van gewoon hoogleraar in de empirische sociologie aan de Rijksuniversiteit te Leiden op vrijdag 11 juni 1982, Samsom, Alphen aan den Rijn, 1982.

Shetter, William Z., *The Netherlands in Perspective, the Organizations of Society and Environment*, Martinus Nijhoff, Leiden, 1987.

Smit, Cees, en Frits Rosendaal, 'Hemofilie en aids: een andere werkelijkheid'. In: Vuijsje en Coutinho (red.), 1989.

Sociaal en Cultureel Planbureau, *Sociale en Culturele Verkenningen*, SCP/VUGA, Rijswijk/Den Haag, 1992, 1993, 1994, 1995, 1996.

Sociaal en Cultureel Planbureau, *Sociaal en Cultureel Rapport*, SCP/VUGA, Rijswijk/Den Haag, 1986, 1988, 1990, 1992, 1994, 1996.

Sociaal en Cultureel Planbureau, *Rapportage Minderheden,* SCP / VUGA, Rijswijk/Den Haag, 1993, 1996.

Socialistiese Partij, brochure *Gastarbeid en Kapitaal,* Rotterdam, 1983.

Stoel, M. van der, *e = md2,* Middelburg, 1991.

Stolk, Bram van, en Cas Wouters, *Vrouwen in tweestrijd tussen thuis en tehuis, relatieproblemen in de verzorgingsstaat, opgetekend in een crisiscentrum,* Van Loghum Slaterus, Deventer, 1983.

Stouthard, Ph.C., en G.P.P. van Tillo (red.), *Katholiek Nederland na 1945,* Ambo, Baarn, 1985.

Swaan, A. de, 'Verschuivingen in gedragsregulatie'. In: *Limperg Dag 1994,* Stichting Moret Fonds/Limperg Instituut, Rotterdam/Amsterdam, 1994.

Swaan, Abram de, *Zorg en de staat, 'Welzijn, onderwijs en gezondheidszorg in Europa en de Verenigde Staten in de nieuwe tijd',* Bert Bakker, Amsterdam, 1990.

Swaan, A. de, 'Overlegeconomie en onderhandelingshuishouding', nabeschouwing bij: Maarten van Bottenburg, *'Aan den arbeid!', in de wandelgangen van de Stichting van de Arbeid, 1945-1995,* Bert Bakker, Amsterdam, 1995.

Swaan, A. de, 'Uitgaansbeperking en uitgaansangst, over de verschuiving van bevelshuishouding naar onderhandelingshuishouding', *De Gids,* 8/1979.

Swaan, A. de, 'De staat van wandaad', lezing voor de Stichting Maatschappij en Krijgsmacht, gepubliceerd in *de Volkskrant,* 14 november 1992.

Tertoolen, G., *Uit eigen beweging. . .?!, een veldexperiment over beïnvloedingspogingen van het autogebruik en de daardoor opgeroepen psychologische weerstanden,* Rijksuniversiteit Utrecht, Utrecht, 1994.

Ultee, Wout, en Ruud Luijkx, *Und Alles kam wie es kommen musste, Jewish-Gentile Intermarriage 1900-1940,* paper voor SISWO sociologendagen, 11 en 12 april 1996.

Von der Dunk, H.W., *Twee buren, twee culturen, opstellen over Nederland en Duitsland,* Prometheus, Amsterdam, 1994.

Vugt, G.W.M. van, en J.F. Boet, *Zuiver handelen in een vuile context,* Gouda Quint, Arnhem, 1994.

Vuijsje, Herman, *Nieuwe Vrijgestelden, de opkomst van het spijkerpakkenproletariaat,* Anthos, Baarn, 1977.

Vuijsje, Herman, *Vermoorde onschuld, etnisch verschil als Hollands taboe,* Bert Bakker, Amsterdam, 1986.

Vuijsje, Herman, en Roel Coutinho (red.), *Dilemma's rondom aids,* Swets & Zeitlinger, Amsterdam/Lisse, 1989.

Vuijsje, Herman, *Lof der dwang,* Anthos, Baarn, 1989.

Vuijsje, Herman, *Mens, erger je niet, privacybescherming en wetenschappelijk onderzoek,* Ministerie van Onderwijs en Wetenschappen, Zoetermeer, 1992.

Vuijsje, Herman, m.m.v. Miriam Bestebreurtje, *Hulpeloze gladiatoren, haalt de openbare gezondheidszorg het jaar 2000?,* De Balie, Amsterdam, 1996.

Wigbold, Herman, *Bezwaren tegen de ondergang van Nederland,* De Arbeiderspers, Amsterdam, 1995.

Woningbedrijf Amsterdam/Algemene Woningbouw Vereniging/Stadsdeel Oost, *Oost*, speciale uitgave t.g.v. vijftig jaar bevrijding, Amsterdam, mei 1995.

Wouters, Cas, *Van minnen en sterven, informalisering van omgangsvormen rond seks en dood*, Bert Bakker, Amsterdam, 1990.

Wouters, Cas, 'Hoe vreemd zijn onze superioriteitsgevoelens?', *Amsterdams Sociologisch Tijdschrift*, oktober 1996, pp. 375/376.

Yankelovich, Daniel, *New Rules, Searching for Self-Fulfillment in a World Turned Upside Down*, Random House, New York, 1981.

Zahn, Ernest, *Regenten, rebellen en reformatoren, een visie op Nederland en de Nederlanders*, Contact, Amsterdam, tweede druk, 1991.

Index

About the Author and Translator

HERMAN VUIJSJE is a Dutch sociologist and writer. He has worked as a journalist for a number of newspapers and magazines. His particular concern is the role that the "politically correct" baby boom generation played at the vanguard of the rapid social changes that began in Holland in the sixties.

MARK T. HOOKER is a Visiting Scholar at Indiana University. He served as a linguist and area specialist with the U.S. Armed Forces and as a Department of Defense civilian. He is the author of *Customs and Etiquette in Holland* (1997) and *The History of Holland* (1999).